Avid Xpress® DV 3.5 Editing

Contents

Preface

Overview and Outline

Module 1: Avid System Overview

Exercise 1: Getting Started

Module 2: Basic Editing

Exercise 2: Basic Editing

Module 3: Fine Tuning

Exercise 3: Trimming

Module 4: Additional Editing Tools

Exercise 4: Subclipping and Storyboarding

Module 5: Saving Your Work

Exercise 5: Backing Up Your Project

Module 6: Editing Dialog

Exercise 6: Editing Dialog

Module 7: Working in the Timeline

Exercise 7: Working in the Timeline

Module 8: Working with Audio

Exercise 8: Fine-Tuning Audio

Module 9: Input

Exercise 9: Inputting Video

Module 10: Preparing Your Bin for Editing

Module 11: Creating Titles

Exercise 10: Creating Titles

Module 12: Outputting the Sequence

Appendix A: Importing and Exporting

Appendix B: Media Management

Glossary

Index

Preface

About This Course

This course was developed by the award-winning team of Avid course developers and education specialists to provide you with an in-depth overview of the concepts and techniques necessary to create a program on an Avid Xpress DV. It documents step-by-step procedures for all basic editing operations, providing many screen captures and explanatory notes as aids to learning.

Instructions for copying the files from the DVD-ROM to your computer are found at the end of the Preface and in a Read Me file on the DVD itself. If you experience any difficulty installing the DVD-ROM or loading the files from it, contact Avid Educational Services at edservices@avid.com.

Who Should Take This Course

This course provides sufficiently detailed instructions on how to operate the Avid Xpress DV system for the beginning user. In addition, it includes a comprehensive feature set that should be useful for the intermediate user.

You might be an experienced or novice editor, graphic designer, or a developer of interactive media. You need not have prior experience with Avid Xpress DV or other Avid systems.

You might be an experienced or novice editor, graphic designer, or a developer of interactive media. You need not have prior experience with Avid Xpress DV or other Avid systems.

Course Prerequisites

This course assumes that you have some basic knowledge of the editing process as an editor, assistant editor, director, producer, or have otherwise gained knowledge of the editing process.

This course also assumes that you are familiar with the Windows or Macintosh computer system software, whichever one you use.

Windows: You should complete an introductory course on Windows XP or have equivalent experience. You should be familiar particularly with the user interface and navigational tools.

Macintosh: You should complete a Macintosh introductory course or have equivalent experience. This should include knowledge of Macintosh computer system software OS X and familiarity with the Macintosh Finder.

Users unfamiliar with the Windows or Macintosh user interface can get up to speed by practicing using the interface before taking the course. You should feel comfortable performing the following tasks on your system: selecting multiple files and other objects; navigating through the file hierarchy; opening, closing, and saving files; and using other common commands and menu items (and preferably using some keyboard shortcuts) such as moving and copying files.

Course Structure and Special Features

This course's **modular structure** generally follows the workflow of a typical project, with one exception. The typical workflow is recording, followed by all phases of editing, and ending with outputting the program. We want you to jump right into editing, and so we moved recording to a later part of the course.

Review questions are found at the end of each module. If you are unsure of the correct answer to any question, you should review the appropriate material in the course before continuing to the exercise or to the next module. (At the end of each question we provide a reference to the relevant section in the module.)

Exercises typically alternate with modules, and use the media that accompanies the course. Most of the exercises provide you with a choice: you can be guided step-by-step through a sequence of tasks, or you can work through a list of tasks on your own, using the preceding module as a reference, if necessary. A **What's Next** section at the end of most exercises provides additional tasks for you to complete if you have extra time after completing the main part of the exercise.

At the back of the book you will find a detailed **index** to help you locate specific items, a **glossary** of terms, and a list of courseware developed by Avid Technology. In addition, two **appendices** cover importing and exporting files and managing your media.

Avid Educational Services

Avid Educational Services offers an extensive range of instructor-led courses and self-study materials. You will find a complete list at the back of the book.

You might find the courses listed below particularly appropriate for your next learning opportunity.

- **Introduction to Avid Xpress DV Effects***

- **Creating Graphics for Avid Xpress DV with Adobe Photoshop***

- **Color Correction for Avid Xpress DV 3.5***

* Available both as an instructor-led course or as a stand-alone book with exercise media on CD.

For More Information

For information about Avid courseware, schedules of up-coming classes, locations of Avid Authorized Education Centers, how to order self-paced books and CDs, visit the Avid website, www.avid.com/training. In addition, to find out more about Avid Educational Services offerings from within North America, call 800 867 AVID (2843), or from elsewhere, call 978 275-2071.

To purchase Avid Educational Services books or CDs from the Avid Store, visit www.avidstore.com.

If you would like to see additional documentation on the use of your system, refer to (or order) the User's Guide for your system. To place an order from within the United States, call Avid Telesales at 800-949-AVID, or from outside the United States, contact your local Avid sales representative.

This Book's Symbols and Conventions

This book uses a few special symbols and conventions so you'll know what type of information we're discussing.

1. Numbered lists, when *order* is important.

    c. Alphabetical lists (within numbered lists), when *order* is important.

    • Bulleted lists, when the order of the items is unimportant.

■ Single step directions when only one step is required.

IMPORTANT comments are written in boldface.

▲ **WARNING is a special type of Important comment. It is set off by this symbol and describes a warning associated with the feature, possibly to avoid.**

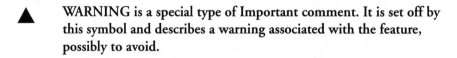 *TIP is set off by this symbol and in italics describes a tip, related step, or an alternative way to perform an action.*

Avid Systems and Computer Platforms

This course book applies to both Windows® XP and Macintosh® OS X systems. Most Avid interface windows and tools look the same on both systems, most procedures are identical, and most menu items and keystrokes are the same. For significant differences, the book includes both the Windows and Macintosh versions.

Throughout the course book, references to Windows stand for Windows XP.

The following table provides the most frequently used equivalent keys and buttons for Windows and Macintosh systems:

Table 1: Windows/Macintosh Equivalents

Windows	Macintosh
Control (Ctrl)	⌘
Alt	Option
Enter key on the main (not numeric) keypad	Return key
Backspace	Delete
Close button (X in upper-right corner of a window)	Close box in upper-left corner of a window to close a window
Control+click multiple items in a window, or click the first item and Shift+click the last item in a range	Shift+click multiple items in a window
Right-click	Shift+Control-click
C: drive	Avid drive (internal hard drive)

Copying the Files from the Avid Xpress DV Editing DVD

The DVD-ROM that accompanies this book contains media formatted for the Avid Xpress DV system. It should not be used on any other Avid system.

This disc does not contain DVD video or audio. (Macintosh only) If the DVD player opens on your Macintosh system, simply close it.

The files on this DVD-ROM are compatible with both the Windows XP and the Macintosh OS X versions of Avid Xpress DV.

If you are installing this media on a Windows XP system, there are additional steps required beyond simply copying the media to the system. Please see the instructions later in this section.

This DVD contains the following:

- <u>Avid Projects</u> - contains the two projects you will use with this course, Avid Editing and Stock Music.

- <u>OMFI MediaFiles</u> - This folder contains the media required for the Avid Xpress DV Editing course. **The space required for the course media is 3.2 GB.**

Copying the Files to Your System:

To copy the Project Files:

<u>Windows</u>:

On the DVD, open the Avid Projects folder. Copy the two folders you find inside (Avid Editing and Stock Music) to the C:/Program Files/ Avid/Avid Xpress DV/Avid Projects. (If the Avid folder is on a drive other than the C: drive, copy to that Avid folder.)

Macintosh:

On the DVD, open the Avid Projects folder. Copy the two folders you find inside (Avid Editing and Stock Music) to the Avid Projects folder on your internal hard drive. (If the Avid folder is on an external drive, copy to that folder.)

To copy the Media Files, you have a couple of options:

- If your drive already has an *OMFI MediaFiles* folder, you can open the DVD's *OMFI MediaFiles* folder and copy the contents into your existing folder. OR:

- If your drive does not have an *OMFI MediaFiles* folder, copy the entire *OMFI MediaFiles* folder from the DVD to your drive.

  NOTE: If you need to spread the media files among multiple drives, simply copy a portion of the folder to the *OMFI MediaFiles* folder on one drive, and then copy remaining files to the *OMFI MediaFiles* folder(s) on other drive(s).

Opening the Project Files

The course book describes how to open and use the projects on this disc. However, if you didn't install Avid Xpress DV on the C: drive, then the first time you open a project in Avid Xpress DV, you will see the following message:

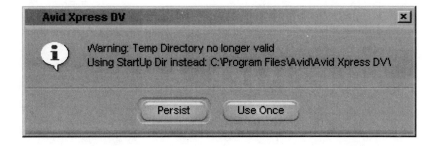

Click Persist, and Avid Xpress DV handles the rest. You will not see this message again.

Note for Windows XP Users:

If you are using a Windows XP system, additional steps are required after you have copied the project and media onto the system.

Files and folders stored on a DVD-ROM are marked as "Read-Only" by Windows XP. When the files are copied to a hard drive, the Read-Only status is maintained. Though it is preferred for media files to remain Read-Only to prevent you from accidentally deleting them, the project files and folders *cannot* be Read-Only.

To remove the Read Only status from the project files:

1. Open Windows Explorer.

2. Navigate to: C:/Program Files/Avid/Avid Xpress DV/Avid Projects. (If you copied the projects to another location, navigate to that location instead.)

3. In the Avid Projects folder, select both the Avid Editing and Stock Music projects.

4. Right-click one of the selected folders and select Properties from the bottom of the pop-up menu.

5. The Properties dialog box appears.

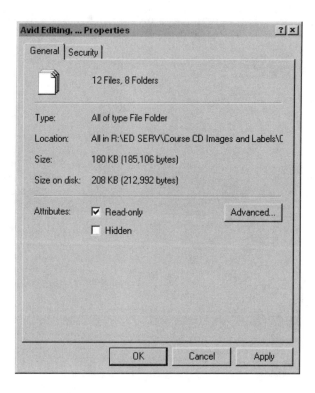

6. Deselect "Read-Only" and click OK.

7. The Confirm Attribute Changes dialog box appears.

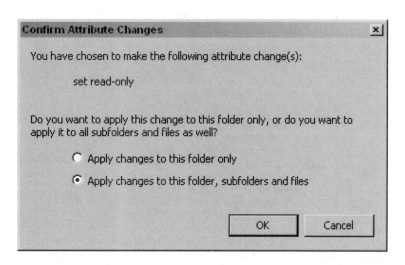

8. Select the option, "Apply changes to this folder, subfolders and files" and click OK.

The projects are now ready for you to use!

Overview and Outline

Overview

This course introduces the concepts and techniques of nonlinear editing and includes all basic features of the Avid Xpress DV system. The course is divided between modules which present the techniques you need to effectively operate the Avid system along with explanatory material, and exercises that provide hands-on practice, with ample time for experimentation with sample material. You will use the Avid system to input and organize source footage, edit sync and non-sync material, trim sequences, adjust audio, create titles, and output work. The final product will be a finished program.

Goals

- Understand Avid Xpress DV software terms and concepts.

- Independently create a finished program using the Avid Xpress DV software interface, including menus, dialog boxes, tools, and buttons.

- Identify and execute basic steps to input information into the system, and to output a finished program.

Course Outline

Module 1:   **Avid System Overview**

- Overview of Avid Xpress DV Hardware
- Basic Editing Process
- Avid Terms and Concepts
- Starting the System
- Launching the Avid Xpress DV Software
- Working in the Project Window
- Working with Bins
- Opening a Bin from Another Project
- Using Online Help

Exercise 1:   *Getting Started*

- Starting the Avid Xpress DV Software
- Working in Bins

Module 2:   **Basic Editing**

- The Editing Interface
- Play Clips
- Mark Edit Points
- Creating a Sequence
- Adding Shots to a Sequence
- Removing Shots from a Sequence

Module 1

Avid System Overview

Before editing on the Avid system, you must understand some basic terminology and something about how the system works. This module introduces you to Avid Xpress DV, its basic editing model, and basic Avid terms and concepts. You should also know how to turn on the Windows or Macintosh system, launch the Avid application, and begin working in a project and bins.

Objectives

After you complete this module, you will be able to:

- Identify the components of the Avid Xpress DV system

- Explain the basic Avid editing process

- Define project, bin, and clip, and other terms related to file organization

- Start the Windows or Macintosh system

- Launch the Avid application

- Create and open an Avid project

- Work in bins

- Open a bin from another project

- Use online help

System Hardware

Let's first take a tour of the hardware components that make up Avid Xpress DV. Regardless of your particular model, the basic components are the same:

- Central processing unit (CPU) — a Windows or Macintosh system, with an internal hard disk

- Onboard OHCI compliant IEEE 1394 format media card to capture and lay to tape video and audio media

- Monitors, for viewing

- Speakers, for listening

- IEEE 1394 capable deck or camera and control connections, to input and output your work. This is supplied by the user.

- Disk drives, for storing your digitized video and audio

Basic Editing Steps

The basic Avid Xpress DV work model is very simple — there are three steps to perform when converting raw footage to master tape:

1. *Input* the source media onto storage disk(s).

    - Record from tapes

    - Import still graphics and animations

2. *Edit* the sequence.

    Editing the sequence (program), could be as simple as stringing a dozen video shots together over some narration and a music track, or it could require a series of five-frame edits, with split edits, dissolves, and audio crossfades. Typically, the process includes the following stages:

    a. Assemble the rough cut.

    b. Trim the shots.

    c. Import graphics.

    d. Add effects.

    e. Add titles.

    f. Adjust the audio.

3. *Output* your material.

- Lay off a program to tape

- Export electronic files, including a QuickTime™ movie, MPEG, or Open Media Framework Interchange (OMFI) file, for use on the web, DVD, or CD-ROM

- Generate an Edit Decision List (EDL) that can be used by a conventional linear online system

Avid Terms and Concepts

The terms presented in this section are used throughout the editing process and are integral to your learning the system.

Project Hierarchy

Avid Xpress DV project items are organized as a hierarchy.

Project Hierarchy

ECO Challenge
Project file

Avid Projects

Avid Projects
folder

☐ ECO Challenge
Project folder

Selects
Bin

Clip

Subclip

Sequence

Project — The project, at the top of the project hierarchy, is an Avid device for organizing your work. When you create a project, the system creates two items: a file and a folder.

- The Project file contains all the information about your current job.

- The Project folder contains all files of your project, including the Project file. It is stored in the Avid Projects folder.

Bin — A bin is the electronic equivalent of the physical bin in which film is stored for retrieval during editing. The bin is simply a file containing clips and sequences. Bins are stored in the Project folder.

Clip — A clip is stored in a bin and contains information about the source of the material — tape name, start and end timecodes, and so on — and about the way you want it to be captured. (A subclip is a subset of a clip.)

Sequence — The sequence is your edited program. You create a sequence by editing clips together. A sequence is stored in a bin, and holds references to its clips.

Media File/Clip Relationship

A key relationship in the Avid system is the one between media files and clips. Understanding this relationship will help you effectively manage your project and media, and troubleshoot problems that may arise.

Media File — A media file is actual recorded video and audio. Media files require substantial storage space, and thus are stored on separate external media drives or on an internal IDE hard drive, within a folder named "OMFI MediaFiles."

Media files should not be stored on the same partition (drive) where the application resides.

Clip — A clip is a pointer to actual media files. The clip does not contain the actual picture and sound data, just references to it.

During the recording process, a media file is created for each track of video and audio in the clip. When you play a clip, the system looks for media files that contain the video and audio. If the media files aren't found, the clip shows the message, Media Offline.

When you play a sequence, the Avid system accesses and plays back the clips that make up the sequence.

Quick Review

Since you should be comfortable with Avid terminology before continuing, please check your understanding by taking this Quick Review.

Please fill in the appropriate term for each definition.

1. _____ Pointer to media files

2. _____ Actual video and audio files

3. _____ Edited program

4. _____ Holder for clips and sequences

5. _____ Holder for bins

Starting the System

It's important to power up the system and all other hardware correctly.

1. Make sure the system is plugged in.

2. Turn on all peripheral hardware such as monitors, speakers, and external drives. (Or use a powerstrip.)

3. Wait about 15-20 seconds for the external drives to spin up to speed.

Starting Avid Xpress DV on Windows

To start the Avid Xpress DV software:

1. Turn on the PC.

   The computer goes through a self-check, and the Windows startup screen appears.

2. Press Control+Alt+Delete and log on.

   The Windows desktop appears.

   The system's internal C: drive contains the Avid application, projects, and bins.

   The external drives hold the media files.

To launch Avid Xpress DV:

1. Locate the Avid Xpress DV application icon in C:\Program Files\Avid\Avid Xpress DV.

2. Double-click the Avid Xpress DV icon.

AvidXpressDV

 You can create a shortcut of Avid Xpress DV, place it on your desktop, and use it to launch the application.

You can also launch via the Start menu, by choosing Start>Programs>Avid>Avid Xpress DV.

Starting Avid Xpress DV on the Macintosh

To start the Avid Xpress DVsoftware:

1. Turn on the Macintosh system.

2. Listen for the tone indicating that the hardware powered-up normally.

3. Wait for the Finder to appear on the screen.

The storage devices in this example are:

* The OS X drive: the Macintosh internal hard drive that contains the Avid application, projects, and bins

* Media: the external media drive that holds the media files

    You can rename media drive storage disks at any time.

To launch the Avid application:

■   Click the Avid icon on the dock (the row of buttons at the bottom of the screen).

AvidXpressDV

Opening a Project

When you launch the Avid application, the Select Project dialog box appears. In this box, you select the project you want to open or create a new one.

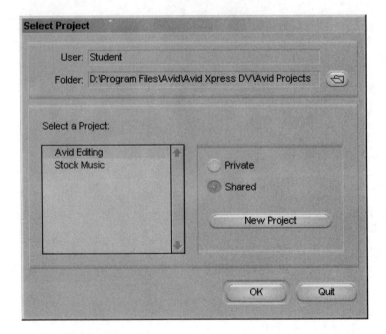

Opening an Existing Project

To open an existing project:

1. Select an Avid Project.

   Avid Xpress DV uses your login name as your Avid User. It appears in the Select Project dialog box.

2. Click OK.

   The project window appears on the monitor.

Creating a New Project

To create a new project:

1. Select the Shared or Private button, depending on whether or not you want other users to have access to your project.

2. Select New Project.

   The New Project dialog box appears.

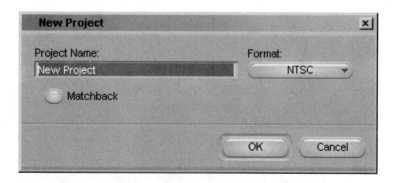

3. Type the name of the project, choose NTSC or PAL from the Format pop-up menu, and click OK.

4. Click OK in the Project Selection dialog box.

   The Project window appears.

When you create a project, the system creates a file that holds all of the information about your project and stores it in a folder that is given the same name. For example, the ECO Challenge project file is stored in a folder called ECO Challenge. The project folder is in turn stored in the Avid Projects folder.

Once you create a project, the project name will appear in the Project Selection dialog box, so you can easily select it.

Working in the Project Window

The Project window shows all the information about your current job, including a list of all the bins that you have ever created in the current project, their size and status (open or closed), folders for organizing bins, and the Trash icon, if you have deleted any bins.

 The Project window must remain open while you are working in a project.

Identifying the Project Window

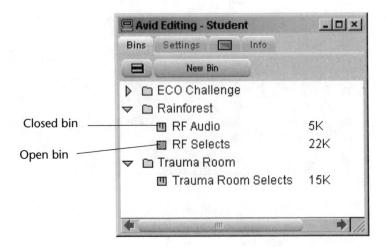

Closed bin

Open bin

You can identify the Project window by these characteristics:

- Just below the title bar are the choices:

- Bins: repository of all source clips and sequences for a project
- Settings: used to customize the way you work in Avid Xpress DV
- Effect Palette (designated by an icon): contains all effects
- Info: information about a project
- New Bin: used to create new bins
- To the left of a bin name is a bin icon; the icon differs for a closed and open bin.
- To the right of the bin name is its size.

Opening and Closing a Bin

While you edit, you will need to frequently access clips (and sequences) from bins.

To open an existing bin:

1. Click the Bins button in the Project window to view the list of bins.

2. Double-click the bin icon next to a bin name.

 (Windows) You can also right-click the bin and choose Open Selected Bins.

The bin opens on the monitor.

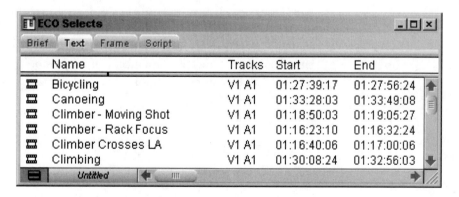

Name		Tracks	Start	End
Bicycling		V1 A1	01:27:39:17	01:27:56:24
Canoeing		V1 A1	01:33:28:03	01:33:49:08
Climber - Moving Shot		V1 A1	01:18:50:03	01:19:05:27
Climber - Rack Focus		V1 A1	01:16:23:10	01:16:32:24
Climber Crosses LA		V1 A1	01:16:40:06	01:17:00:06
Climbing		V1 A1	01:30:08:24	01:32:56:03

It's a good idea to close bins that you are not using; you will keep your desktop neat and consume less memory.

To close a bin:

■ In the Bin window, click the X in the upper-right corner (Windows) or the box in the upper-left corner (Macintosh).

When you close a bin, you also close all open objects within it.

 (Windows) You can also right-click the bin and choose Close Selected Bins.

To display an open bin that is hidden from view:

■ Choose the bin from the Windows menu.

Open bins

Creating a New Bin

It is good practice to create separate bins for source clips and sequences. To have fast and easy access to your clips, it is better to create more bins with fewer objects than to create few bins with many objects.

You might want to organize source footage by storing different types of shots in different bins. For instance, you might store all Scene 1 clips in a Scene 1 bin, or store the clips for separate characters in separate bins.

To create a new bin:

1. Click New Bin in the Project window.

   A new, empty bin opens on the Bin monitor. It has the name of your project with the word Bin appended to the name. The new bin is also listed in the Project window. It is highlighted, ready for you to type a new name.

2. To name the bin, type the new name, and press Enter (Windows) or Return (Macintosh).

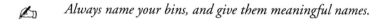 *Always name your bins, and give them meaningful names.*

Activating a Bin

To work in a bin (or any other Avid window), you must activate it. Click anywhere in the bin and notice that the Title bar becomes purple.

Creating Folders in a Project

For organization purposes, you can add folders to a project, and drag and drop bins into folders, or folders into folders. For example, you might want to create a Source Tapes folder, where each bin contains the footage of a different source tape, and a Content folder where the bins are organized by subject.

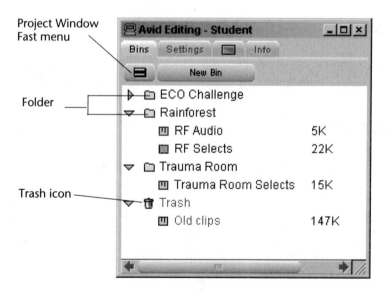

Creating a Folder

1. Choose New Folder from the Project Window Fast menu.

A new untitled folder appears.

2. Type a new name, and press Enter (Windows) or Return (Macintosh).

Opening and Closing Folders

1. Click the triangle (pointing to the side) next to a folder to view its contents.

2. Click the triangle (pointing down) again to close the folder.

Moving a Bin into a Folder

To move a bin into a folder, click and drag the bin icon to the folder triangle. When you release the mouse, the bin appears in the folder.

Deleting a Bin or Folder

1. Click the bin or folder you want to delete to select it.

2. Press the Backspace key (Windows) or Delete key (Macintosh).

    The deleted item is stored in the Trash until you empty it or move it out of the Trash. (If this is the first item you've deleted during this session, the Trash bin appears in the Project window after you delete.)

 (Windows) You can also right-click the bin and choose Delete Selected Bins.

Viewing Contents in the Trash

You can move bins and folders out of the Trash. (To view items in the Trash, you must move them out of the Trash first.)

1. If you don't see the Trash contents, click the Trash triangle so that it points down.

2. Click and drag the desired items from the Trash to the Project.

3. Double-click the bin or folder to view it.

Emptying the Trash

1. Choose Empty Trash from the Project Window Fast menu.

   An alert box appears.

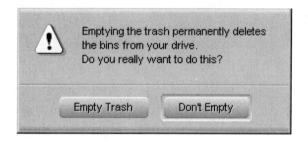

2. Click Empty Trash to delete the bins from the Trash.

   The Trash bin disappears from the Project window.

Working with Settings

The Settings button in the Project window opens a list of features that a user can customize, such as the automatic saving frequency.

To view or change settings:

1. Click the Settings button in the Project window.

The Project Settings window opens.

2. Double-click the name of a setting to open a window that lists the options you can adjust.

   Settings are further discussed later in this module and in Module 4.

Locating the Project Window

Unlike bins, which you can close while you work in a project, the Project window must remain open. Sometimes, however, it becomes hidden from view. To locate the Project window, do one of the following:

• Choose Project from the Tools menu or press Control+9 (Windows) or ⌘+9 (Macintosh).

• Click any unobstructed part of the Project window to bring it forward.

Closing the Project Window

When you want to leave the project, click the close box in the Project window. The Select User and Project window dialog box appears. From there, you can quit the Avid application or open another project.

Working in Bins

The bin contains the clips, sequences, and subclips you create.

Bin windows open on the Bin monitor. There is technically no limit to the number of bins you can open in a project. To improve bin management, we recommend that you have no more than 100 clips in a bin at any time; however, it is usually better to have far fewer clips in a bin.

Using SuperBins

Earlier in the module, you learned how to open bins. Avid Xpress DV also enables you to make efficient use of the screen real estate by using SuperBins. The SuperBin feature lets you open multiple bins in a single Bin window, keeping them open with only one bin visible at a time.

Enabling the SuperBin

You enable the SuperBin in the Bin settings.

1. Click the Settings Tab in the Project window.

2. Double-click Bin in the Settings scroll list.

The Bin Settings dialog box appears.

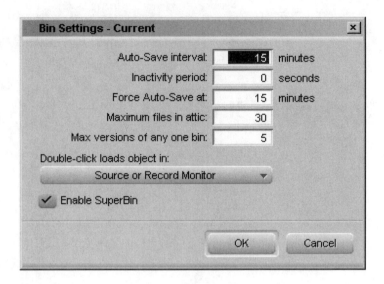

3. Click Enable SuperBin, and click OK.

4. Click the Bins tab in the Project window.

Opening Bins in the SuperBin

To open bins in the SuperBin:

1. Click a Bin icon in the Project window.

The bin opens in the SuperBin. The SuperBin icon appears in the upper-left corner, and the title is SuperBin: *bin name.*

Ways to use SuperBin include:

- To view a previously opened bin in the SuperBin, click the SuperBin icon and choose the bin from the menu of open bins. You can also click the open bin in the Project window.

  The bin reappears in the SuperBin.

- To move bins in and out of the Superbin, double-click the open bin's icon in the Project window.

- To move clips and sequences into the Superbin, drag the clip or sequence from an open bin window into the SuperBin.

- To move clips and sequences from the Superbin into another bin, drag the clip or sequence from the SuperBin to a bin icon in the Project window.

To copy clips and sequences between the SuperBin and another bin, press the Alt key (Windows) or Option key (Macintosh) as you drag.

- To close one or more bins in the SuperBin, select the bin(s) in the Project window. Then right-click anywhere in the Project window and choose Close Selected Bins. If no other bins are in the SuperBin, the SuperBin closes.

- To delete one or more bins in the SuperBin, select the bin(s) in the Project window. Then right-click anywhere in the Project window and choose Delete Selected Bins. If no other bins are in the SuperBin, the SuperBin closes.

- Close the SuperBin the way you would close any bin, by clicking the X in the upper-right corner (Windows) or the box in the upper-left corner (Macintosh).

Selecting Clips in a Bin

To select clips in a bin, do one of the following:

- To select all the clips in the bin for digitizing, choose Select All from the Edit menu, or press Control+A (Windows) or ⌘+A (Macintosh).

- To select specific clips in the bin, hold down the Control (Windows) or Shift (Macintosh) key and click the icon for each clip.

- To select a range of clips, click the first clip and Shift+click the last clip in the range (Windows).

Bin Views

You can display the bin in four views — Text view, Brief view, Frame view, and Script view. As you become more experienced on the system, you may find you prefer one view over the others. On the other hand, you will probably find it useful to use different views for different situations.

Text View

Text view lists clips and sequences along with statistical information. Text view gives you fast access to data about your clips as you edit.

Brief View

Brief view displays five and only five statistical columns: Name, Start [timecode], Duration [of clip], Tracks [of clip], and Offline [indicates that the clip's associated media is offline].

Frame View

Frame view displays the head (first) frame of each clip and sequence in the bin. This view is handy for getting a quick glimpse of the content of each clip. It can also be used to create storyboards.

Script View

Script view combines the features of text view with frame view. The frames are displayed vertically on the left side of your screen and there is a box next to each for typing in a portion of the script. Text from word processing programs can be cut and pasted into this box. This view can be used to create annotated storyboards.

Click and type in this box.

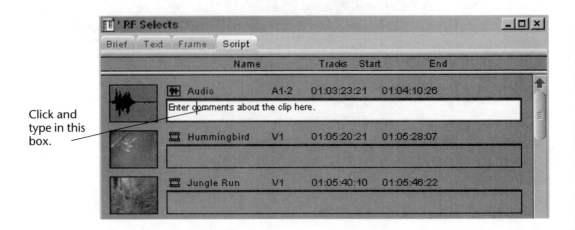

Displaying a Bin View

To display Brief, Text, Frame, or Script view, click the appropriate tab in the upper-left corner of the bin.

Brief view ——————  ———— Script view

Text view   Frame view

Frame View Options

You can adjust several Frame view properties to improve the display.

Changing Frame Size

To make your frames smaller or larger:

1. Click the Frame tab in the upper-left corner of the bin to place the bin in Frame view.

2. Choose one of the following:

   • To make the frames bigger, choose Enlarge Frame from the Edit menu, or use the keyboard equivalent Control+L (Windows) or ⌘+L (Macintosh).

   • To make the frames smaller, choose Reduce Frame from the Edit menu, or use the keyboard equivalent Control+K (Windows) or ⌘+K (Macintosh).

Cleaning Up the Frame View Display

To clean up the Frame view of your bin, try the following options:

■ Choose Fill Window from the Bin menu.

   This arranges the clips so that you can see most, if not all, of them within your current window. The clips are arranged in the bin in the order they are found in Text view.

   Some clips may now be off screen.

■ Choose Align to Grid from the Bin menu.

Adjusting the Size of the Bin Window

To adjust the size of the Bin window, do one of the following:

- (Windows) Move the mouse over the lower-right corner (or any edge) of the bin and drag the mouse when the cursor becomes a double-sided arrow, or click the Maximize button in the upper-right corner of the Bin window.

- (Macintosh) Drag the box in the lower-right corner of the bin or click the zoom box in the upper-right corner of the Bin window.

Changing the Representative Frame

By default, the first frame of the clip or sequence is displayed in Frame view. This may not be the best frame to display. To change the representative frame:

1. Select the clip or sequence (by clicking the clip *frame*).

2. Do any of the following:

    - Jog through the clip using the Jog keys:

        - 1 key: 10 frames back

        - 2 key: 10 frames forward

        - 3 key: 1 frame back

        - 4 key: 1 frame forward

    - Play through the clip using the Play (5) key. Press 5 again or the Space bar to stop.

    - Use the Home (First Frame) key on the keyboard to see the first frame in the clip or sequence, or use the End (Last Frame) key to see the last frame.

To change the frame of multiple clips all at once, select the clips and then perform the operation. For example, select all clips in a bin and press the 2 key three times to move forward 30 frames.

Rearranging Clips

In Frame view, it is sometimes useful to rearrange clips in the bin into a storyboard prior to editing them together.

1. Create a clear area in the bin by making all your frames smaller and/or making the bin larger.

2. Select the first clip for your storyboard.

3. Drag the clip to a clear part of the bin.

4. Repeat this procedure for other clips you want in your storyboard until you have them in the order you want.

Printing a Storyboard

If your system is connected to a printer, you can print this storyboard by choosing Print Bin from the File menu.

 You can also print a list of the text in Text view or the frames and the text in Script view.

Bin Fast Menu

The Bin menu is duplicated within the bin as the Bin Fast menu. Whenever we mention the Bin menu, you may prefer to use the Bin Fast menu, located in the bottom left corner of each bin.

Bin Fast menu

Opening a Bin from Another Project

Sometimes you will want access to material from another bin, but you will not want to permanently bring the material into the project. For example, you might have a separate project with bins of stock footage or sound effects, or other commonly used material. You can easily open a bin from another project.

1. With any bin highlighted, choose Open Bin from the File menu.

   The Select a Bin dialog box appears.

2. If you do not see the name of the bin you are looking for, look in other Project folders.

3. When you locate the bin in the dialog box, click on it and click Open.

   The bin opens in your project, and a folder, "*Other Bins*," appears in the Project window in italics. The bin is listed inside this folder, with the originating project in the column to the right of the bin name. Remember you are simply borrowing this bin from the other project.

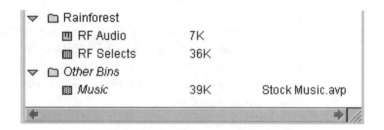

Using Online Help

The Avid application includes an online help feature which you can use to look up specific features and functions. Choose Avid Xpress DV Help from the Help menu or press F1 (Windows) or the Help button on the keyboard (Macintosh).

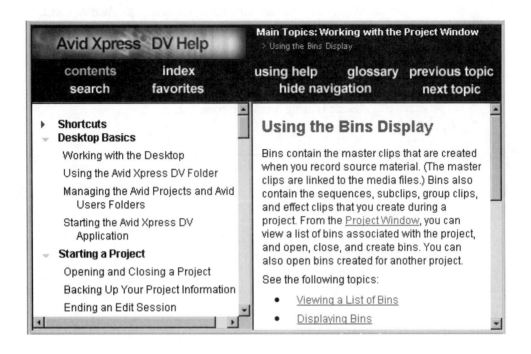

Review Questions

1. What are the main hardware components of Avid Xpress DV? See "System Hardware" on page 1-2.

2. Fill in the missing step of the Avid Xpress DV editing model. See "Basic Editing Steps" on page 1-2.

   a. Input footage

   b. Edit the sequence

   c. _____

3. Where are the Project files stored? See "Project Hierarchy" on page 1-3.

4. Match the following terms with their definitions.

Table 2: Match terms

Term	Definition
1. media file	a. an edited program
2. bin	b. repository for bins
3. clip	c. a file containing clips and sequences
4. project	d. digitized media
5. sequence	e. pointer to a media file

5. When turning on your system, which should you turn on first, the external drives or the computer? See "Starting the System" on page 1-6.

6. Label the following components in the Project window.

   a. Closed bin

   b. Open bin

   c. Tab to use to reach options you can customize

   d. Fast menu

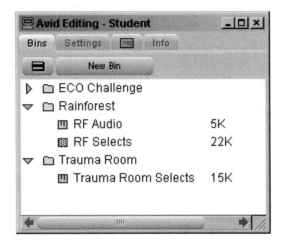

7. What happens if you close the Project window while you are working? See "Working in the Project Window" on page 1-10.

8. Where are the Frame view, Brief view, Text view, and Script view tabs?

   a. Project window

   b. Bin window

   c. Timeline

   d. All of the above

9. Which bin view(s) could you use to check the Start Timecode of a clip? See "Working with Settings" on page 1-15.

10. What dialog box appears when you close the Project window? See "Locating the Project Window" on page 1-16.

11. What key on the keyboard do you press to advance the representative frame of a clip in the bin by ten frames? See "Changing the Representative Frame" on page 1-24.

Exercise 1

Getting Started

In this exercise you start to use the Avid system interface, and get ready to work on the Rain Forest (RF) sequence. We have already created a project and a bin with digitized audio and video clips for you to use.

This exercise provides you with a choice: you can be guided step-by-step through a sequence of procedures, or you can work through a list of procedures on your own, using the preceding module as a reference, if necessary. If this is your first time on an Avid system, we recommend the first way, which goes carefully through each step of a procedure.

For the first way, see Getting Started (Guided) on this page; for the second way, see "Getting Started (Outlined)" on page 41.

Getting Started (Guided)

The first step is to start the Avid system hardware and software. You may have already done these steps.

1. Power on your storage disks.

2. Power on all other hardware except the PC or Macintosh. Include decks, audio processing hardware, speakers, and monitors.

Getting Started (Windows)

1. Press Control+Alt+Delete to log on at the Windows start up screen.

   The Windows desktop appears.

   The system's C: drive contains the Avid Xpress DV application, projects, and bins.

   The external drives hold the media files.

2. If a shortcut of the Avid Xpress DV application appears on the desktop, double-click it and proceed to the next section.

   If not:

3. Locate the Avid Xpress DV application icon in C:\Program Files\Avid\Avid Xpress DV.

4. Double-click the Avid Xpress DV application icon to launch it.

AvidXpressDV

Getting Started (Macintosh)

1. Press the Power On key — at the top-right corner of the keyboard — to turn on the Macintosh.

   The Finder desktop appears.

2. Click the Avid icon on the dock (the row of buttons at the bottom of the screen).

AvidXpressDV

Opening a Project

A few moments after the application is launched, a dialog box opens on the Bin monitor.

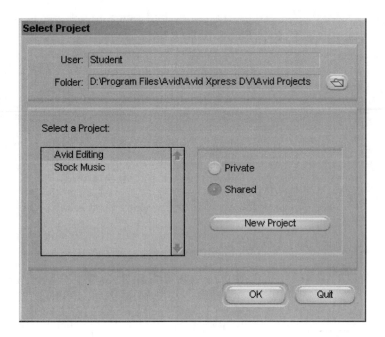

This is the Project Selection dialog box where you can open an existing project or create a new one. For this exercise, we'll open an existing project.

1. If not already highlighted, click the **Avid Editing** project.

    The User, displayed in the dialog box, is your login name.

2. Click OK.

    The project opens.

    The monitor shows the Project window, and the Composer and Timeline windows.

    The menu bar now shows a different set of commands — ones specific to the Avid Xpress DV application.

Opening New and Existing Bins and Folders

You store clips and sequences in bins, and optionally, you can store bins in folders.

Let's create a bin to hold your finished sequences and move it into the Rain Forest folder.

1. Click on the New Bin button in the Project window.

   The new bin opens and is given the name of your project with the word Bin appended to the name. Let's rename this bin.

2. It is already highlighted in the Project window, so all you need to do is type the new name. Name the bin **RF Sequences** and press Enter (Windows) or Return (Macintosh).

3. Drag the bin to the **Rain Forest** folder.

4. Open the Rain Forest folder by clicking the triangle next to the folder name so it points down.

   To begin working, you'll also need to open the bin that was created for you containing the digitized clips.

5. In the Rain Forest folder, double-click the bin icon to the left of **RF Selects** to open the bin.

Viewing the Bin

The information in the bin can be viewed in four ways: Text view, Brief view, Frame view, and Script view. The following illustration shows clips displayed in Text view.

1. To switch to Brief view, click the Brief tab in the upper-left corner of the bin.

Brief view always displays the same five statistical columns.

2. To switch to Script view, click the Script tab in the upper-left corner of the bin.

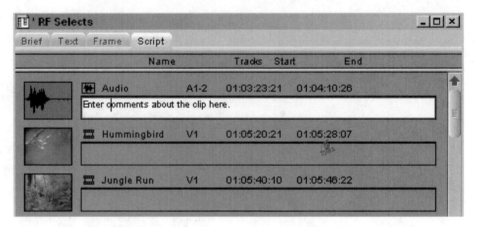

3. To add information about a clip, click in the box to the right of the frame and type some text.

4. To switch to Frame view, click the Frame tab in the upper-left corner of the bin.

5. To make the frames bigger, choose Enlarge Frame from the Edit menu, or use the keyboard equivalent Control+L (Windows) or ⌘+L (Macintosh).

6. To make the frames smaller, choose Reduce Frame from the Edit menu, or use the keyboard equivalent Control+K (Windows) or ⌘+K (Macintosh).

7. Click the Maximize button (Windows) or Zoom box (Macintosh) of the Bin window (upper-right corner).

The bin zooms to fill the screen. Some clips may appear off screen.

8. Choose Fill Window from the Bin menu.

    This arranges the clips so that you can see most, if not all, of them within your current window.

Changing the Representative Frame

Although the clips used in this project are easily identified by their name, you might sometimes find it helpful to use a more representative frame to identify a clip. By default, clips are represented with their first frame. For practice, let's modify one of the clips in the bin.

1. Select the **hummingbird** clip by clicking on the clip's *frame* (not the name).

2. Press the Jog 10-Frames Forward key (the 2 key above the Q key) several times until you see the hummingbird appear in the frame.

3. When you edit, you will often find it useful to rearrange clips in the bin in Frame view (for example, to storyboard clips, which we cover later). For now, simply move the **hummingbird** clip to the bottom of the bin. (If it doesn't fit there, figure out a way to make it fit.)

4. Close all open bins.

Using the SuperBin

Let's enable the SuperBin so you can use your desktop space efficiently.

1. Click the Settings Tab in the Project window.

2. Double-click Bin in the Settings scroll list.

The Bin Settings dialog box appears.

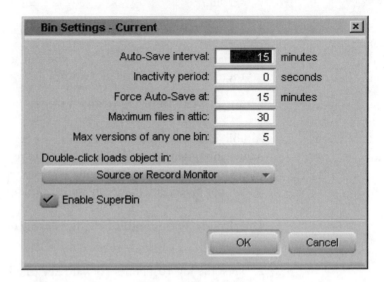

3. Click Enable SuperBin, and click OK.

4. Click the Bins tab in the Project window.

Practice Opening Bins in the SuperBin

To open bins in the SuperBin:

1. Click once on a bin icon (next to the bin name) in the Project window.

The bin opens in the SuperBin. The SuperBin icon appears in the upper-left corner, and the title is SuperBin: *bin name*.

2. Open another bin in the SuperBin.

   Now two bins are open (look at the bin icons in the Project window to confirm), but only the last one you opened is visible.

3. To view a previously opened bin in the SuperBin, click the SuperBin icon and choose the bin from the menu of open bins. The bin reappears in the SuperBin.

4. Move one of the open bins out of the SuperBin by double-clicking the bin's icon in the Project window.

5. Close the SuperBin the way you would close any bin. Close the other open bin.

Opening a Bin from Another Project

The objective of this part of the exercise is to familiarize you with the process of opening bins, moving through the file hierarchy, and generally making you feel more comfortable with the structure of projects, bins, and sequences.

The exercise is simple: We have created a project, a bin within that project, and a couple of music clips within that bin. Your task is to find and open the bin, without leaving the Avid Editing project. The only clue you get is the name of the bin: **Music**. Try to do this exercise without help. **If you have difficulty, use the following directions.**

1. With the Project Window or any bin highlighted, choose Open Bin from the File menu.

   The Select a Bin dialog box appears.

   If you do not see the name of the bin you are looking for, continue looking in other project folders, as follows:

2. In the Select a Bin dialog box, press the down arrow and navigate to the Avid Projects folder.

3. Double-click the **Stock Music** folder to see its contents.

   You should see the bin, **Music**, in this folder.

4. Double-click the bin to open it.

   Remember you are simply borrowing this bin from the Stock Music project.

What's Next

If you have more time, you can practice some of what you learned by doing the following:

1. Create a New Project. (How do you get to the New Project dialog box?)

2. Open the new project.

3. Open the RF Selects bin from within the new project, and then repeat for the RF Audio bin.

4. Place the RF Selects bin in Frame view, and change the representative frame of various clips.

5. Practice using the SuperBin.

6. Close the bins and close the project.

Getting Started (Outlined)

Complete this sequence of procedures, referring to Module 1, if necessary. All of the procedures in this exercise are stepped out in Module 1.

1. Power on the system hardware.

2. Launch Avid Xpress DV.

3. Open the **Avid Editing** project.

   The User, displayed in the dialog box, is your login name.

4. Open the **Rain Forest** folder.

5. Create a new bin, name it "Sequences," and move it into the **Rain Forest** folder.

6. Open the **RF Selects** bin within the Rain Forest folder.

7. View the **RF Selects** bin in Text view and Brief view.

8. View the **RF Selects** bin in Script view, and add comments about a clip.

9. View the **RF Selects** bin in Frame view, and do the following:

   a. Make sure all clips are visible in the bin.

   b. Make any size adjustments to the frames so they are just the right size for viewing.

   c. Arrange the clips nicely in the bin and make sure they are all still visible.

   d. Change the image displayed in each frame so that it shows a good, representative image.

   e. Move a clip to another part of the bin.

10. Activate the SuperBin and practice using it.

11. Close the **RF Selects** and the **Sequences** bins.

12. For the final part of the exercise, from within the Avid Editing project, open the **Music** bin from the **Stock Music** project.

13. If time still remains, see "What's Next" on page 40.

Module 2

Basic Editing

Now that you know how to navigate around a project and bins, it's time to edit! The basic procedure for editing on an Avid system involves viewing a source clip, marking the portion of the clip you want to edit into the sequence, and then adding the clip to the sequence by splicing or overwriting. You can also remove a clip (or a portion of one) from the sequence by extracting or lifting.

Nonlinear editing means that you can add and remove material from a sequence in any order, at any time. You can start by building a middle section before tackling the open, build all the scenes from one location before moving to another, edit scenes as the material comes in from the shoot, and so on. The possibilities are endless, and the sooner you become used to the nonlinear work process the better you will be as an editor.

This module covers how to use the Avid Xpress DV system's basic editing functions to create a rough cut of a sequence.

Objectives

After you complete this module, you will be able to:

- Identify components of the editing interface

- Play clips, mark edit points, and create a new sequence

- Add shots into a sequence by splicing and overwriting

- Remove shots from a sequence by lifting and extracting

The Editing Interface

The editing interface is where you review your footage and do your editing.

The interface consists of:

- Pop-up monitors, which are windows, larger than the frames in Frame view, where you view and mark the footage you intend to use in your sequence. You can have several pop-up monitors open at the same time, so that you can view and compare several shots.

Wildlife · V1 · 01:04:46:24 — Close box, Zoom box, Timecode display, Position indicator, Position bar, Tool bar with buttons

Tool Palette Fast menu

- The Composer monitor, which displays your sequence. This is where edits are assembled and reviewed. A sequence is played in the Composer monitor the same way a clip is played in the pop-up monitor. The control buttons, keyboard commands, Tool Palette

Fast menu, and use of the blue Position indicator in the Composer monitor and pop-up monitors are identical.

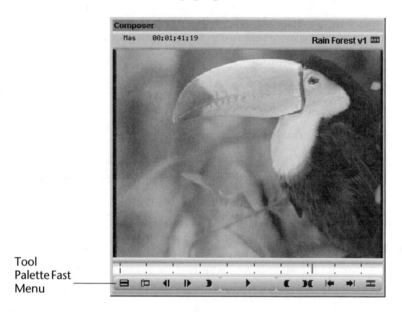

Tool Palette Fast Menu

- The Timeline, which is a graphical representation of your sequence and the place where you do your editing. The Timeline window shows your sequence as bars of audio and video against a timecode line.

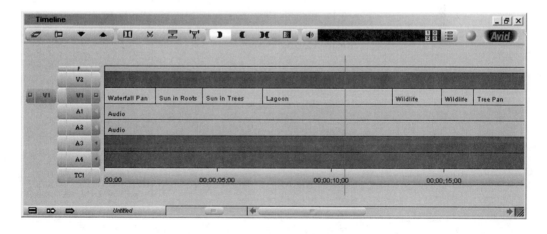

Using the Toolset

You can use predesigned work environments, called Toolsets, to set up your desktop to perform some frequently used tasks. In this module, you should become familiar with Basic and Source/Record Editing.

1. Choose one of the following options from the Toolset menu or press the keys listed:

   - Basic (the default) (Shift+F8)

     This toolset displays a basic set of windows: Project window, bin(s) (if open), the single monitor Composer window, and the Timeline.

   - Source/Record Editing (Shift+F9)

     This toolset displays the following windows: the Project window, the SuperBin (if activated) in Frame view, the Source/Record monitor, and the Timeline.

   In Exercise 2, you will switch to the Source/Record Editing Toolset and use that toolset for subsequent exercises.

   - Effects Editing (Shift+F10)

     This toolset displays tools used to create effects. This toolset will not be used in this course.

   - Audio Editing (Shift+F11)

     This toolset displays tools used to adjust audio.

   - Recording (Shift+F12)

     This toolset displays tools used to record media.

2. (Option) To customize a toolset:

   a. Choose the toolset you want to customize from the Toolset menu.

   b. Arrange, add, and remove windows on the desktop.

   c. All toolsets except Source/Record Editing use the single-monitor Composer window. If you want to use the Source/Record dual-monitor window, click and drag the left side of the Composer window. When you release the mouse, the Source/Record monitor appears.

d. Choose Save Current from the Toolset menu.

Any time you return to this toolset this arrangement appears.

3. To remove the customization, choose Restore Current to Default from the Toolset menu.

4. To return to the toolset for editing, choose Source/Record Editing from the Toolset menu.

Playing Clips

The basic editing procedure starts with loading a source clip into a monitor and playing the clip, so you can decide what portion of the clip you want to add to your sequence. As you will see, the system provides many ways to play and jog through the clip.

If you are using the Source/Record Editing Toolset, you load clips in the Source monitor instead of the pop-up monitor. During this course, we will refer mostly to the Source monitor, and assume you are using the Source/Record Editing Toolset. If we want to discuss pop-up monitors, we will explicit say so. Also, if you choose to use the Basic Toolset, simply substitute pop-up monitor for Source monitor, wherever you see it in the text.

Loading a Source Clip

To load a source clip into the Source monitor:

1. Open the bin in which the clip resides.

2. Click and drag the clip from the bin into the Source monitor, or double-click the desired clip image (Frame view) or clip icon (Text view).

To load clips and other Avid objects listed in a bin, double-click on the icon, not the name.

The clip appears in the Source monitor.

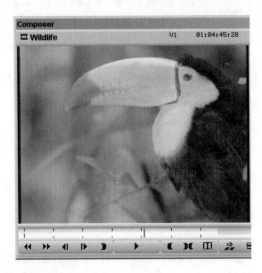

The Track Selector panel appears in the Timeline, indicating the video or audio tracks the loaded clip contains. In this example, the selected source tracks are V1, A1, and A2.

Source track monitors — Source tracks

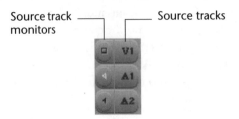

Working with Pop-Up Monitors

You load a clip into a pop-up monitor just as you do into the Source monitor.

1. Choose the Basic toolset.

2. Double-click the desired clip image (Frame view) or clip icon (Text view).

The clip appears in the pop-up monitor.

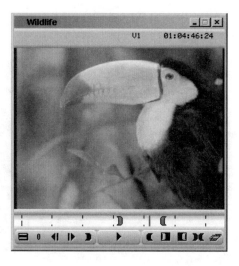

Opening Several Clips at Once

It may save you time to open several clips at once. To open several clips in pop-up monitors simultaneously:

1. In an open bin, hold down the Control key as you click on each clips, or lasso the clips if they're consecutive, to select them.

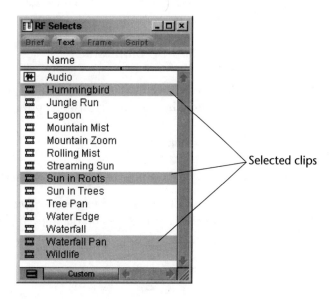

Selected clips

2. Alt+double-click one of the selected clips.

   A pop-up monitor appears for each clip.

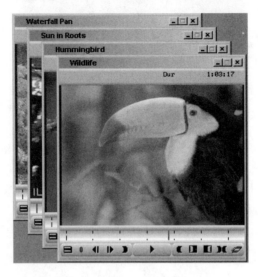

Resizing a Pop-up Monitor

1. Move your cursor to the lower right corner of the pop-up monitor. The cursor turns into a bi-directional arrow.

2. Click and drag down and to the right (or up and to the left) to resize the pop-up monitor.

Closing Pop-Up Monitors

While you are working on a project, it's a good idea to keep your desktop tidy by periodically closing pop-up monitors.

To close a single pop-up monitor:

1. Select the pop-up monitor you want to close.

2. Choose Close from the File menu. You can instead, for Windows, click the Close box (X) on the upper-right corner of the pop-up

monitor; or for Macintosh, click on the small close box in the upper-left corner of the pop-up monitor.

To close all open pop-up monitors:

1. Select any pop-up monitor.

2. Choose Close All Pop-up Monitors from the Windows menu.

Playing Clips

The Avid system provides a variety of ways to play and jog through footage. You should practice using all methods during this course and in your work before selecting the combination most comfortable for you.

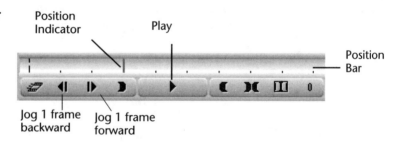

Here are some basic ways to move through the clip, using buttons, their keyboard equivalents, and the blue Position indicator.

• To play the clip, click the Play button below the Source monitor.

• To stop the clip, click the Play button again or press the Space bar on the keyboard.

• To go to the start of the clip, press the Home (First Frame) key or click at the start of the Position bar.

• To go to the end of the clip, press the End (Last Frame) key or click at the end of the Position bar.

- Jog through the footage forward or backward in 1-frame increments by:

  - Clicking the Jog 1-frame forward and backward buttons

  - Pressing the 4 and 3 keys

- Jog through the footage forward or backward in 10-frame increments by:

  - Pressing the Alt key (Windows) or Option key (Macintosh) while clicking the Jog 1-frame forward and backward buttons

  - Pressing the 2 and 1 keys

- To scroll through the clip, click and drag the blue Position indicator in the Position bar.

- To move to a specific spot in the clip, click that spot in the Position bar.

  The Position indicator automatically moves to that spot.

The following table provides a list of motion control buttons (and their keyboard equivalents) covered in this module.

Table 3: Motion Control Buttons & Keys

Function	Button	Key
Play		5 ~ (Tilde)
Stop		5 again Space bar
Jog 1 frame forward		4 Right arrow
Jog 1 frame backward		3 Left arrow

Function	Button	Key
Jog 10 frames forward	Alt/Option + ![4]	2 Alt+Right arrow (Windows) Option+Right arrow (Macintosh)
Jog 10 frames backward	Alt/Option + ![3]	1 Alt+Left arrow (Windows) Option+Left arrow (Macintosh)
Go to first frame (head)	IL	Home
Go to last frame (tail)	JI	End

Marking the Edit Points in a Clip

You define a shot that you want to add to the sequence by marking IN and OUT points in a clip.

One of the advantages of working in nonlinear editing is that you can loosely mark these IN and OUT points and refine them later in the editing process. When assembling the initial cut, you don't have to worry about being frame accurate; the Avid system provides several ways to fine tune the edit after the shot has been added to the sequence.

1. Play a clip in the Source monitor, and stop at the start of the material you want to add to the sequence.

2. Click the Mark IN button in the row of buttons below the Source monitor.

Mark IN ——————————————— Mark OUT

3. Continue playing your clip and stop at the end of the material to be added to the sequence.

4. Click the Mark OUT button.

5. Play the clip from the IN to the OUT point by pressing the Play IN to OUT (6) key to confirm your marks.

6. Reposition an IN or OUT mark by placing the Position indicator where you want the mark to be and then click the Mark IN or Mark OUT button. (You don't need to clear the previous mark first.)

Marking Buttons and Their Keyboard Equivalents

The following table provides a list of Marking buttons and their keyboard equivalents.

 Most of the buttons appear below the Source monitor. If they don't, you have to map them from the Command Palette, which will be covered later in the course.

Table 4: Marking Buttons & Keys

Function	Button	Key
Mark IN		I E
Mark OUT		O R
Mark Clip		T
Play IN to OUT		6
Go to IN		Q
Go to OUT		W
Clear IN Mark		D
Clear OUT Mark		F
Clear Both Marks		G

Creating a New Sequence

You can create a sequence by defining a shot and making your first edit. Because this is nonlinear editing, this shot need not be the first one in your sequence—if you even knew which one that would be!

■ Open or create the bin that will hold the sequence you are about to create.

You should create different bins for sequences than for clips.

Making the First Edit

1. Play a clip that you want to use in a new sequence and set the Mark IN and OUT points.

2. Click the Source track selectors for the tracks you want to use for the edit.

 Source tracks

3. Click the Splice button (yellow arrow) in the Tool Palette Fast menu (below the Source/Record monitors) to make your first edit.

Creating a New Sequence

1. If multiple bins are open when you click the Splice button, the Select a Bin dialog appears. To choose the destination bin for your sequence, click the bin name and press Enter or Return, or click New Bin and press Enter/Return.

The new sequence appears in the selected bin, with its default name, *Untitled Sequence.n.* The sequence name also appears above the Record monitor.

2. Name your sequence by doing the following:

   a. If you don't see the bin in the monitor, choose it from the Windows menu.

   b. Click the sequence name to select it (so it is highlighted in black).

   c. Type in the new name and press Enter on the numeric keypad.

3. Play the sequence in the Record monitor.

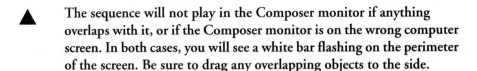 **The sequence will not play in the Composer monitor if anything overlaps with it, or if the Composer monitor is on the wrong computer screen. In both cases, you will see a white bar flashing on the perimeter of the screen. Be sure to drag any overlapping objects to the side.**

If you are using the Source/Record Editing toolset, the sequence plays in the Record monitor (the right window within the Composer monitor). In this course we usually use the term Record monitor, assuming that you are using the Source/Record Editing toolset. If we want to discuss the Composer monitor, we will explicitly say so. Also, if you choose to use the Basic toolset, simply substitute Composer monitor for Record monitor, wherever you see it in the text.

Adding Shots

You can add shots to the sequence by splicing or overwriting.

Splicing

When you splice, footage from a clip is inserted into the sequence at a point you specify, without replacing material already in the sequence.

Any shots in the sequence after the edit point ripple down, lengthening the sequence.

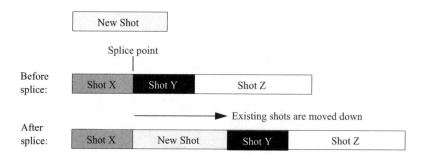

You use splice edits in two main situations:

- When you first assemble shots in your sequence, you can add shots one after the other. You use splice edits to add the first shot, then the second shot, then the third shot, and so on.

- You also use splice edits to insert a shot between two other shots. Let's say you assemble ten shots and then decide to insert a shot between shots 6 and 7. You use splice edit to insert the shot.

To splice a shot into your sequence:

1. Load your clip into the Source monitor.

2. Mark an IN and OUT in the source clip to define a shot.

   If you don't mark the clip, the entire clip will be selected. (If the Position indicator is not at the head of the clip, the mark IN will appear at the Position indicator, and the mark OUT will appear at the end of the clip.)

3. Place the Position indicator in the Timeline where you want to splice the shot into the sequence, and mark an IN.

   If you don't mark an IN, the system splices the new shot into the sequence before the current frame (the location of the blue Position indicator).

4. Click the source and record track selectors for the tracks you want to use for the edit. The selected tracks are highlighted.

In this example, material from source tracks V1 and A1 will be edited onto tracks V1 and A1 in the Timeline.

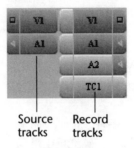

Source   Record
tracks   tracks

5. Click the Splice button (yellow arrow) in the Tool Palette Fast menu (below the Source/Record monitors), or press the V key, to insert the shot into the sequence at the Position indicator.

Overwriting

When you overwrite, you replace (write over) existing sections of the sequence with new material. Overwrite edits do not change the length of the sequence unless the new footage extends beyond the existing sequence.

The overwrite function is typically used to create three-point edits, where you mark three IN/OUT points, in one of the following combinations:

• Method 1: Overwriting a specific segment in the Timeline. You mark an IN *and* OUT in the Timeline, and you mark an IN *or* OUT in the clip

    This type of overwrite edit is very common, and is often used to create cutaways. For example, if your sequence contains a long clip of one person talking, you can add visual variety to the segment by overwriting other images over the "talking head." You mark the portion of the Timeline to overwrite, and mark an IN or OUT point in the clip. The system calculates the exact number of frames to write over the talking head.

- Method 2: Overwriting a specific segment of a clip into your sequence. You mark an IN *and* OUT in the clip, and you mark an IN *or* OUT in the Timeline

  This type of overwrite is used when you know you want to add a particular shot into a sequence and it's less important to specify the exact segment to overwrite. For example, you would use this method if you want to insert a particular line of dialog or a sound effect.

To overwrite a shot into your sequence:

1. Load your clip into the Source monitor.

2. Mark three IN and OUT points in the source clip and the Timeline.

   - If you use Method 1, mark an IN *and* OUT in the Timeline and mark an IN *or* OUT in the clip.

     The selected segment is highlighted in the Timeline. The insert shot will replace (overwrite) this segment.

     The system figures out how many frames to insert in the segment to replace the exact number of frames marked in the Timeline. If the clip does not contain sufficient footage, the screen displays the message, "Insufficient source material to make this edit."

   - If you use Method 2, mark an IN *and* OUT in your clip and mark an IN *or* OUT in the sequence.

     The marked clip is added into the sequence, at the IN or OUT point you marked.

   If you marked four IN and OUT points, the system defaults to the record OUT and ignores the source OUT.

3. Click the source and record track selectors for the tracks you want to use for the edit.

4. Click the Overwrite button (red arrow) in the Tool Palette Fast menu (below the Source/Record monitors), or press the B key, to overwrite

the marked section of the sequence with the material you selected in the clip.

The shot is inserted into the sequence. The total length of the sequence does not change unless the inserted shot extends beyond the end of the sequence.

Adding Audio to Your Sequence

Adding audio to your sequence from a source clip is just like adding video.

Follow the steps given for adding video to a sequence, but remember to turn off any video track selectors in the track panel, and turn on desired audio track selectors before you make the edit.

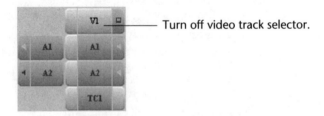

Turn off video track selector.

Removing Material from a Sequence

You can use remove footage from your sequence, and either close or retain the gap that results.

- *Lifting* removes material from the Timeline and leaves video black or silence to fill the gap; it's often used if you want to maintain the rhythm of a sequence or the synchronization of the picture and audio tracks. This action is the inverse of overwriting; both operations maintain the integrity of the sequence.

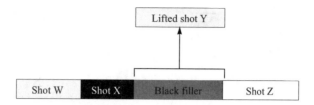

- *Extracting* removes material from the Timeline and closes the gap left by its removal. This action is the inverse of splicing; both operations affect the length of the sequence.

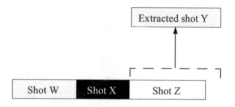

To lift or extract material from the sequence:

1. Mark an IN and OUT at the start and end of the material in the sequence that you want to lift or extract.

   Or use the Mark Clip button (or T key) to quickly select a whole clip for removal. (The Mark Clip button is found in the Timeline toolbar.) Based on the record tracks you have selected and the location of the blue Position indicator, the Mark Clip function automatically finds the IN and OUT of a clip in the sequence.

2. Select the appropriate record tracks.

3. Lift or extract by doing one of the following:

   - Click the Lift button in the Timeline tool bar or press the Z key to lift the selected material from the sequence and leave black or silence in the gap.

      Lift

- Click the Extract button in the Timeline tool bar or press the X key to remove the selected material and close the gap.

 Extract

Edit Buttons and Their Keyboard Equivalents

The following table provides a list of Edit buttons and their keyboard equivalents.

Table 5: Edit Buttons & Keyboard Equivalents

Function	Button	Key
Splice		V
Overwrite		B
Extract		X
Lift		Z
Undo		Control+Z (Windows) ⌘+Z (Macintosh)
Redo		Control+R (Windows) ⌘+R (Macintosh)

Essential Basic Tools

This section provides a number of basic tools and operations that you will use frequently as you edit.

Tool Palette

To display the Tool Palette, click on the Fast menu just below the line separating the Source and Record windows. The Tool Palette can be *torn off* by dragging it anywhere on the monitor. It provides easy access to commonly used editing buttons. You are already familiar with some of these buttons; you will learn others in later modules.

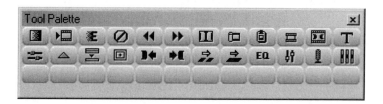

To display more or fewer buttons (and to display more empty buttons), drag a corner of the palette in or out.

Snapping to an Edit Point in the Timeline

You will often need to park the blue Position indicator at the exact head or tail of a shot in the Timeline. One of the best and quickest methods to do this is to snap to a transition point. You never have to worry if you're a frame off. Also, the technique is not track sensitive, so you don't have to select a track first.

To snap to a transition point in the Timeline, do one of the following:

• Control+click (Windows) or ⌘+click (Macintosh) near the desired transition to snap to the *head* frame of the shot (or IN or OUT mark).

- Control+Alt+click (Windows) or ⌘+Option+click (Macintosh) near the desired transition to snap to the *tail* frame of the shot (or IN or OUT mark).

This method is not track sensitive.

To mark a series of shots, Control+click (Windows) or ⌘+click (Macintosh) at the head of the first shot for the IN and Control+Alt+click (Windows) or ⌘+Option+click (Macintosh) at the tail of the last shot for the OUT.

Undo/Redo

The Avid system allows you to undo and redo up to 32 previous editing changes. You can undo the previous operation, or a series of operations. Thus, if you perform a series of operations to perform one task, you can easily revert to the sequence as it was before you went down that path.

- To undo the previous operation, select Undo from the Edit menu or press Control+Z (Windows) or ⌘+Z (Macintosh).

- To redo the previous operation, select Redo from the Edit menu or press Control+R (Windows) or ⌘+R (Macintosh).

  Each Undo removes the effect of the previous action; Redo negates the previous Undo. You can move forward and backward through your last 32 commands with Undo and Redo.

- To Undo or Redo everything back to a particular command, choose that command from the Undo/Redo List submenu of the Edit menu. (The Redo options, when present, are located at the top of the list.)

  The gray bar marks the place in the list where you are right now.

Zooming In and Out

The Zoom slider enables you to zoom in on a section of the Timeline centered around the blue Position indicator, and then zoom back to your original display.

1. Place the blue Position indicator in the area you want to expand.

2. Drag the Zoom slider to the right.

Zoom slider

The Timeline expands horizontally to show more detail. If you zoom in far enough, the Position indicator splits into a solid blue line and a dotted blue line (or "shadow"), marking the beginning and end of the current frame.

3. Move the Zoom slider back to the left to display the entire sequence.

Closing and Opening Tools and Windows

In the previous module, you learned how to locate the Project window if it is hidden from view. Other windows and tools that make up the Avid system can also be hidden from view or closed, just like any other Windows or Macintosh window. Since you might close these windows accidentally, you must know how to open and close them.

1. Click anywhere in the Timeline window to highlight it.

2. Choose Close from the File menu.

The window disappears.

3. Choose Timeline from the Tools menu.

The Timeline window reappears.

Review Questions

1. What are the main components of the editing interface?

2. Label the following buttons:

3. How do you load a clip into the Source monitor? See "Loading a Source Clip" on page 2-5.

4. When you create a new sequence, in what two places does the name appear? See "Creating a New Sequence" on page 2-13.

5. You have opened a bin and you want to change the name of the clip. Precisely where do you click on the clip before typing a new name? See "Creating a New Sequence" on page 2-13.

   binoculars LA

6. Provide the missing steps for this overwriting procedure: (See "Overwriting" on page 2-16.)

   a. Mark an IN and OUT in the clip.

   b.

   c. Select the source and record tracks.

   d.

7. What's the difference between Splice and Overwrite? See "Adding Shots" on page 2-14.

8. When would it be appropriate to Splice? See "Splicing" on page 2-14.

9. When would it be appropriate to Overwrite? See "Overwriting" on page 2-16.

10. If you just edited a shot by splicing it and now you want to remove it, but leave filler in its place, which of the following should you do?

    a. Select Undo from the Edit menu.

    b. Mark the clip, then extract.

    c. Mark the clip, then lift.

11. How is Lift similar to Overwrite?

12. How is Extract similar to Splice?

13. How do you snap the Position indicator to the head frame of an edit? See "Snapping to an Edit Point in the Timeline" on page 2-21.

14. What keys do you press to undo the last step? See "Undo/Redo" on page 2-22.

Exercise 2

Basic Editing

In this exercise, you edit together the Rain Forest footage that you saw in the previous exercise. You will also add a narration, spoken by a woman's and childrens' voices. The exercise goes carefully through each basic editing procedure, and also gives you a chance to practice procedures on your own.

✍ *Tables of Motion Control, Marking, and Editing buttons and their keyboard equivalents appear at the end of the exercise. Please refer to them as needed, and try to become as familiar with them as possible by the end of the exercise.*

We provide you with two versions of the exercise; perform the one that best suits your abilities and work style. For a more guided exercise, see "Editing the Rain Forest Sequence (Guided)" on this page. For a less guided exercise, see "Editing the Rain Forest Sequence (Outlined)" on page 38.

Editing the Rain Forest Sequence (Guided)

At the end of the exercise, you'll find tables of Play, Mark, and Edit buttons and their keyboard equivalents that you might want to use as you edit this sequence. Most of the buttons, but not all, were covered in the module.

■ The **Avid Editing** project should already be open. If not, open it now.

Using the Toolset

For the remainder of the course, you will view clips in the Source monitor instead of the pop-up monitor. So let's switch now to the Source/Recording Editing toolset.

1. Choose Source/Recording Editing from the Toolset menu.

   From now on, when you double-click a clip, it loads in the Source monitor.

2. In the Project window, open the **Rain Forest** folder and the **RF Selects** bin. View the bin in Text or Frame view. (The RF Selects bin should be in the SuperBin.)

3. If you think you'll usually want to view your bins in Text view, you can change the Toolset display:

   a. Place the RF Selects bin in Text view.

   b. Choose Save Current from the Toolset menu.

   Any bin you open will automatically be in Text view.

Let's start by editing in the audio clip.

1. In the bin, press and hold the icon (Text view) or frame (Frame view) for the clip named **audio** and drag it to the Source monitor. Then release the mouse button.

   The clip opens in the Source monitor and has voice-over on track A1 and music on track A2. No picture appears because this clip only has audio. Notice that audio track selectors A1 and A2 now appear in the Timeline.

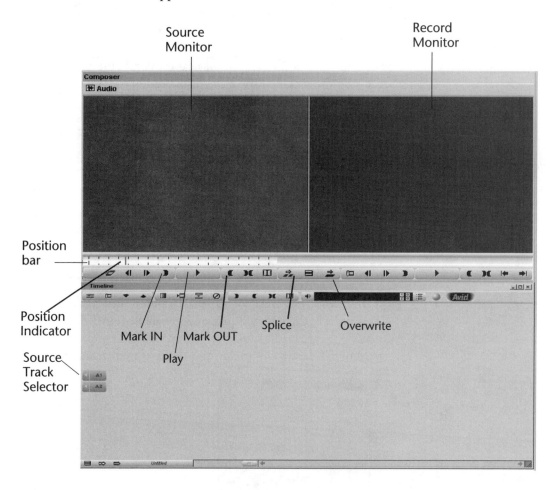

Source Monitor

Record Monitor

Position bar

Position Indicator

Mark IN

Mark OUT

Play

Splice

Overwrite

Source Track Selector

2. Click the Play button under the Source monitor.

   Notice that a vertical blue line below the image scrolls along as the clip plays. This line is called the **Position indicator** and the horizontal bar in which it is located is called the **Position bar**.

3. The clip will play through to the end unless you press the Space bar on the keyboard or click Play again.

4. Drag the Position indicator forward and back in the Position bar to see how quickly you can move through the clip.

5. To go to the first frame of the clip, click the mouse at the very beginning of the Position bar or press the Home/First Frame key (between the main keyboard and the numeric keypad).

6. Click the Mark IN button.

7. Click the blue position indicator near the end of the clip. Click Play, and stop (by clicking Play again) at the end of the voice-over line, "And keep your promise."

8. Click the Mark OUT button.

   You have now marked the audio you will use in the sequence.

9. Click the Splice button, which is the yellow arrow in the Tool Palette's Fast menu.

   If more than one bin is open, the Select a Bin dialog box appears.

10. If the Select a Bin dialog box appears, double-click **RF Sequences**. This is the bin in which your sequence will be stored. Remember, making that first edit is the first step in creating a sequence, so you need to tell the system where you want to store that sequence.

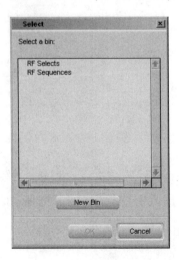

Congratulations! You've made your first Avid edit!

A graphical representation of your edit appears in the Timeline. The system will continue building this Timeline as you edit.

Naming the Sequence

Now it is time to name your sequence.

1. Click the RF Sequences bin to load it into the SuperBin.

   Your sequence bin pops to the front and contains your newly created sequence. By default, the system names it **Untitled Sequence.01**.

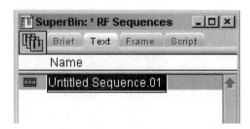

2. If the sequence name is not highlighted as above, click the name **Untitled Sequence.01** once to highlight it.

3. Type **Rain Forest v1**, and press Enter on the numeric keypad.

Playing the Sequence

■ Play through the sequence and listen to the audio track. The narration is transcribed for you.

Rain Forest Narration

WOMAN

If we don't save the rain forest, what will happen?

CHILDREN

The trees will all fall down. (pause)

There won't be a place for the animals to live. (pause)

The plants that cure people will disappear. (pause)

The birds can't fly home. (pause)

Our planet will get too hot. (pause)

We won't be able to breathe. (pause)

Will I become extinct? (pause)

WOMAN

We promise our children the world. Let's show them we mean it….
Adopt an acre of the rain forest, and keep your promise.

Overwriting Video

Now we'll start laying in some video on top of the lines of narration.

Getting Started

1. Open the **RF Selects** bin.

2. Spend a few minutes screening the clips in this bin. Make a mental note of the clips that may fit some of the VO lines. For example, the Hummingbird video clip fits nicely with the VO, "The birds can't fly home."

You will now locate each individual line of voice-over, and edit a video clip for each one on the video track. Start anywhere in the sequence you like. Because this is non-linear editing, there is no need to start at the beginning of the sequence. Later in the exercise you will add video in the areas without voice-overs; for now, leave them black.

In the Sequence

1. In the sequence, find a line of audio voice-over.

2. Click the Mark IN button under the Record monitor at the start of this line of VO.

3. Mark an OUT at the end of the line of VO.

4. Press the 6 (Play IN to OUT) key to confirm your marks.

Identifying the Source Material

1. In the bin, double-click the video clip you want to edit over this VO line. (If you are editing over the first VO line, choose a shot with motion, such as *sun in roots*. It will be helpful to have a shot with movement for the next exercise.)

    The clip is loaded into the Source monitor.

2. Drag the Position indicator to the right, then to the left, to locate the part of the clip you'd like to use.

    Notice that the video timecode display above the Source monitor updates as you scroll.

3. Mark an IN at the beginning of the section you'd like to use. If you want to use the head of the clip, mark the IN point at least 15 frames into the clip, so you can trim the shot or add a dissolve in a later exercise.

    You do not need to mark an OUT. The OUT will be determined by the duration of the marks you have placed in your sequence.

Performing the Overwrite

1. Turn off A1 and A2 in the Track Selector panel, because the next edits are video-only.

2. Click the Overwrite button, which is the red arrow in the Tool Palette Fast menu.

In the Timeline you'll see two audio tracks, plus the section of video you just added.

3. Click the blue Position indicator in the Timeline, a little before your newest edit.

4. Play through your edit.

5. Click Play again to stop playback, or press the Space bar.

Repeat the Procedure

■ Continue adding video to the other segments of voice-over in the sequence, by repeating the same procedure: mark a VO segment in the Timeline, locate appropriate video in the bin, load it into the Source monitor, and edit it over the audio.

You should have gaps between video segments where there is no narration.

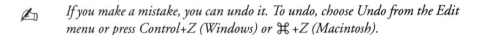

If you make a mistake, you can undo it. To undo, choose Undo from the Edit menu or press Control+Z (Windows) or ⌘ +Z (Macintosh).

Overwriting Video on Your Own

Now we'll overwrite a few shots of video, between the third and fourth voice-over lines.

1. Locate the line, "There won't be a place for the animals to live."

2. Hold down Control (Windows) or ⌘ (Macintosh) and click the mouse in a frame of black just after that VO.

Notice that a frame of black appears in the Record monitor and a bracket appears in the left corner. The bracket indicates that the Position indicator is parked on the first frame of black.

There is about a four second gap between this line and the next.

3. Overwrite three animal shots from the **Wildlife** clip into this gap, without leaving any space between the shots in the sequence.

 If you like, zoom into the area.

Each time you overwrite a shot, think about whether to mark the IN and OUT points in the Source or in the Timeline. Why might you want to use the Mark Clip button in the Timeline for the last shot you overwrite? (The Mark Clip button is found in the Timeline toolbar.)

4. Play the section.

Filling in the Gap Between the First and Second VO Lines

Now fill in the gap between the first and second lines of voice-over. **Do not be concerned about editing to the music at this point; in the next exercise you will trim this section to a beat of the music.**

1. Place the blue Position indicator within the black section between the first and second voice-over lines.

2. Click the Mark Clip button to mark this segment of black.

3. In the Source monitor, mark an IN or OUT in the clip you want to overwrite into the sequence.

4. Overwrite the clip.

5. Play the section.

Changing a Shot

Nonlinear editing makes it easy for you to experiment and try different shots at any time. Review the cut so far, and find a shot (or part of a shot) on the video track that you would like to replace.

1. Use the Overwrite procedure to replace a shot or part of a shot in the sequence.

2. Play the segment, and if you do not like the results, try another clip.

Adding a Slug

You realize you don't like the shot you added between the first and second voice-overs, but you don't have time to replace it. You can lift out the shot and the gap remains for you to fill in later. (Actually, you'll fill in the gap in the next exercise.)

1. Mark the second video clip in the sequence.

2. Click the Lift button in the Timeline tool bar or press the Z key to lift the selected material from the sequence and leave black in the gap.

 Lift

What would happen to the Timeline if you extracted the segment instead of lifting it?

Closing and Opening Tools and Windows

It is easy to forget that the windows and tools that make up the Avid system can be closed or hidden from view like any other window. Since you might close these windows accidentally, you must know how to open and close them.

1. Click anywhere in the Timeline window to highlight it.

2. Choose Close from the File menu, or click the Timeline window's Close button (Windows) or Close box (Macintosh).

The window disappears.

3. Choose Timeline from the Tools menu.

The Timeline window reappears.

Unlike the other windows, the Project window must be open at all times. If you close the Project window, the entire project closes and the Project Selection dialog box appears. So, only close the Project window if you want to open another project or quit the Avid application.

✍ *If you cannot see your Project window, choose Project from the Tools menu to bring it forward.*

Closing and Reopening Bins

1. Select your **RF Sequences** bin by clicking it, or if you cannot see it choose it from the Windows menu.

2. Choose Close from the File menu.

The bin disappears. But notice that your sequence is no longer in your Record monitor or in your Timeline. This is because the system allows you to see or work on a sequence only if the bin it resides in is open. Let's reopen that bin.

3. Open the RF Sequences bin.

4. Double-click the Sequence icon (showing three film frames) in the bin.

Your sequence is loaded back into the Record monitor and your Timeline is restored.

What's Next

If time remains, do any of the following:

• Reload your Rain Forest sequence into the Timeline and continue to overwrite video into the sequence. **However, leave gaps between the two voice-overs, "If we don't save the rain forest..." and "The trees will all fall down"; and between the two voice-overs, "Our planet**

will get too hot" and "We won't be able to breathe." We will fill in
those gaps in the next exercise.

- Replace one shot (video only) with another, using Overwrite.

- Practice the Motion Control and Mark buttons. These are listed in
  tables in the next section. Also, practice using keyboard equivalents
  to the buttons. The more familiar you become with the buttons and
  keys on this first day, the easier the future exercises will be.

Editing the Rain Forest Sequence (Outlined)

As you go through this exercise, it's important to start thinking
"nonlinear." Don't worry about marking IN and OUT points exactly,
and don't build the shots in consecutive order. Nonlinear editing makes
it easy to experiment and change your mind; use these advantages to the
fullest!

If necessary, refer to Module 2 or the guided exercise for complete
procedures.

Make sure you practice the following operations, buttons, and keys as
you go through the exercise (see the table at the end of the exercise for
appropriate buttons and their keyboard equivalents):

- Play, Stop, and Jog buttons and keys

- Blue Position indicator to navigate through the Timeline

- Control+click (Windows) or ⌘+click (Macintosh) to snap to the
  head of a shot in the Timeline

- Alt+Control+click (Windows) or Option+⌘+click (Macintosh) to
  snap to the tail of a shot in the Timeline

- Go to IN, Go to OUT

- Mark IN and OUT, and Mark Clip

- Splice

- Overwrite

- Lift

- Extract

- Explicit save

- Undo

Creating and Editing the Sequence

1. Open the **RF Sequences** bin; this is where you will store your sequence.

2. Open the **RF Selects** bin and load the **audio** clip in the Source monitor.

3. Mark an IN at the head of the **audio** clip, and an OUT after the voice-over line, "And keep your promise."

4. Click the yellow Splice button to make your first edit. (If a dialog box appears asking you to choose a bin, choose the **RF Sequences** bin.)

   The new sequence appears in the Timeline, containing the **audio** clip on tracks A1 and A2.

5. Name the new sequence in the RF Sequences bin.

6. Play the audio track. To follow the narration, see "Rain Forest Narration" on page 32.

7. Build the video track on track V1, using clips in the **RF Selects** bin, by doing the following:

   a. Screen clips in the **RF Selects** bin.

   b. Add video over each line of voice-over in the sequence, by performing this procedure for each line of voice-over: mark a VO segment in the Timeline, locate appropriate video in the bin, load it into the Source monitor, turn on the correct source and record track selectors, and edit the video over the audio.

      You should have gaps between video segments where there is no narration.

c. Overwrite video between the lines of voice-over in the sequence. (Make sure to turn on the correct source and record track selectors.)

✍ *If you make a mistake, you can undo it. To undo, choose Undo from the Edit menu or press Control+Z (Windows) or ⌘+Z (Macintosh).*

8. To remind yourself that Avid system windows behave like any window on a computer, close the Timeline window and then re-open it.

9. Close the **RF Sequences** bin and note the consequences.

10. Load the sequence you were editing into the Record monitor.

Using Motion Control and Mark Buttons

The following tables list various buttons (and their keyboard equivalents). Practice using them now, because recognizing them and understanding what they do will help you during the rest of the course, and also make you a more productive and efficient editor.

Most of the buttons are readily available; if not they are available in the Command Palette, which will be covered later in the course. You can, of course, always use the keyboard equivalents.

These buttons only affect the active Source or Record monitor, which is the monitor with the lighter gray position bar.

Table 1: Motion Control Buttons & Keyboard Equivalents

Function	Button	Key
Play	▶ 5	5 ~ (Tilde)
Stop	▶ 5	5 again Space bar

Function	Button	Key
Jog 1 frame forward		4 Right arrow
Jog 1 frame backward		3 Left arrow
Jog 10 frames forward	Alt/Option +	2 Alt+Right arrow (Windows) Option+Right arrow (Macintosh)
Jog 10 frames backward	Alt/Option +	1 Alt+Left arrow (Windows) Option+Left arrow (Macintosh)
Go to first frame (head)		Home
Go to last frame (tail)		End

Table 2: Marking Buttons & Keyboard Equivalents

Function	Button	Key
Mark IN		I E
Mark OUT		O R
Mark Clip		T
Play IN to OUT		6
Go to IN		Q
Go to OUT		W

Function	Button	Key
Clear IN Mark		D
Clear OUT Mark		F
Clear Both Marks		G

Table 3: Edit Buttons & Keyboard Equivalents

Function	Button	Key
Splice		V
Overwrite		B
Extract		X
Lift		Z
Undo		Control+Z (Windows) ⌘+Z (Macintosh)
Redo		Control+R (Windows) ⌘+R (Macintosh)

Module 3

Fine Tuning

After you build the rough cut of your program, you can see where it drags, where you want to add emphasis, and how you want to build the rhythm of shots. Then you can go back to individual shots to tighten or extend them. You add dissolves to smooth transitions and to modify the rhythm of a scene. This module covers techniques for fine-tuning a sequence by trimming, and how to add dissolves to a sequence. Additional techniques will be covered in later modules.

A table of Trim buttons and keyboard equivalents is found at the end of Exercise 3.

The only effects covered in this course are dissolves. If you would like to know more about creating and using effects, consider taking the following Avid course:

- **Introduction to Avid Xpress DV Effects.***

* Available both as an instructor-led course or as a stand-alone book with exercise media on CD.

Objectives

Upon completion of this module, you will be able to:

- Locate an audio edit cue

- Trim footage

- Add dissolves

Locating an Audio Edit Cue

Locating an exact audio edit cue is crucial when working with audio. You may need to locate audio such as a specific word, sound effect, or the exact beginning or end of a phrase of music. The Avid system provides several tools to help you locate audio cues.

Monitoring Audio

In the Track Selector panel, you can determine which tracks will be edited into your sequence, as well as do patching and other functions. The little box next to each track selector controls how audio is monitored.

You can choose among the following features:

- To monitor an audio track, the speaker icon next to the desired track must be visible. If it's not, click the little box to the right of the desired track. (You can monitor up to eight tracks at once.)

- To solo a track, Control+click (Windows) or ⌘+click (Macintosh) the speaker icon next to the desired track. The monitor box turns green.

- To prepare to scrub audio digitally, Alt+click (Windows) or Option+click (Macintosh) the speaker icon next to the desired track. The speaker icon turns gold.

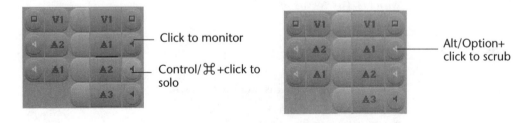

Click to monitor

Control/⌘+click to solo

Alt/Option+click to scrub

Selecting the speaker is different from selecting the track. You can deselect a track and still listen to it by turning on its speaker icon.

Adjusting Speaker Volume

If you want to change the volume from your speaker or headphones, you can use the Master Volume button.

1. From the Timeline, click and hold the Master Volume button.

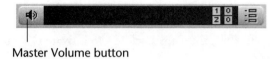

Master Volume button

2. Drag the volume slider to the level you prefer, and release the mouse.

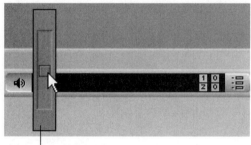

Volume Control slider

Digital Audio Scrub

The Digital Audio Scrub feature helps you locate an audio edit cue in either the source clip or the sequence. When you jog through footage using this feature you can hear the audio in a kind of slow motion, with the digital nature of the scrub giving the audio a stuttering quality.

To use Digital Audio Scrub:

1. Place your Position indicator at the desired location in the source clip or sequence.

2. Alt+click (Windows) or Option+click (Macintosh) the speaker icon next to the track you want to scrub. The speaker icon turns gold.

The Avid system uses as many tracks as possible to scrub, including tracks where the speaker icon is not gold. As long as a track is on, it may be included for scrubbing. The gold icons indicate which tracks will be played if the system has to drop tracks during audio scrubbing. By default, the Avid system selects the top two audio tracks unless you make a selection.

If you want to scrub only one track, solo that track.

3. Press the Caps Lock key to activate Digital Audio Scrub.

4. Use the Jog buttons to scrub around the edit cue to find it.

5. Turn off Caps Lock when finished scrubbing.

For good work habits, always turn off Caps Lock when finished scrubbing. You can also use the Shift key as a temporary audio scrub that turns off automatically when you lift your finger from the Shift key.

Shuttling with Three-Button Play

One of the most powerful and flexible shuttling tools is a three-key combination called *three-button play* or *J-K-L*, located on the J, K, and L keys on the keyboard. The L key functions as play forward, the J key functions as reverse playback, and the K key functions as a pause key.

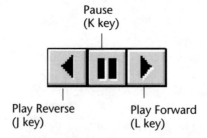

Pause
(K key)

Play Reverse
(J key)

Play Forward
(L key)

You can use the JKL keys to play footage at standard speed, more slowly, or more quickly. This feature is also used to scrub audio, it provides an analog scrub with no stuttering quality.

To shuttle forward or backward, you have several options.

- Press the L key to play forward and the J key to play backward at standard speed (30 fps NTSC/25 fps PAL). Each additional press on the L or J key increases shuttle speed 2x, 3x, 5x, 8x. Press the K key to stop playback.

- Press the K key with either the L or J key to play forward or reverse at 8 fps (approximately quarter speed). Release the L or J key to stop playback.

- Hold down the K key and tap the L or J key to go forward or back one frame at a time.

- You can rock back and forth over an area of a clip by pressing the K key with the middle finger and alternately pressing the J and L keys.

- When you use the combination K/J or K/L, you can scrub a single audio track by soloing that track.

- The maximum speed at which the system can play audio is triple speed.

- In 1x forward speed (30 fps NTSC or 25 fps PAL), you can scrub all 8 audio tracks.

  At two times normal speed, you can scrub 8 tracks (Windows) or 2 tracks (Macintosh).

  At three times normal speed, you can scrub 2 tracks.

  You cannot scrub audio at higher than triple speed.

✍ *Some editors use the J-K-L keys almost exclusively to move through footage and the I and O keys to mark footage so they can play and mark footage within a small area of the keyboard.*

✍ *Three-button play keys can be assigned to alternate keyboard locations. Right-handed operators may want to move three-button play to the left side of the keyboard. (Mapping buttons will be covered in a later module.)*

Trimming

After you create a series of straight cuts, you can enter Trim mode to remove or add frames to the incoming or outgoing material on either side of the transition.

Trimming is one of the most powerful tools of your editing system. It will enable you to improve your sequence in a variety of ways. Good use of trimming can speed or relax the viewer's heartbeat, change your audience's reaction to a character, clarify (or mystify) an action, and undoubtedly enable you to go from a good to a great sequence.

Specifically, you can use trimming to:

- Move a transition point between two shots

- Fine tune the length of a shot

- Smooth continuity of movement from shot to shot

- Create split edits

- Edit the picture to a beat of music, or create other correspondences between picture and sound

Trim mode creates a full-screen display that is dedicated to trimming.

Trim Mode

Outgoing
(A) side

Incoming
(B) side

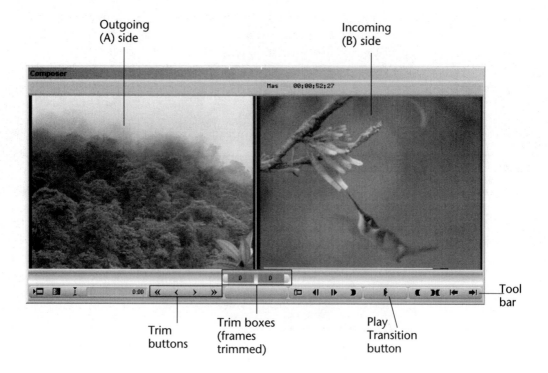

Tool
bar

Trim
buttons

Trim boxes
(frames
trimmed)

Play
Transition
button

Different Types of Trimming

When you trim, you affect the outgoing (A) side or the incoming (B) side of the transition (using single-roller trimming), or both (using dual-roller trimming).

Explaining Single-Roller Trims

Single-roller trimming trims one side of a transition. Single-roller trims:

- Adjust the length of a shot.

- Reveal additional frames or remove existing frames from one side of a transition.

- Expand or shrink the duration of the clip and the sequence.

You use single-roller trims, for example, to "trim the fat" from a shot, to let another shot "breathe," or to smooth continuity of movement from shot to shot. You also use it to fix upcut audio, to shorten or lengthen a pause, and in general to improve the pace of a scene.

The Importance of Handle

It's intuitively obvious that the system can trim away frames from a clip in a sequence, but how does it add frames? Where does it get the frames?

Remember when you marked an IN and OUT in the source clip, and then added that segment to the sequence? The footage before the IN point and after the OUT point is still available. (Of course, if your IN and OUT points were at the very beginning and end of the source clip, you have no extra footage available for trimming. When we get to the digitizing module, you'll be reminded to capture "loose" to avoid having nothing to trim.)

A source clip may be three minutes long. However, you may add a shot from that clip to the sequence that's only ten seconds long. That leaves 2 minutes and 50 seconds of extra material in the clip. That material can be added to the sequence by trimming.

This extra material that is not used in the sequence is called **handle**. Any media that exists as part of the clip **before** the shot used in the sequence is called **incoming handle**. Media that exists as part of the clip **after** the shot used in the sequence is referred to as **outgoing handle**. The following illustration shows the incoming (before) and outgoing (after) handle for the *runners* shot in a sequence.

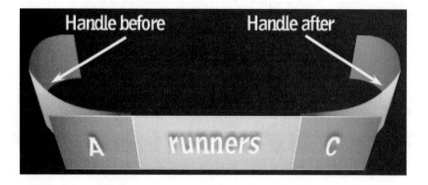

Trimming the A & B Sides of a Transition

When you trim, you trim at an edit (also called cut point or transition) in a sequence. Each edit point is preceded and followed by a shot.

- The shot before the edit is the **outgoing shot** or **A Side** of the edit.

- The shot after the edit is the **incoming shot** or **B Side** of the edit.

 Do not confuse outgoing and incoming shots of an edit with incoming and outgoing handle of a clip.

One of the most important things to do when performing a single-sided trim is to focus on how you want the shot to change, and then know how to execute the change that you want.

For example, if a shot seems too long and you want to shorten it before the next shot comes, you need to know that you want to trim the **outgoing** shot by **removing** frames. You would therefore trim the A side to the left.

Trimming on the A Side

You can perform single-roller trim on the A side to extend or shorten the edit.

- When you extend the edit on the A side:
  - The edit point moves to the right.
  - Frames are removed from the handle and added to the tail of the shot.
  - The sequence is lengthened.

- When you shorten the edit on the A side:
  - The edit point moves to the left.
  - Frames are removed from the tail of the shot and added to the handle.
  - The sequence is shortened.

The following illustrations show what happens when you use single-roller trim to shorten or extend the edit on the A side.

Single-Roller Trim:
Shortening the edit on the A side

Single-Roller Trim:
Extending the edit on the A side

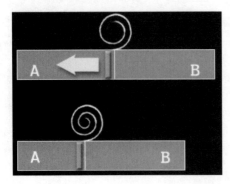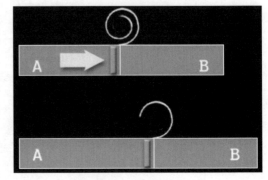

The following graphics illustrate what happens to the Timeline when you use a single-roller trim to extend the edit on the A side.

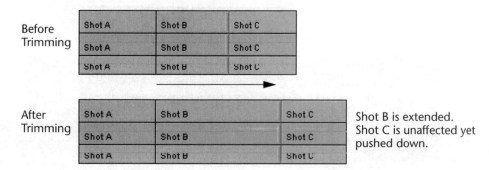

Before Trimming

After Trimming

Shot B is extended. Shot C is unaffected yet pushed down.

Trimming on the B Side

Trimming the Outgoing (A) shot is fairly intuitive; trimming the Incoming (B) shot is not. Pay special attention to what happens when you trim the B shot.

You can perform single-roller trim on the B side to extend or shorten the edit point.

- When you extend the edit on the B side:

    - The edits downstream move to the right.

    - Frames are added to the head of the shot and removed from the handle.

    - The sequence is lengthened.

- When you shorten the edit on the B side:

    - The edits downstream move to the left.

    - Frames are removed from the head of the shot and added to the handle.

    - The sequence is shortened.

The following illustrations show what happens when you use single-roller trim to extend or shorten the edit on the B side.

Single-Roller Trim:
Extending the edit on the B side

Single-Roller Trim:
Shortening the edit on the B side

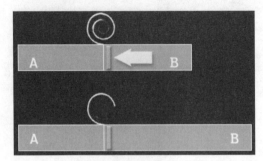 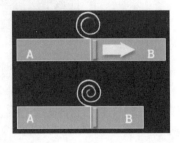

The following graphics illustrate what you see in the Timeline when you use a single-roller trim to shorten the shot on the B side.

Before Trimming

After Trimming

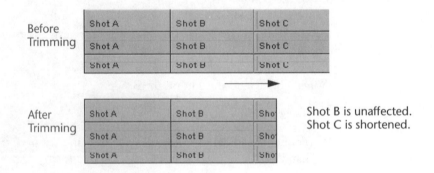

Shot B is unaffected.
Shot C is shortened.

Trimming Examples

Here are a couple of examples of trimming transitions using single-roller trimming.

- A person makes a gesture at the end of the shot, but the gesture is not completed. To show the entire gesture; you want to extend the tail of the shot.

    a. Select the transition in the Timeline between this shot and the following shot.

b. Click the picture of the outgoing (A side) frame.

c. Trim the tail of the outgoing shot by moving forward the appropriate number of frames (typing a positive number).

- A person enters the frame but takes too long to reach a table in the middle of the room. You want to remove footage from the head of the shot.

    a. Select the transition in the Timeline between this shot and the preceding shot.

    b. Click the picture of the incoming (B side) frame.

    c. Trim the head of the incoming shot by moving forward the appropriate number of frames (typing a positive number).

Performing a Single-Roller Trim

This section explains how to enter Trim mode, make the trim, and exit Trim mode.

Entering Trim Mode

1. In the Timeline, park the Position indicator near the transition you want to trim.

2. Click the record track selectors for the tracks you want to trim.

 When you use single-rolling trimming with synced material, select all synced tracks to maintain sync.

3. To enter Trim mode:

    - Click the Trim Mode button in the Timeline toolbar or press the left bracket ([) key.

     Trim Mode button

Performing a Single-Roller Trim

To perform a single-roller trim:

1. Click the picture of the outgoing (A side) or incoming (B side) frame.

Click A side or B side.

The pink Trim mode rollers in the Timeline move to the corresponding side to be trimmed, the mouse pointer becomes a Single-Roller icon, and the corresponding Trim box (in the Trim window) is highlighted.

Trimming the outgoing side

2. Use the Trim buttons to add frames to or remove frames from the selected material at the selected transition.

Trim 10 frames back   Trim 10 frames forward

Trim 1 frame back   Trim 1 frame forward

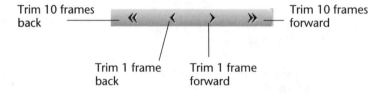

3. To play the currently selected transition repeatedly, click the Play Transition button or press the 5 key.

 Play transition

The system plays the number of outgoing and incoming frames currently set in the Preroll and Postroll boxes in the Trim mode window.

4. To stop, click the Play Transition button again, or press the 5 key or Space bar.

5. Trim additional frames until you like the result.

Exiting Trim Mode

To exit Trim mode and return to Source/Record mode:

■ Click anywhere in the Timecode (TC1) track in the Timeline.

Dual-Roller Trimming

Dual-roller trimming trims both sides of a transition. Use dual-roller trimming to move the transition point earlier or later in the sequence, adding frames to one shot while subtracting the same number of frames from the adjacent shot. The combined duration of the two clips being trimmed does not change; and because both sides of the transition are equally affected, sync is maintained throughout the sequence.

The following illustrations show what happens when you use dual-roller trim to move the edit point earlier in the sequence.

Dual-Roller Trim:
Before Trim

Dual-Roller Trim:
After Trim Backward

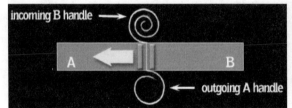
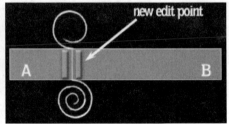

The following table explains what happens when you make a dual-roller trim. Unlike a single-roller trim, a dual-roller trim affects both the outgoing and incoming sides of a transition, and the length of the sequence does not change.

Table 6: Dual-Roller Trimming Guidelines

	Trims Outgoing (A) Shot & Incoming (B) Shot
Trim Backward	Removes frames from the tail, adds frames to the head, and the transition moves to left; sequence length does not change.
Trim Forward	Adds frames to the tail, removes frames from the head, and the transition moves to right; sequence length does not change.

Entering Trim Mode

You enter Trim mode the same way as in single-roller trimming. See "Entering Trim Mode" on page 3-13.

Performing a Dual-Roller Trim

To perform a dual-roller trim:

1. When you enter Trim mode, you are automatically in dual-roller trimming. If you are in single-roller trim mode, click on the transition line between the frames to prepare for a dual-roller trim.

Click on the line between frames.

Both pink Trim mode rollers appear in the Timeline, the mouse pointer becomes a Dual-Roller icon, and both Trim boxes are highlighted.

Rolling Mist · Hummingbird — Trimming both sides

2. Use the Trim buttons to add frames to one side of the selected transition and remove them from the other.

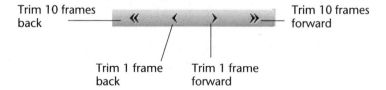

Trim 10 frames back — Trim 10 frames forward

Trim 1 frame back · Trim 1 frame forward

3. To play the currently selected transition repeatedly, click the Play Transition button or press 5.

4. To stop, click the Play Transition button again, or press the 5 key or Space bar.

Exiting Trim Mode

You exit Trim mode the same way as in single-roller trimming. See "Exiting Trim Mode" on page 3-15.

Additional Trim Features

Now that you know the essential theory and practice of trimming, here are a few features to round out your knowledge.

Methods for Adding and Removing Frames

Use any of the following methods to trim by adding frames to one side of the selected transition and/or removing them from the other:

• Use the Trim buttons in the Trim window.

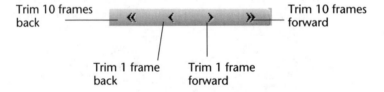

Trim 10 frames back   «   ‹   ›   »   Trim 10 frames forward

Trim 1 frame back   Trim 1 frame forward

• Use the numeric keypad on the right side of the keyboard in one of the following ways:

• Type a plus sign (+) and the number of frames (from 1-99) you want to move the edit forward, then press Enter.

• Type a minus sign (-) and the number frames (from 1-99) you want to move the edit back, then press Enter.

- Type a number larger than 99 to enter a timecode (for example, to enter 1 second and 2 frames, type 102). Or with Caps Lock off, type an f after a large number to enter it as a frame count (for example, to enter 200 frames, type 200, f, and press Enter).

▲ **The (+) and (-) keys only refer to the direction of the trim. They do not necessarily indicate that frames will be added or removed. For example, a (+) operation on the B side of an edit will actually remove frames from the head of the B shot instead of adding them.**

- Trim using the Timeline:

  - Click a trim roller(s) in the Timeline, then drag the roller(s) forward or back in the sequence.

    If you are performing a one-sided trim, make sure the Trim cursor is pointed in the direction you want to trim.

  ✍ *You can use this method to snap to the previous or next transition.*

  - Press and hold the Control (Windows) or ⌘ (Macintosh) key while dragging to snap to IN and OUT marks.

    As you trim, the Trim boxes display the number of frames that have been trimmed from the outgoing and incoming sides of the transition.

The following table shows the equivalent methods for adding and removing frames, or to put it another way, moving backward and forward in time as you trim. The actions in the left column move a transition to the left in the Timeline; the actions in the right column move a transition to the right in the Timeline.

Table 7: Trimming Backward and Forward in the Clip

Moving Backward in Time	Moving Forward in Time

Negative (-) numbers	Positive (+) numbers
Drag Trim roller(s) left	Drag Trim roller(s) right

Scrubbing Audio While Trimming

■ To scrub audio while you trim, press the Caps Lock key and solo the track you want to scrub.

 Don't forget to turn off Caps Lock when finished scrubbing.

Adding Dissolves

The Avid system uses the same basic method to create dissolves and fades. You can add a dissolve at any transition from Trim mode or from Source/Record mode.

To add dissolves at a transition point:

1. Place the Position indicator on or near a transition in the Timeline.

2. Select the track(s) on which you want to add the dissolve.

3. Click the Add Dissolve button on the Timeline toolbar. Or press \ (back slash) on the keyboard.

The Quick Transition dialog box appears.

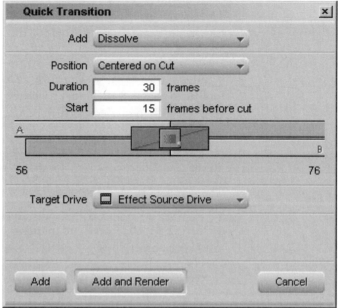

4. In the Quick Transition dialog box, specify the following fields:

   • **Duration**: (number of frames to use for the dissolve's duration). The default is
     30 fps for NTSC and 25 fps for PAL.

   • **Position**: The position of the dissolve in relation to the cut: Starting, Centered, or Ending.

   To fade up at the beginning of a sequence set the dissolve Position parameter to Starting at Cut. To fade down at the end of a sequence, set the dissolve Position parameter to Ending at Cut.

   To add a dissolve, enough source media must exist on each side of the cut to last the duration of the transition. This extra media, as you know, is referred to as handle. If you attempt to add a dissolve where there is not enough handle, the system automatically adjusts to give you the longest possible transition. You can then adjust the duration or position, if desired, within the Quick Transition dialog box.

5. Choose the target drive where you want to store the media for rendered dissolves.

   The default is Effect Source Drive, which stores the effect media file on the same disk as media for the clip on the A side of the transition.

6. (Option) Click the Real-Time Effects button on the Timeline toolbar to enable Real-Time Preview of Video Effects. The button turns green. (To disable this feature, click the button again, and it turns blue.)

7. Click Add or Add and Render. You might want to Add video dissolves and Add and Render audio dissolves. Please note the following points:

   • Audio dissolves need to be rendered.

   • Video dissolves play back without rendering.

   • If you select Add and Render, the system renders the dissolves.

   • If you select Add, the system adds the dissolves without rendering them; video dissolves play back (if you enabled Real-Time Preview of Video Effects), and audio dissolves do not.

Adding Audio Crossfades

On the Avid system, an audio crossfade is simply a dissolve applied to an audio transition. Audio crossfades will often eliminate pops in transitions. A crossfade of short duration (2-10 frames) can be used to smooth audio transitions. They may be especially important when making transitions between audio coming from different locations.

Depending on the duration of the audio dissolves, the dissolves may have added undesired audio or cut off the desired audio. You may need to tweak the dissolves individually until you are satisfied.

Adding Dissolves from Trim Mode

If you are in Trim mode and want to add a dissolve to a transition you've been working on, add it in Trim mode. Also, if you have trimmed to the best of your ability and the transition is still a little rough, try adding a short dissolve to see if it helps.

To add a dissolve in Trim mode:

1. In Trim mode, select the transition and the track(s) where you want to add the dissolve.

2. If necessary, change the position by clicking the Position button and selecting the appropriate choice. (By default, the system creates a centered dissolve.)

Position   Duration

3. Enter the duration in the Duration box and press Enter.

   This adds (but does not render) the dissolve at the selected transition and a Dissolve effect icon appears in the Timeline when you move the Position indicator from that transition.

4. If necessary, render the effect:

   a. Click the Render Effect button in the Tool Palette.

   b. When the dialog box appears, click OK.

Insufficient Handle

If you attempt to add a dissolve from the Trim window and there is not enough handle, the Insufficient Source dialog box appears.

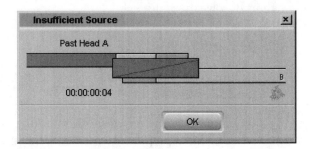

The Insufficient Source dialog box shows you which side does not have enough handle and tells you how many frames are missing.

You can adjust the dissolve in the dialog box and click OK. Or you can adjust available handle on the clips using Trim mode, and then add the dissolve again with the new handles.

Deleting a Dissolve

To remove an effect from the Timeline:

1. In Source/Record mode, place the Position indicator on the transition where you want to delete the dissolve.

2. Select the track that the effect is on.

3. Select the Remove Effect button in the Timeline toolbar.

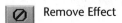 Remove Effect

The dissolve is removed from the transition.

Adding Multiple Dissolves

To add a dissolve or audio crossfade to multiple transitions at once:

1. Mark an IN before the first transition where you want to add a dissolve and mark an OUT after the last transition where you want to add a dissolve.

2. Place the Position indicator near one of the transitions within the IN and OUT marks.

3. Click the appropriate track selectors.

4. Click the Add Dissolve button.

5. Enter the duration and choose the relative position of the dissolve.

6. Check Apply to All Transitions.

7. Click Add or Add and Render.

Review Questions

1. How do you solo an audio track? See "Locating an Audio Edit Cue" on page 3-2.

2. In Trim mode, when only the B side is selected, and you enter +6 frames, will you add or subtract frames from the head of the shot? See "Explaining Single-Roller Trims" on page 3-7.

3. If the system is prepared to perform a single-roller trim, how can you activate dual-roller trimming at the same transition? See "Dual-Roller Trimming" on page 3-16.

4. What is one major difference between single-roller and dual-roller trimming?

5. A person completes a line of dialog, and you would like to add a brief pause before cutting to the listener. How would you trim the shot? See "Explaining Single-Roller Trims" on page 3-7.

6. What do you select in the track selector panel if you want to trim V1 only but also want to monitor the audio only on track A2 as you trim? See "Explaining Single-Roller Trims" on page 3-7.

7. In the following table, two of the four boxes have mistakes; two are correct. Please identify the mistakes and correct them.

Table 8: Trimming Guidelines

	Trim Outgoing (A) Shot	Trim Incoming (B) Shot
Trim Backward	Adds frames to the tail; transition moves to left and sequence is shortened	Removes frames from the head; transitions downstream move to left and sequence is shortened
Trim Forward	Adds frames to the tail; transition moves to right and sequence is lengthened	Removes frames from the head; transitions downstream move to left and sequence is shortened

8. Fill in the Frame counters to move the transition backward 20 frames without affecting the duration of the sequence.

9. What are these buttons?

10. How do you add multiple dissolves? See "Adding Multiple Dissolves" on page 3-25.

Exercise 3

Trimming

In this exercise, you will trim the Rain Forest sequence that you began in the previous exercise and add some dissolves.

For a more guided exercise, see "Fine-Tuning the Sequence: Guided" on this page. For a less guided exercise, see "Fine-Tuning the Sequence (Outlined)" on page 38.

 At the end of the exercise, you'll find a table of Trim buttons and their keyboard equivalents that you might want to use as you work on this exercise.

Fine-Tuning the Sequence (Guided)

In the first part of the exercise, you trim shots, make a cut occur on the beat of the music, and using trimming to fill in a gap in the sequence.

Duplicating the Sequence

Before you start reworking the sequence, it's a good idea to *duplicate* it— this backup copy functions as a protection dub. If you make a mistake during the second cut, you can always go back to the original.

1. Open the **RF Sequences** bin.

2. Select the sequence (make sure to click its icon, not its name), and choose Duplicate from the Edit menu.

A copy appears in the bin. The word **Copy01** is appended to the sequence name.

3. Change the name of the copy to **Rain Forest v2**.

4. Make sure Source/Record Editing is chosen in the Toolset menu.

5. Double-click the copied sequence to load it into the Record monitor.

Trimming Wildlife Shots

In the last exercise, you added three shots from the Wildlife clip into your sequence. You can trim any of those shots, making them enter earlier or cut out later.

1. In the Timeline, lasso the transition of the **Wildlife** shot that you want to trim by positioning the cursor **above** the Timeline, pressing the mouse button, and dragging a lasso around the transition on only track V1. (Before lassoing, you may want to use the Zoom slider to zoom in on that section of the Timeline.)

The system enters Trim mode, and selects the transition you lassoed.

The Trim mode windows show the last frame of the outgoing shot on the left and the first frame of the incoming shot on the right. Notice the new buttons in the Tool bar.

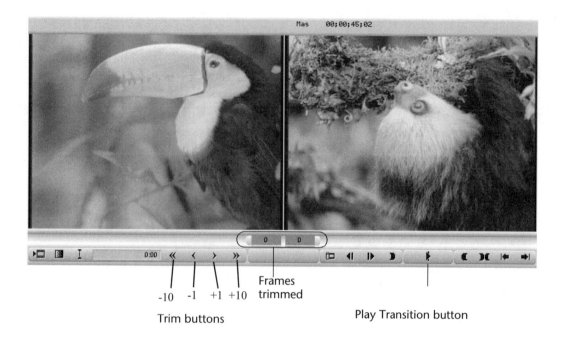

Trim buttons
-10 -1 +1 +10
Frames trimmed

Play Transition button

2. Confirm that only the V1 record track selector is on.

3. Click the Play Transition button, and decide whether you want to trim to the right or left.

4. To stop the playback loop, press the Space bar or click the Play Transition button again.

5. Without pressing the mouse, move it over the highlighted transition, until it becomes a left-sided or right-sided roller.

6. Press the mouse and drag the transition to the right or left, depending on what you want to trim. As you start to drag, the cursor

becomes a hand. Notice the display that keeps track of the frames you have trimmed. Release the mouse.

Dragging to the right adds frames to the tail of the outgoing shot and removes frames from the head of the incoming one. Dragging to the left removes frames from the tail of the outgoing shot and adds frames to the head of the incoming one. In both cases, the duration of the video track remains the same.

7. Play the transition again and, if necessary, use the -1 and +1 frame trim keys to adjust the trim.

8. When you are finished, to return to edit mode: click anywhere in the Timecode (**TC1**) track in the Timeline.

9. Go to the area before the trim, and play through your cut.

10. Repeat the procedure to trim other **Wildlife** shots.

Cutting to Music

Now, let's make a cut occur on a beat of the music.

1. Listen to the beginning of the sequence. Notice that at approximately
4 1/2 - 5 1/2 seconds into the sequence (between the first and second lines of voice-over), the music becomes rhythmic. Let's make the video cut to the first beat of this rhythmic passage.

2. If you want to change the volume from your speaker:

  a. From the Timeline, click and hold the Master Volume button.

  b. Drag the volume slider to the level you prefer, and release the mouse.

3. Enter Trim mode at the **video** transition to the video for the voice-over line, "The trees will all fall down."

4. Click the Play Transition button. To stop the playback loop, press the Space bar.

5. To prepare for audio scrubbing, Alt+click (Windows) or Option+click (Macintosh) the speaker monitor for track A2 (the music track) and press the Caps Lock key to turn on Digital Scrub.

6. Click the Trim 1 Frame key repeatedly until you add approximately 2/3 of a second to the head the incoming clip, so the cut occurs on the beat. With Digital Audio Scrub on, you should be able to hear a marked change in audio level, which indicates the beat of music.

   Think before you act: Do you want to use the + or - Trim keys to make this trim? Why?

7. Play the transition again and, if necessary, use the Trim keys to trim the cut so that it occurs on the beat.

Trimming Out Black Frames

This transition works, but now there are a few frames of black between the shot you just trimmed and the previous one. Let's trim out the black frames.

1. Drag a lasso around the previous edit, or press the A (Rewind) key to move to the previous transition in Trim mode.

   Notice that the incoming shot is a black frame.

2. Drag the Trim roller to the right until it won't move farther.

   The incoming shot is no longer a black frame.

3. Press the Caps Lock key to turn off Digital Audio Scrub.

   It's a good practice to turn off Digital Scrub when finished using it.

4. When you are finished, exit Trim mode.

5. Go to the start of the sequence, and play through your changes.

Trimming Out Black Frames by Joining Two Clips

In some cases you may not want to fill a gap in the Timeline by adding another clip, but would instead prefer to simply join the two video clips on either side by making each a little longer. Let's try that for the gap between two voice-overs: "The planet will get too hot" and "We won't be able to breathe."

1. Place the Position indicator on or near the **video** edit at the end of the VO line "Our planet will get too hot." to enter Trim mode.

2. Select track V1 and deselect all others.

3. Click the Trim button to enter Trim mode. The Trim Mode button is located in the Timeline toolbar.

 Trim Mode button

You are now set to perform a dual-roller trim at this transition.

4. Drag the Trim rollers to the right about halfway to the next edit.

5. Without leaving Trim mode, press the S (Fast Forward) key to advance to the next edit.

6. This time drag the pink rollers to the left, until the system prevents you from dragging any more.

7. Release the mouse.

   The gap is now closed.

8. Click the Play Transition button.

9. Press the Space bar to stop playback.

10. Continue trimming this edit to your liking.

11. Exit Trim mode, and play the section you just trimmed.

Trimming Earlier

Play the video edit with the corresponding audio "The birds can't fly home." It begins a little abruptly, so let's bring shot with the bird — or whichever shot you have put there — in a little earlier.

1. Enter Trim mode at the appropriate edit point.

2. Perform the appropriate dual-roller trim to bring the shot in earlier.

3. Play the trim.

4. Exit Trim mode, and play the section you just trimmed.

Adding Dissolves

In this part of the exercise, you add fades and multiple dissolves.

Fading Up

In this part of the exercise, you will fade up the beginning of the sequence.

1. Use the Home/First Frame key to go to the start of your sequence.

2. Make sure only the V1 record track selector is on.

3. Click the Real-Time Effects button on the Timeline toolbar to enable Real-Time Preview of Video Effects. The button turns green.

4. Click the Add Dissolve button on the Timeline toolbar.

The Quick Transition dialog box appears.

5. For the Position parameter, choose Starting at Cut.

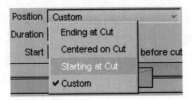

6. For the Duration parameter, use 30 frames (NTSC) or 25 frames (PAL).

7. Click Add.

Will you be able to play the fade?

Fading Down

Follow a similar procedure to fade down the video track at the end of the sequence. (Choose Ending at Cut for the Position.)

Adding Multiple Dissolves

Add dissolves on at least two consecutive transitions on track V1.

1. Mark an IN before the first transition where you want to add a dissolve and mark an OUT after the last transition where you want to add a dissolve.

2. Select only the V1 record track selector.

3. Place the Position indicator near one of the transitions within the IN and OUT marks.

4. Click the Add Dissolve button.

A dialog box appears.

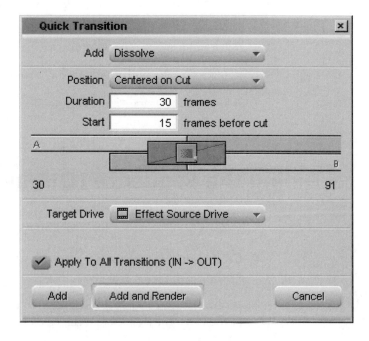

5. Choose the position, Centered on Cut.

6. Enter a duration.

7. Check the Apply to All Transitions checkbox.

8. Click Add.

9. Play that portion of the sequence to see the results.

What's Next

If time permits, try any of the following:

- If gaps remain in the sequence, fill them by using one of the following methods:

    - Overwrite shots into the sequence to fill the gaps.

    - In some cases you may not want to fill a gap in the Timeline by adding another clip, but would instead prefer to simply join the two video clips on either side by making each a little longer. Use Trim mode to extend the shots on both sides of the gap.

- Continue trimming this edit to your liking, by dragging the Trim roller and using the Trim buttons.

- Replace one clip with another using Overwrite.

- Add a dissolve from within Trim mode.

Periodically play through your cut.

Fine-Tuning the Sequence (Outlined)

Use Digital Audio Scrub when you perform some of the trims.

1. Create a duplicate of the **RF sequence** you began in the last exercise. Name the duplicate sequence.

2. Perform at least two dual-roller trims to further improve the rhythm of the video track and to cut the video to a beat of the music.

3. Practice navigating from edit to edit within Trim mode by using the A (Rewind) or S (Fast Forward) keys.

4. Periodically exit Trim mode and play through your cut.

5. When you finish using Digital Audio Scrub, turn off Caps Lock.

Now, see how to fill a gap in the sequence by extending shots in Trim mode:

1. To prepare, lift the last one or two seconds of any shot in the sequence. Then, trim the material back in the sequence by dragging the Trim rollers in the Timeline.

2. Lift an unwanted shot. Fill the gap in the Timeline by joining the two video clips on either side by making each a little longer. Do this by dragging the Trim rollers in the Timeline.

In this exercise, performing single-roller trims is optional because this isn't the best sequence to use single roller trims. Do you know why? (Stop and think before you read on.) Because single-roller trims will remove the correspondence between the video and the voice-over segments that you created in the previous exercise. You might want to practice single-roller trims toward the end of the sequence to avoid loss of sync in the earlier part of the sequence.

Creating Dissolves

In this part of the exercise, you add a fade in and out and several dissolves to the sequence.

1. Fade up the V1 track at the beginning of your Rain Forest sequence.

2. Fade out the V1 track at the end of the sequence.

3. Add dissolves to two or more consecutive transitions on the V1 track.

4. Add a dissolve from within Trim mode.

Using Trim Buttons

The following table lists various buttons (and their keyboard equivalents). Practice using them now, because recognizing them and understanding what they do will help you during the rest of the course, and also make you a more productive and efficient editor.

Table 4: Trim Keys & Buttons

Function	Button	Key
Enter Trim Mode	🔲	[(left bracket)
Trim 1 frame back	‹	, (comma)
Trim 1 frame forward	›	. (period)
Trim 10 frames back	‹‹	M
Trim 10 frames forward	››	/

Function	Button	Key
Play transition		5
Exit Trim Mode		1, 2, 3, 4

Module 4

Additional Editing Tools

This module presents some powerful tools to aid you in the editing process, including ways to change settings, subclip and storyboard, and how to use locators.

Objectives

After you complete this module, you will be able to:

- View and change settings
- Navigate effectively through the sequence
- Map buttons to the keyboard or a command palette
- Create subclips
- Perform storyboard editing
- Use locators

Viewing and Changing Settings

The Settings button in the Project window opens a list of features that you can customize and save for your particular work style, for example, you can change the automatic saving frequency.

To view or change a setting:

1. Click the Settings button in the Project window.

   The Project Settings window opens.

2. Double-click the name of a setting to open a window that lists the options you can adjust.

   For example, you can use Bin settings to change the default setting of the automatic save feature, which regulates the frequency with which the Avid system automatically saves your work.

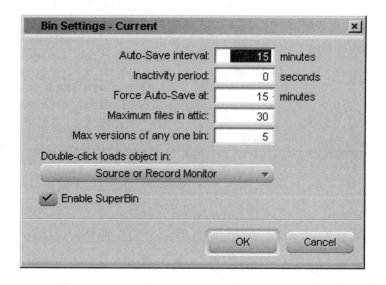

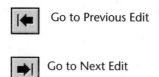 *User settings can be copied to a floppy disk and used on another system. However, keep in mind that you might not be able to use your settings on an older version of the Avid system.*

Additional Navigation Tools

Moving From One Transition to Another in the Timeline

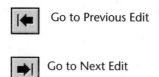 *These buttons work in Source/Record mode and Trim mode.*

By default, the Go to Previous Edit button (or [key) and Go to Next Edit button (or] key) go to the head (that is, the first frame) of each clip in the sequence on the selected tracks. These buttons are found below the Record monitor.

Go to Previous Edit

Go to Next Edit

If you press the Alt (Windows) or Option (Macintosh) key while clicking the button, the Position indicator moves to the head of the closest clip regardless of track selection.

Using the Clip Name Menu

The Record monitor has its own Clip Name menu. Click and hold the Clip Name menu to display the sequence name and several other options.

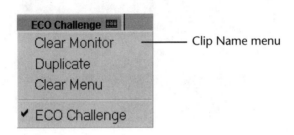

Clip Name menu

Using the Timecode Display

Above the Source and Record monitor is a Timecode display that shows data about the source of the frame currently displayed in the monitor. This display lists Timecode data about the sequence and also about the source clips that make up the sequence.

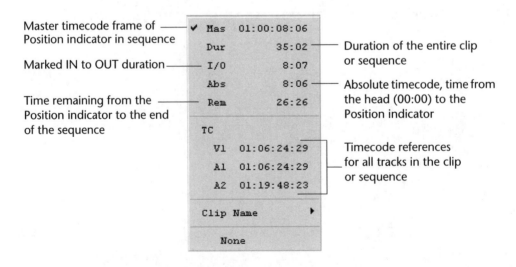

Master timecode frame of Position indicator in sequence

Marked IN to OUT duration

Time remaining from the Position indicator to the end of the sequence

Duration of the entire clip or sequence

Absolute timecode, time from the head (00:00) to the Position indicator

Timecode references for all tracks in the clip or sequence

To adjust the Timecode display, press the Timecode display and choose a timecode type from the pop-up menu. The first five timecodes give you information about the sequence loaded in the Timeline.

- Mas (M on the interface): displays the location of the Position indicator on the sequence's Timecode track (known as Master timecode)

- Dur (D): displays the duration of the entire clip or sequence

- I/O (IO): displays the marked IN to OUT duration

- Abs (Ab): displays the time from the head (00:00) to the Position indicator (known as Absolute timecode)

- Rem (R): displays time remaining (from the Position indicator to the end of the sequence)

- Below the dotted line, the source timecode references for all tracks in the clip or sequence are listed.

Seeking Frames

After loading a clip or sequence into a monitor, you can go to a specific frame by typing its video timecode. You can also move forward or backward from your current position in a clip or sequence by entering a frame offset.

 The monitor's timecode display determines the way the system references the numbers you type into the monitor. For example, if you want to reference the V1 (video) timecode of a clip, you must select V1 in the Timecode display. If you instead display I/O timecode, the system won't be able to find a frame using the following method.

Finding a Frame

1. Load a clip or sequence into a monitor.

2. Make sure the monitor is active (the active monitor has the brighter position bar).

3. If you are using a keyboard without a separate numeric keypad (for example, if you use a laptop), activate numlock by pressing the numlock or another function key with the numlock function.

4. Enter the SMPTE timecode using the numeric keypad on the right side of the keyboard (or the regular keypad with numlock activated, if using a laptop). Type the hours, minutes, seconds, and frames, omitting leading zeros. Example: type 1230200 to enter 01:23:02:00.

   Or, if you find a timecode that starts at the same hour as the current timecode, just type the last digits. For example, if the current timecode is 1:05:12:13 and you type 423, the system finds the frame at 1:05:04:23.

   As you start typing, an entry field opens in the middle of the monitor, showing the numbers you type. (The system inserts the colons.)

5. Press Enter on the numeric keypad.

   The Position indicator locates the specified frame.

▲ **Whenever you use the numeric keypad, you must press Enter on the numeric keypad after typing the number. Do not use the Enter key on the main keyboard.**

▲ **The system beeps if it can't find specified timecode number in the clip or sequence. Check the Timecode display and make sure the appropriate timecode is shown.**

6. If you are using a keyboard without a separate numeric keypad, deactivate numlock if necessary to activate the standard keyboard.

Typing a Frame Offset

You can also use the "frame offset" feature to move the Position indicator from its current frame forward (or backward) a specified number of frames. (This procedure is similar to the method for adding and removing frames using the numeric keypad in Trim mode, covered in the previous module.)

To type a frame offset with a clip or sequence loaded in a monitor:

1. Make sure the monitor with the clip or sequence is active.

2. Activate numlock, if necessary (see the previous section).

3. Enter the SMPTE timecode using the numeric keypad, and type a plus sign (+) before the number to move forward or a minus sign (-) before the number to move backward from the current position.

4. Enter the number of frames for the offset by doing one of the following:

   • Type numbers between 1-99 frame.

   • Enter 100 or a higher number to move forward or backward a specified number of seconds and frames.

   • With Caps Lock off, type an f after a large number to enter it as a frame count (for example, to enter 200 frames, type 200, then f).

   When going forward or backward, enter one less frame than desired, since the system counts the current frame. For example, if you want to move forward 3 seconds and 10 frames, type 309.

5. Press Enter.

6. If you press Enter again, the system remembers the last entry and advances the same number of frames.

7. Deactivate numlock, if necessary (see the previous section).

Match Frame

The Match Frame function locates the frame currently displayed in the Record monitor, by loading the master clip that contains it into the Source monitor, and locating the frame with the blue position indicator. An IN point is marked at that location to prepare for making an edit.

This function is useful when you need to view earlier or later source footage from a clip in the sequence, or when you need to re-edit a clip into your sequence.

1. Move to the frame in your sequence that you want to match.

2. Select the track in the track panel that you want to match and deselect higher tracks.

3. Click the Match Frame button in the Tool Palette.

You can also use Match Frame to locate the frame currently displayed in the *Source* monitor. You would use this, for example, if a subclip is currently in the Source monitor and you want to locate the same frame in the master clip.

With the subclip in the Source monitor, press the Alt/Option key with the Match Frame button to load the master clip into the Source monitor.

Useful Application

If a portion of a clip is in your sequence, and you want to see what you left out, park near the beginning or end of the clip and use Match Frame to load the master clip into the Source monitor.

Mapping User-Selectable Buttons

The Command Palette provides a central location for all user-selectable buttons. You can map buttons to any row of buttons, command palette, or the keyboard. You can also map menu commands to various buttons and keys.

The Command Palette groups buttons by editing category: Move, Play, Edit, Trim, FX, Other, and More. Tabs are displayed for each category and the buttons that perform those functions are displayed within each tab. The Command palette windows you will find most useful in this course appear below.

Move Buttons

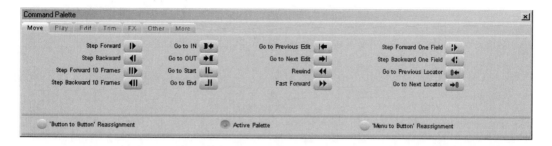

Play Buttons

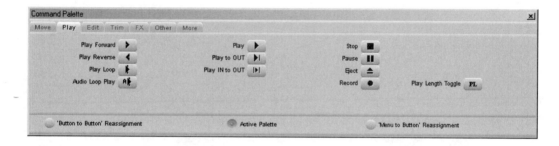

Edit Buttons

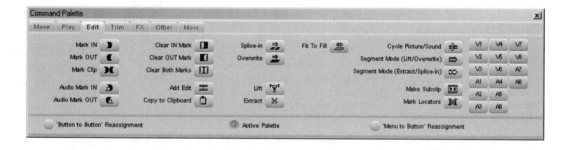

Trim Buttons

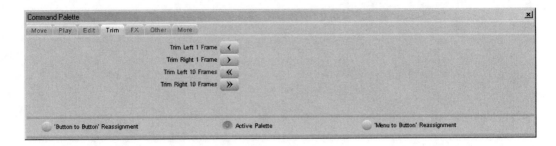

Other Buttons

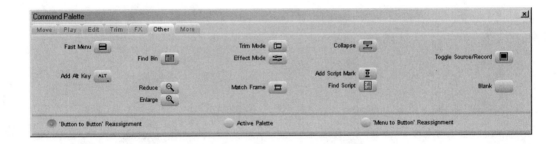

Mapping User Selectable Buttons

To remap buttons or keys using the Command Palette:

1. Open the Keyboard settings from the Project window if you want to map a button to the keyboard.

2. Choose Command Palette from the Tools menu.

The Command Palette appears.

Click a tab.

Click the Button to Button Reassignment radio button.

3. Click the **Button to Button** Reassignment box if it's not selected.

4. Click the tab for the category that contains your user-selectable button.

5. Click and drag the button from the Command Palette to the keyboard palette or to a location on a row of buttons, for example, under a monitor or in the Tool Palette.

   (Windows only) You can't map to the F1 key.

   If you hold the Shift key down when you drag the button to the keyboard palette, you can map to Shift+[key]. This also works for other modifiers in addition to Shift.

6. Close the Command Palette when you are finished.

As you get used to editing on the system and find that you constantly use certain features, you might want to map them to keys on the keyboard.

All of your interface modifications are saved as User settings and can be copied to a removable disk and used on another system. However, keep in mind that you might not be able to use your settings on an earlier version of the system.

Mapping Menu Commands

To map menu commands:

1. Open the Keyboard settings from the Project window if you are going to map a menu item to the keyboard.

2. Choose Command Palette from the Tools menu.

   The Command Palette appears.

3. Click the **Menu to Button** Reassignment box.

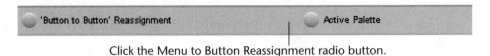

Click the Menu to Button Reassignment radio button.

4. Click a button on the keyboard or a row of buttons.

   The pointer changes to a small white menu.

5. Choose a command from a menu.

   The initials for the command appear on the button.

Menu command (in this example, Tools>Command Palette) mapped to keyboard

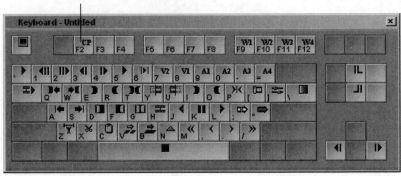

6. Close the Command Palette when you are finished.

Subclipping and Storyboarding

Mastering the following editing methods will help you work more efficiently on the Avid system.

Creating a Subclip

Subclipping is used to divide portions of one clip into shorter clips, called subclips. The original master clip used to create a subclip remains intact. In addition, a subclip edited into a sequence can be expanded to reveal more material from the original master clip. Subclipping is a great tool for organizing your footage into manageable units and for creating storyboards.

 Before you start creating subclips, adjust the Bin window to its largest size. This gives you the maximum target area to use to drag clips back to the bin.

To create a subclip:

1. Load the clip into the Source monitor.

2. Play the clip.

3. Mark an IN where you would like the subclip to begin and an OUT where you would like it to end.

4. To confirm the marks, press the Play IN to OUT (6) key.

5. To create the subclip:

    • Alt+drag the *picture* from the Source monitor to the destination bin.

    A new item appears highlighted in the bin, called *clip name.Sub.n*, where *n* is the number of subclips you have created from that clip. Notice that the subclip icon is a small version of the clip icon.

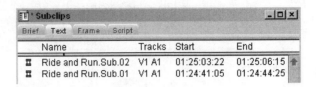

▲ **If the icon looks like a regular master clip you did not press the modifying key while dragging the picture from the Source monitor. Dragging the picture without pressing this key results in the entire master clip being copied to your bin.**

Subclipping a clip does not restrict your access to the material in the master clip when trimming or performing other editing functions.

6. Name the subclip.

When creating subclip names, it's just as important to follow a good naming scheme as when creating clip names. This will help you keep track of your footage and make the subclip easy to locate when needed.

✍ *To create a subclip, you can also click the Make Subclip button in the Tool Palette.*

 Make Subclip

Useful Applications

Use subclipping to:

- Break up an interview into one subclip per question.

- Break up a dialog scene into separate passages of dialog.

- Isolate interesting cutaways.

- Create storyboards.

Creating a Storyboard

You can storyboard clips in your bin and edit them into the sequence in the order your storyboard indicates, in one operation. You simply mark the parts of the clips you want to use, arrange them in the bin, and then make the batch edit.

Storyboarding can be used effectively with subclipping, particularly if the master clips are long and will be used more than once in the storyboard.

1. Place the bin in Frame view.

2. Arrange the clips in your bin, from left-to-right and top-to-bottom, in the order you want them to appear in your sequence. (If you need to make more room available in your bin, reduce the size of the clips by pressing Control+K in Windows or ⌘+K in Macintosh.)

3. For each clip:

   a. Play or jog through the clip using any motion control keys on the keyboard, including Play (5), Jog (1, 2, 3, and 4), JKL, and Home and End keys.

   b. Press the IN (I) and OUT (O) keys at the start and end of the material you want to use in your sequence.

   You must press the I and O keys while the footage is playing.

   If you need to manually select source tracks, open the clip in the Source monitor, mark an IN and OUT point, and select source tracks. Also, open the clip if you need to see Timecode information. You cannot do these things by playing through clips in Frame view.

   To move to the next and preceding clip in the bin, press the right and left arrow keys just left of the numeric keypad.

4. Choose one of the following to prepare the sequence:

   • If you are adding the clips to an existing sequence, mark an IN point or place the Position indicator at the location in the Timeline where you want to add the storyboarded clips and turn on the desired Record track selectors.

- Otherwise, create a new sequence. (Choose New Sequence from the Clip menu, and if prompted choose a bin.)

5. In the bin, select all the desired clips by Shift-clicking each one individually, or by dragging a lasso box around them all.

6. To splice the clips into the sequence:

- Drag the clips to the Position indicator (or edit point or IN/OUT mark) in the Timeline. (If you have created a new sequence, drag the clips into the Timeline window.)

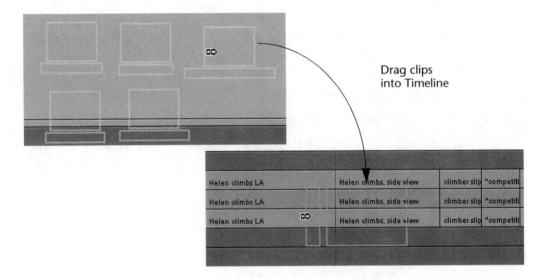

Drag clips
into Timeline

When the clips are dragged over the Timeline, the cursor changes to a yellow arrow.

The clips are automatically spliced into your sequence at the Position indicator.

To overwrite instead of splice the clips into the sequence, select the red button at the bottom of the Timeline before you drag the clips. The cursor changes to a red arrow.

Red button

Useful Applications

Use storyboard editing to:

- Scan easily through a bunch of clips (by storyboard editing them into a sequence). Save the sequence so you can scan through the clips at any time.

- Quickly assemble a rough cut.

- Assemble an entire long program from multiple sequences for output and to time the show. To do this most effectively:

  a. Number each "act" of your show so they are in story order in Text view.

  b. Load each act into the Source or Record monitor, select all tracks, and remove IN and OUT marks.

  c. Create a new sequence.

  d. Display the bin in Frame view, and arrange the sequences in "act" order.

  e. Storyboard edit the acts into one long sequence.

You can also use this technique to quickly add one or more clips into the Timeline. If you don't care about the order of the clips, you can also use this technique with the bin in Text view.

Using Locators

While marking footage you can also add Locators, electronic bookmarks that allow you to find and identify specific frames during editing. You can enter text into the comment field attached to each Locator. For example, you can use locators to:

- Identify shots that will be added later

- Provide the correct spelling for titles

- Identify where music cues or sound effects will need to be added at a later time

- Include notes for a colorist, audio mixer, or graphic artist

- Identify all remaining tasks. Thus, when all of your locators are gone, the program should be finished.

Adding Locators While Editing

Follow these instructions to add Locators to a sequence or clip:

1. Open a clip or sequence.

2. If you want to add locators to your sequence, map an Add Locator button from the More tab of the Command Palette to a button in the Tool Palette or to a key.

3. Cue to the frame where you want to add the locator. Do one of the following:

   - To add a locator to a clip, click the Add Locator button in the toolbar under the Source monitor.

   - To add a locator to the sequence, click the Add Locator button that you just mapped.

An oval appears at the bottom of the frame in the monitor, in the Position bar (on the highest highlighted track), and if you have added the locator to the sequence, in the Timeline.

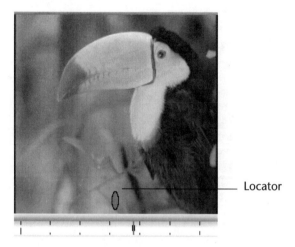

Locator

4. To add comments, click the Locator oval in the Record or Source monitor image. The Locator Window appears, allowing you to view and enter information for the current locator or other locators found in your sequence.

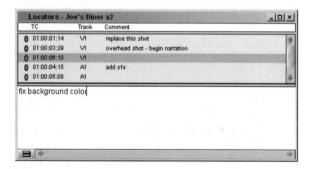

5. Type the information. The amount of information you can enter is unlimited.

6. Close the window.

The information is stored with the marked frame, and the first line of the information appears at the bottom of the clip in the monitor.

Moving to Locators

■ Use the Fast Forward and Rewind buttons in the Tool Palette to move to the next or previous locator. You can also use the Move to Previous Locator or Move to Next Locator buttons if they are mapped (from the Move tab of the Command Palette) to a button or key.

 Track selectors are ignored when using these options.

Removing Locators

To remove a Locator:

1. Go to the frame that contains the Locator.

2. Press the Delete key on the keyboard.

   The Locator is removed.

Review Questions

1. How do you customize specific features (menus, buttons, and so on) of the Avid system to suit your work preferences? See "Viewing and Changing Settings" on page 4-2.

2. When you change a setting, how can you use the setting on a different Avid system? See "Viewing and Changing Settings" on page 4-2.

3. How would you go to a frame in the sequence one second before the current location of the blue Position indicator? See "Seeking Frames" on page 4-5.

4. How would you map the Clear IN button to a blank button in the Tool Palette? See "Mapping User Selectable Buttons" on page 4-10.

5. Describe how you might use locators. See "Using Locators" on page 4-17.

Exercise 4

Subclipping and Storyboarding

Storyboarding, and optionally, subclipping, is one method for quickly creating a first cut. In this exercise, you will storyboard a brief montage that will be used as the opening of a sequence.

In this exercise you begin a sequence that you'll work on in the next few exercises, using documentary footage from ECO Challenge, Utah, an annual multi-activity sporting competition. The final sequence, when finished, will be a 40-second advertising spot promoting the Canyonlands Outdoor Adventure School in Utah.

We provide you with two versions of the exercise; perform the one that best suits your abilities and work style. For a more guided exercise, see "Subclips and Storyboards (Guided)" on next page. For a less guided exercise, see "Subclips and Storyboards (Outlined)" on page 33.

Subclips and Storyboards (Guided)

You will first create subclips from a master clip. You will then arrange the subclips in a storyboard, and edit them into a new sequence.

Changing Settings

The Auto-Save interval regulates the frequency with which the Avid system automatically saves your work. The default is 15 minutes.

To change the Auto-Save interval:

1. Click the Settings tab in the Project window.

The Project Settings window opens.

2. Double-click the Bin settings.

3. Change the Auto-Save interval, which regulates the frequency with which the Avid system automatically saves your work. Click OK.

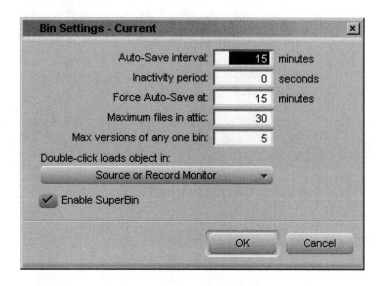

4. Click the Bins button in the Project window.

Mapping Buttons and Keys

Before subclipping and storyboarding, let's map some commands to buttons and keys. You'll then be able to use them in this and later exercises.

To map the Make Subclip button to a button in the Tool Palette:

1. Choose Command Palette from the Tools menu.

   The Command Palette appears.

2. Click the **Button to Button** Reassignment button if it's not selected.

Click the Button to Button Reassignment radio button.

3. Click the Edit tab.

4. Open the Tool Palette Fast menu. Drag your mouse off to the right of the palette. This will "tear off" the menu and leave it as a free standing palette of buttons when you release the mouse.

   If the Tool Palette has no blank buttons, drag the palette to the side so it stays open. Then drag one of its corners to enlarge it and display blank buttons.

5. Click and drag the following buttons from the Command Palette to a blank button in the Tool Palette.

   • Clear IN

   • Clear OUT

Mapping Menu Commands

The Fill Window menu command can be used to arrange the clips neatly. This command will be useful when you create your storyboard later in the exercise. You'll map this menu command to a key on the keyboard.

1. Open the Keyboard palette from the Settings option in the Project Window.

2. In the Command Palette, click the **Menu to Button** Reassignment button.

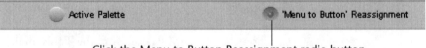

Click the Menu to Button Reassignment radio button.

The pointer changes to a small white menu.

3. Click the F8 button on the keyboard palette.

4. Choose Fill Window from the Bin menu.

The initials for the command appear on the button.

Menu command
mapped to keyboard

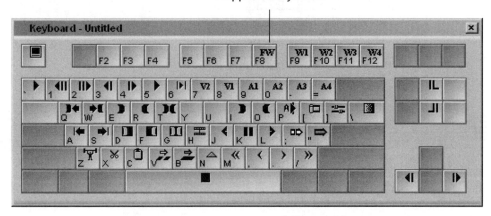

5. Close the Command palette and Keyboard palette.

6. Now, whenever you want to use the Fill Window command, press the F8 key. (You must be in Frame view to use this feature.)

Subclipping

When you are editing you want to know the content of your shots quickly. Subclipping is a great tool for giving you faster access to the contents of longer shots. In this part of the exercise, you will create subclips of a long clip, **Climbing**, to make the material more manageable.

After creating the subclips, you will storyboard edit some of them into a video montage of approximately 15 seconds.

Getting Started

1. Create a new bin and name it **Activities**. This bin will hold your subclips. Do not close the bin.

2. Move the bin into the **ECO Challenge** folder.

3. Open the bin called **ECO Selects**.

Creating Subclips

The Climbing clip is quite long, and contains separate shots. Let's create five subclips for this clip.

1. Load the **Climbing** clip from the **ECO Selects** bin into the Source monitor.

2. Mark an IN and OUT point for the first shot in the Climbing clip. Practice using the
J-K-L keys to move through the clip. *Don't worry about being frame accurate; subclipping can be done quickly. Remember you still have access to the entire clip when you trim.*

3. Alt+drag the *picture* from the Source monitor to the **Activities** bin. Release the mouse.

   A subclip appears in the bin. Its name is **Climbing, Sub.01**.

4. The subclip name is highlighted, so type a name and press Enter. Choose a meaningful name, for example: "**cl: rotate & zoom out on climber.**"

   Since you will be naming several shots with similar content, you might want to name all of the subclips of climbing with a common beginning or end, such as "cl: [name]" or "[name], cl." The reason for this will be clearer later in the course when we discuss organizing bins.

5. Create subclips for four additional shots in the climbing clip, renaming each subclip when it appears in the bin.

Storyboard Editing

In the previous section, you made your footage more accessible by creating subclips. For this part of the exercise, you will use some of these subclips to create a **15-second montage of climbing shots**. In the next exercise you will add a narration and music under this montage, and it will be the beginning of your ECO Challenge sequence.

This section takes you through the following steps: First, you will decide which subclips you want to include in the montage, and organize them into a storyboard. Then, you will mark the sections you want to use. Finally, you will edit the subclips as a batch into a new sequence.

When building the video montage, do not worry about choosing the perfect shots. Remember, this is a practice exercise. It is more important to take the time to understand what you are doing and have fun!

Arranging the Storyboard

1. Create a bin to hold your ECO Challenge sequence. Name it **ECO Sequences**. Leave the bin open.

2. Make sure the **Activities** bin is in Frame view. (With SuperBin, you can no longer see the ECO Sequences bin, but it is open.)

3. If you want to change the frame size, click once in the bin to highlight it and press Control+K (Windows) or ⌘+K (Macintosh) to shrink or Control+L (Windows) or ⌘+L (Macintosh) to enlarge.

4. Move the subclips you want to use to a clear area at the bottom of the bin, positioning them from left to right, and top to bottom, in the order you want them to appear in the sequence. You should use at least five subclips in your montage. (Keep in mind the 15-second limit, but we give you time to shorten or lengthen the montage at the end of the exercise.)

   You can quickly arrange clips in a storyboard, without paying attention to neatness or lining up frames exactly.

5. Press the F8 key to line up the subclips.

Marking the Storyboard Clips

For each subclip you will use in your storyboard:

1. Play or jog through the clip using any motion control keys on the keyboard, including Play (5), Jog (1, 2, 3, and 4), JKL, and Home and End keys.

2. Press the IN (I) and OUT (O) keys at the start and end of the material you want to use in your sequence. (Do not worry about being frame-exact. You will have a chance to trim the clips in the next section.)

   You must press the I and O keys while the footage is playing.

Creating the Storyboard

1. Select all of the subclips in your storyboard by dragging a lasso around them. Press and hold the mouse button in the gray space just to the left of the left-most subclip, then drag down and to the right. A box forms as you move.

2. Release the mouse button when the box touches all the storyboarded subclips.

   The storyboarded subclips are all highlighted.

3. There should not be a sequence in the Timeline. If there is one, clear it by choosing Clear Monitor from the Clip Name menu in the upper-right corner of the monitor.

 Closing the bin that holds the sequence will achieve the same result.

Editing the Storyboard into a New Sequence

1. Drag one of the subclips into the (empty) Timeline window. All the other subclips follow. Release the mouse.

2. If the Select a Bin dialog box appears, choose the **ECO Sequences** bin.

3. A new sequence appears in the Timeline, with all the subclips from your storyboard. The sequence is stored in the ECO Sequences bin. (If the sequence appears instead in the Activities bin, move it into the ECO Sequences bin.)

4. Name the sequence **ECO Challenge v1**.

5. Play the sequence.

Revising the Sequence

Now you should shorten or lengthen your montage to approximately 15 seconds.

1. To display the entire duration of the sequence in the Timecode display, press the Timecode display above the Record monitor and choose Dur from the pop-up menu.

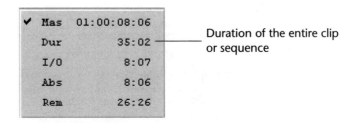

✔ Mas	01:00:08:06	
Dur	35:02	— Duration of the entire clip or sequence
I/O	8:07	
Abs	8:06	
Rem	26:26	

2. If it is exactly 15 seconds in duration, proceed to the next section, What's Next.

Use Single-Roller Trimming to shorten or lengthen the transitions. Here is the basic procedure. Refer back to the Trimming module if you need more instruction.

1. Play the sequence and decide on a shot you want to shorten or lengthen. Plan how you will trim the shot: Which transition will you trim? Will you trim the incoming or outgoing shot? Will you trim forward or backward?

2. Enter Trim mode at the appropriate transition.

3. Click the picture of the outgoing (A side) or incoming (B side) frame.

   The pink Trim mode rollers in the Timeline move to the corresponding side to be trimmed, the mouse pointer becomes a Single-Roller icon, and the corresponding Trim boxes above the Timeline are highlighted.

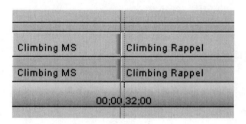

4. Use the Trim buttons (or another method you learned) to add frames to or remove frames from the selected material at the selected transition.

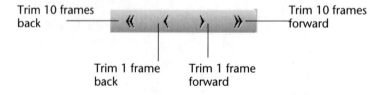

5. Play the transition.

6. Stop play.

7. Adjust the trim further, if necessary.

8. When you are satisfied, press the A (Rewind) or S (Fast Forward) key go to another transition while staying in Trim mode. (Or if you prefer, exit Trim mode and enter it again at another transition.)

9. Trim other transitions by repeating this procedure.

10. Exit Trim mode.

What's Next

If time remains, do any of the following:

- Map additional buttons and menu items to the keyboard.

- Practice the navigational tools introduced in Module 4, particularly J-K-L.

- Change other User settings you would find helpful.

Subclips and Storyboards (Outlined)

Changing Settings

1. In the Bin settings, change the Auto-save interval from 15 to 10 or 20 minutes.

2. Change any other User settings you would find helpful.

Customizing your Keyboard

Map the Clear IN, and Clear OUT buttons (and any others) from the Command Palette to a blank button or key on the keyboard.

Map the Fill Window menu item from the Bin menu (and any others) to a key on the keyboard. You can later use this key to neaten your storyboard of clips in the bin.

Subclipping

In this section you will subclip and storyboard a long clip, **Climbing**. You will use some of the subclips in a 15-second montage that will play at the start of the ECO Challenge sequence you will work on for several exercises.

1. Create a new bin to hold the subclips and name it **Activities**. Move it into the ECO Challenge folder.

2. Create at least five subclips for the **Climbing** clip, giving them meaningful names. The clip is found in the **ECO Selects** bin in the **ECO Challenge** folder.

Practice using two methods for creating subclips.

Storyboarding

1. Arrange the subclips you want to use in a storyboard, and use your Fill Window key to neaten the storyboard. You should use at least 5 subclips for the 15-second montage.

2. Mark the sections you want to use by doing the following:

   a. Play or jog through the clip using the motion keys.

   b. Press the IN and OUT keys at the start and end of the material you want to use in your sequence.

3. Drag the subclips as a batch into the (empty) Timeline window.

4. Create a new sequence and store it in a bin that will hold your ECO Challenge sequences.

Revising the Sequence

1. Display the entire duration of the sequence in the Timecode display above the Record monitor.

2. If the montage is not exactly 15 seconds long, use single-roller trimming to shorten or lengthen the sequence. (See the trimming module if you need further guidance).

When you finish this part of the exercise, and if you have more time, see "What's Next" on page 33.

Module 5

Saving Your Work

This module shows you how to save and back up your projects.

Objectives

After you complete this module, you will be able to:

- Save projects
- Back up projects and bins

Saving Your Work

When you are working on a computer-based editing system, it is important to save and back up your work. Although the Avid system automatically saves for you at regular intervals, you should get into the habit of explicitly saving your bins to protect your work in case of power outages or other mishaps.

Auto Save

The Avid system automatically saves changes to your work every 15 minutes. When this occurs, any open bins are updated with changes you have made since the last save and copies of these bins are placed in the Attic (which we cover in the appendix).

Explicit Saves

An explicit save is one where you, the user, save something you are working on. An asterisk (Windows) or diamond (Macintosh) in the title bar of your bin indicates that a change has been made since your last save.

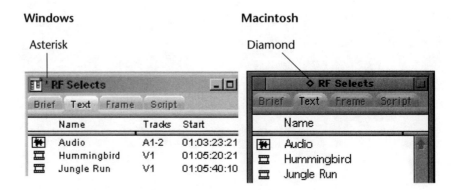

Saving a Bin

When you explicitly save a bin, a backup copy is placed in the Attic folder and your original bin file is updated.

To save a bin:

1. Click the bin to activate it.

2. Choose Save Bin from the File menu, or press Control+S (Windows) or ⌘+S (Macintosh).

   If you save the SuperBin, all bins opened in it are saved.

   The Save Bin command is dimmed if the active bin has already been saved.

Saving All Bins in a Project

1. Click the Project window to activate it, but don't select any individual bins listed in the window.

2. Choose Save All from the File menu, or press Control+S (Windows) or ⌘+S (Macintosh).

   The system saves all the open bins for the project as well as your settings.

   If your goal is to save changes to the sequence you are working on, make sure you know which bin it is in, and save that bin. If you are not sure and don't want to take the time to locate the sequence, save all your bins.

Ending the Session

When you end the session, it's a good idea to back up your project and bins onto a floppy disk, particularly if you have made a lot of changes. The following procedures outline the process for ending the session for the Windows and Macintosh systems.

Ending the Session for Windows

The following procedure explains how to back up your project to disk:

1. Choose Exit from the File menu to exit Avid Xpress DV and return to Windows.

2. Respond to the prompt asking if you want your work saved.

   The system saves the project, closes the Avid application, and puts you back to the desktop.

3. Insert a floppy disk into the disk drive.

   If you have a large Project folder, consider backing up to a removable drive, such as a CD-ROM drive, or use multiple floppy disks.

4. If the disk is unformatted, format it by double-clicking the "My Computer" icon and choosing Format from the File menu.

5. Open the C: drive.

6. Open the Program Files folder, Avid folder, and Avid Projects folder.

7. Back up the entire project or selected bins to the floppy disk.

   • If backing up the entire project, drag the Project folder with bins and projects enclosed to the floppy disk.

   • If backing up selected bins, double-click the Project folder that contains the bin(s) you want to back up, and drag the bin icon(s) to the floppy disk.

   You can also right-click the appropriate folder, select Copy, and right-click the destination drive and select Paste.

8. When the system finishes copying the files, eject the disk.

9. Exit Windows and turn off the system.

10. Turn off the rest of your hardware.

✍ *For safety, you should save at least a week's worth of work on separate disks rather than backing up on a single disk.*

Ending the Session for Macintosh

1. Choose Quit from the File menu.

   The system saves the project and closes the Avid application.

2. Insert a floppy disk into the disk drive.

✍ *If you have a large Project folder, consider backing up to a removable drive, such as a CD-ROM drive, or use multiple floppy disks.*

3. If the disk is blank, click Initialize both times the prompt appears in the dialog box, and name the disk if prompted.

4. Open the Avid drive.

5. Open the Avid Projects folder.

6. Back up the entire project or selected bins.

   • If backing up the entire project, drag the Project folder with bins and projects enclosed to the floppy disk.

   • If backing up selected bins, double-click the Project folder that contains the bin(s) you want to back up, and drag the bin icon(s) to the floppy disk.

7. When the system finishes copying the files, eject the disk.

8. Choose Shut Down from the Special menu.

9. After a few seconds, turn off the rest of your hardware.

✍ *For safety, you should save at least a week's worth of work on separate disks rather than backing up on a single disk.*

Review Questions

1. How do you explicitly save the sequence you are working on? See "Explicit Saves" on page 5-2.

2. What does an asterisk or diamond in the title bar of your bin indicate? Circle one of the following. See "Explicit Saves" on page 5-2.

   a. That the active bin was just saved by the auto command.

   b. That the bin has been altered since your last save.

3. You need to abruptly end your session. Do you need to explicitly (manually) save your work before leaving the Avid application? Please explain. See "Ending the Session" on page 5-4.

4. (Windows) True or False: To back up a bin, you can right-click the appropriate file, select Copy, and right-click the destination folder or drive and select Paste. See "Ending the Session" on page 5-4.

Exercise 5

Backing Up Your Project

In this exercise, you will back up your project and bins. You should do this at the end of each session, whether for this course or in your own work.

We provide you with two versions of the exercise; perform the one that best suits your abilities and work style. For a more guided exercise, see "Ending the Session (Guided)" on this page. For a less guided exercise, see "Ending the Session (Outlined)" on page 8.

Ending the Session (Guided)

When you are ready to end the session, back up your project and bins onto a floppy disk. The following procedures outline the process for ending the session for the Windows and Macintosh systems.

Ending the Session for Windows

The following procedure explains how to back up your project to diskette:

1. Choose Exit from the File menu to exit the Avid application and return to Windows.

2. Respond to the prompt asking if you want your work saved.

   The system saves the project, closes the Avid application, and puts you back to the desktop.

3. Insert a floppy disk into the disk drive.

4. If the disk is unformatted, format it by double-clicking the "My Computer" icon and choosing Format from the File menu.

5. Open C:\Program Files\Avid\Avid Xpress DV\Avid Projects folder.

6. To back up the entire **Avid Editing** project, drag the Avid Editing Project folder with bins and project files enclosed to the floppy disk (3 1/2 Floppy (A:) in Windows Explorer or "My Computer").

You can also right-click the appropriate folder, select Copy, and right-click the destination drive and select Paste.

7. When the system finishes copying the files, eject the disk.

8. Exit Windows and turn off the system.

Ending the Session for Macintosh

1. Choose Quit from the File menu.

   The system saves the project and closes the Avid application.

2. Insert a floppy disk into the disk drive.

3. If the disk is blank, click Initialize both times the prompt appears in the dialog box, and name the disk if prompted.

4. Open the Avid drive.

5. Open the Avid Projects folder.

6. To back up the entire Avid Editing project, drag the Avid Editing Project folder with bins and project files enclosed to the floppy disk.

7. When the system finishes copying the files, eject the disk.

8. Choose Shut Down from the Special menu.

Ending the Session (Outlined)

■ At the end of the session, be sure to back up your project to floppy disk.

Module 6

Editing Dialog

Working with synced dialog requires that you pay close attention to your edits, especially when trimming. Avid Xpress DV provides a host of tools to help you maintain sync and to regain sync should you lose it.

This module stresses a problem-solving approach to the intricacies of working with dialog and audio.

Objectives

Upon completion of this module, you will be able to:

- Trim dialog
- Create split edits
- Prevent breaking sync and regain sync

Trimming Dialog

You use single-roller trimming to trim the shots in a scene until you like the rhythm of the dialog (at this point, you are not considering the visuals). This focus on dialog cutting is often referred to as the radio edit. The dialog should flow smoothly, with an appropriate speed and rhythm for the scene. Remember, single-roller trims reveal or remove frames from the outgoing or incoming shot of a transition.

To review single-roller trim:

1. Enter Trim mode.

2. Activate the Record track selectors for the synced tracks.

3. Click the picture of the outgoing (A side) or incoming (B side) frame.

4. Add frames to or remove frames from the selected material at the selected transition, by using the Trim buttons (or any other method you have learned).

5. Click the Play Transition button or press the 5 key.

6. To stop, click the Play Transition button again, or press the 5 key or Space bar.

7. Exit Trim mode.

Creating Split Edits

After you have trimmed the dialog of a scene using single-roller trimming, the dialog sounds good. However, the sequence is still a series of straight cuts, where the video and audio start and end at the same point. This can be monotonous for the viewer. Also, if you look at the visuals, you will undoubtedly see things to correct at the beginning and end of shots, such as an incomplete action or an inappropriate expression.

Split edits to the rescue! You use split edits to trim the audio and video separately, to vary the rhythm of a dialog scene and to fix problems. A split edit (also called an L-cut or overlap cut) is one in which the video and audio start or end at different points. For example, you might use a split edit to linger on Character A's reaction while hearing Character B begin to respond. You can create a split edit by using dual-roller trimming.

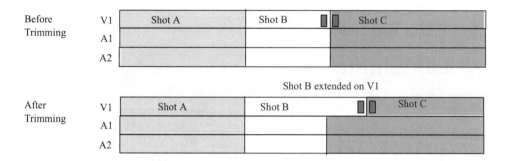

Before Trimming

Shot B extended on V1

After Trimming

Useful Applications

In dialog editing, use split edits to:

- Extend the video of Character A so it overlaps with the beginning of Character B's audio.

  Conversely, split edits are also used to extend one person's audio over the video of a different person.

- Vary the rhythm and tempo of the edit.

Creating Split Edits Using Dual-Roller Trims

1. Start by editing a sequence using straight cuts.

2. Enter Trim mode at the transition where you want the split edit to occur.

3. Turn off the track selector(s) for either audio or video, depending on whether you want to extend the video over the audio or the audio under the video.

4. With both sides of the transition selected, slide the edit point right or left on the Timeline.

   You can also use any other trim method to adjust the edit point.

5. Play your edit while still in Trim mode.

6. Exit Trim mode.

Maintaining Sync

Working with dialog and other synced sound brings with it the possibility of losing sync. If you understand the common ways of breaking sync and the tools Avid Xpress DV provides to keep sync, you can save yourself a lot of time and avoid problems.

Common Ways of Breaking Sync

- Trimming only one side of a transition, without selecting all tracks

- Extracting frames from only the video or audio track

- Splicing in only audio or video

- Moving only audio or video when using segment editing (to be covered in the next module)

Ways to Prevent Breaking Sync

- When trimming a single track, always trim with both sides of the transition selected.

- Whenever you add to or subtract frames from one track, also add to or subtract them from the other. It is especially helpful to remember this rule when trimming, splicing, or extracting.

- Alternatively, whenever you want to add to or subtract frames from one track, use lift or overwrite instead of extract or splice.

- Work with Sync Locks turned on.

Trimming with Sync-Locked Tracks

Sync-locking tracks enables you to lock several tracks of audio in sync with one another, or lock the audio to the video. When it is enabled, Sync Lock is applied to the entire sequence.

Sync Lock maintains sync by preventing you from removing footage from only some of the locked tracks. This feature will also add filler to non-selected locked tracks to maintain sync when you add material. (If filler is added to an audio track, you will probably need to fill the gap with "nat" sound.)

Sync-locked tracks only aid single-roller trims, because dual-roller trims cannot break sync between tracks.

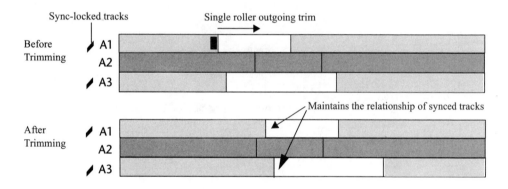

Turning Sync Lock On

To trim with sync-locked tracks:

1. In the Timeline, click the box to the left of each Record track selector that you want to keep in sync. The sync lock icon appears next to each track.

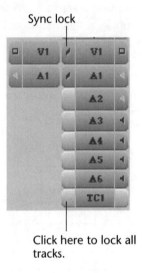

Sync lock

Click here to lock all tracks.

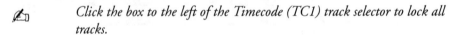 *Click the box to the left of the Timecode (TC1) track selector to lock all tracks.*

2. Enter Trim mode and perform any necessary single-roller trims. You will see following results:

   • When you lengthen the A side or B side of an edit with sync locks turned on, any sync-locked tracks whose segments are not included in the trim will have "filler" added to maintain the sync relationship.

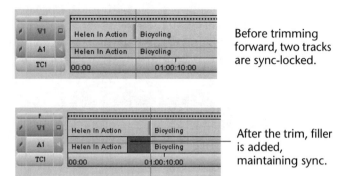

Before trimming forward, two tracks are sync-locked.

After the trim, filler is added, maintaining sync.

- When you shorten the A side or the B side of an edit with sync-locks turned on, the system prevents the edit from happening. The Avid system does not allow you to remove material to maintain sync. Instead you receive an audible alert sound indicating that the system cannot maintain the sync relationship without sacrificing the integrity of other edits.

    Here's an explanation of why the system lets you add, but not remove, material when using sync locks:

    - Adding filler to other tracks to maintain sync is an obvious change to the timeline. The editor should notice the change and be able to make a fix, if necessary.

    - Removing material from the other tracks is not easily detected by an editor and may go unnoticed. The system prevents an editor from making this mistake and forces the editor to make a conscious decision about how to fix the edit.

3. Turn off Sync Lock by clicking the sync lock icons.

    Sync locks are automatically disabled when you end the editing session.

🖎 *You might want to use Sync Lock while you are learning to use Avid Xpress DV. It can also be useful in complex sequences that have extensive sound effects or video effects (because these tracks tend to have a lot of filler).*

Fixing Broken Sync Using Sync Breaks

By default, the Timeline displays sync breaks whenever they occur during editing. These appear at break points as positive or negative numbers indicating the number of frames out of sync. Sync-break offset numbers appear only in the affected track(s).

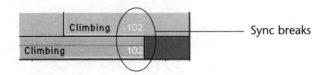 Sync breaks

 Sync Breaks show the amount that two tracks from the same clip are out of sync, for example, the video is out of sync with the sync sound, or audio from the same source master clip.

Sync Break information is not displayed if the audio and video tracks come from different sources.

Using Trim Mode to Correct Sync

In Trim mode, you can restore the frames to sync by performing one or more single-roller trims on the out-of-sync track(s). To reverse the sync break, you trim the exact number of sync-break frames displayed in the Timeline. Dual-roller trims do not remove sync breaks.

To fix broken sync:

1. Enter Trim mode at the first transition that displays a number.

2. Using single-roller trim, add or subtract the appropriate number of frames.

   - If the number shown in the Timeline is negative, you know that track is delayed by that number of frames. You will need to add to one side of the edit on one track.

   - If the number shown in the Timeline is positive, it is ahead of the other track by that many frames. You will need to remove frames from one side of the edit on one track.

☞ *To determine whether the video or audio is out of sync, listen to the area before and into the material that goes out of sync (it may help to close your eyes and pay attention to the rhythm of the audio).*

☞ *If both audio and video are out of sync, first adjust one and then sync up the other.*

▲ **Simply removing the white numbers does not mean the original edit has been fixed. A sync break can be fixed while altering the original edit. To make sure that your sequence is in sync, play it and carefully review the repaired section for errors.**

Review Questions

1. To create a split edit, would you use a single-roller or dual-roller trim? See "Creating Split Edits" on page 6-2.

2. Describe a situation where you would want to hold on Character A's image while cutting to Character B's dialog?

3. Describe a situation where you would want to hold on Character A's dialog while cutting to the visual of Character B?

4. Which type of edit are you more likely to break sync with: a splice or an overwrite edit? See "Common Ways of Breaking Sync" on page 6-4.

5. What's wrong with this single-roller trim?

6. You are cutting a dialog sequence, and so far you have been cutting tight on the dialog. At the climax of the sequence, a character hears shocking news. You would like to show the person's reaction before he speaks. To add footage to the head of the shot (underline the appropriate choices):

   a. Select the transition in the Timeline between this shot and the [*preceding/following*] shot.

   b. Select the Trim window for the [*outgoing/incoming*] shot.

   c. Trim the head of this shot by [*adding/removing*] the appropriate number of frames (typing a *negative/positive* number).

7. A person speaks a line of dialog, followed by one word of the next sentence. To remove the extraneous word (underline the appropriate choices):

   a. Select the transition in the Timeline between this shot and the [*preceding/following*] shot.

   b. Select the Trim window for the [*outgoing/incoming*] shot.

   c. Trim the tail of this shot by [*adding/removing*] the appropriate number of frames (typing a *negative/positive* number).

Exercise 6

Editing Dialog

You are developing an educational CD-ROM that uses "real-life" situations to teach students math and science. Your assignment is to edit a dialog scene that takes place in a hospital's Trauma Room, a room in the Emergency wing. The scene's characters include Susan and Fred, a doctor and nurse working in the Trauma Room; Jennifer Bates, an unconscious patient; and Mrs. Bates, Jennifer's mother.

This exercise has two parts: You begin by quickly editing the scene; then you trim the shots to improve the rhythm of the dialog and to create split edits.

Getting Started

If you have quit Avid Xpress DV:

1. Launch Avid Xpress DV.

2. In the Project Selection dialog box, highlight the **Avid Editing** project and click OK.

Once in the Avid Editing project follow these steps:

1. Close any ECO Challenge bins that are open.

2. Create a new bin and name it **Trauma Room Sequences**. Do not close the bin.

3. Move the bin into the **Trauma Room** folder.

4. Open the bin called **Trauma Room Selects**.

5. Watch all of the scene's clips.

   There are several basic shots: Master Shot, Fred's single, and Susan's single. There are also a few cutaway (B-roll) shots.

To create a new sequence:

1. Choose New Sequence from the Clip menu.

   In the dialog box that appears, choose the **Trauma Room Sequences** bin.

2. Name your new sequence something meaningful like Trauma Room Cut 1.

Part 1: Assembling the Sequence

You have a choice of how to build this sequence. The instructions for three methods are outlined below. As you proceed, keep in mind the following points:

Don't worry about being frame accurate; initial assembling can be done quickly. After you edit the first cut, you will trim it.

Mark your IN and OUT points quickly. Remember you can edit rough and then fine-tune later.

- Method 1: Use the Splice function to add shots one at a time into the sequence, following the order of the script.

- Method 2: Start by laying down the master shot, and then overwrite shots from the Fred and Susan clips. If time permits, add material from the cutaways.

- Method 3: Use subclipping and storyboarding:

   a. Create another new bin and name it **Trauma Room Subclips**.

   b. Move the bin into the **Trauma Room** folder.

   c. Create subclips for each line (or several lines) of dialog, and store them in the **Trauma Room Subclips** folder.

d. Create a good naming scheme for your subclips.

For example: **MS: I'm getting vitals** stands for Master Shot, followed by a few words of dialog.

e. Create a storyboard of the subclips you want to use and batch edit them into your new sequence.

f. If time permits, add material from the cutaways.

Part 2: Fine Tuning the Dialog

While you will not be given specific tasks in this part of the exercise, you should perform the following activities:

1. Before creating split edits, use Trim mode (using single-roller trimming and activating all record track selectors) to trim the shots until you like the rhythm of the dialog.

2. Create one or more split edits using Trim mode.

3. If you did not finish the rough cut and you have finished creating split edits, continue editing and refining the remainder of the sequence.

Do not use sync locks for this exercise. If you lose sync, fix it by using Trim mode or Undo (Control+Z (Windows) or ⌘ +Z (Macintosh)).

Script for "Trauma Room"

▲ The characters occasionally ad lib, so the words they speak may be
somewhat different from the words on the page.

ACT ONE

SCENE D

(Susan, Fred, Mrs. Bates, Jennifer Bates)

INT. TRAUMA ROOM

*Susan, the doctor, and Fred, the nurse, examine
Jennifer, while Mrs. Bates (Jennifer's mother)
stands by.*

SUSAN

What's up?

FRED

I'm just getting her vitals in. She's 110
pounds, age 15, and respiration is 28.

MRS. BATES

Is 28 high?

SUSAN

Yes, 28's higher than normal.

FRED

Pulse is 125.

MRS. BATES

How's that? I mean is 125 a good pulse or what?

SUSAN

Mrs. Bates, we need to look at the entire
situation before we can make a decision....
Anything else, Fred? How's her blood pressure?

FRED

BP's 90 over 60.

SUSAN

90 over 60, okay. What about her temperature?

FRED

Temperature is 38 Celsius.

SUSAN

38 Celsius, fine. Anything else?

FRED

Yeah, not responding to stimuli.

SUSAN

Right, let's move on this right away. I want a
glucose reading with a finger stick, a complete
blood count, and a chem 7 panel.

FRED

Glucose, blood count, and a chem 7. Got it.

SUSAN

Oh, and Fred, check the blood gases, too. I'm
going to run down to the lab and see if I can't
light a fire under these guys to get them done
stat. And Fred? Make sure she doesn't go into a
coma.

Module 7

Working in the Timeline

For basic editing, you load clips into the Source monitor and edit the material into a sequence in the Record monitor. To revise and fine-tune the sequence, you can edit in the Timeline.

This module explains the different ways you can use the Timeline to edit.

Objectives

After you complete this module, you will be able to:

- Add and patch tracks
- Edit segments in the Timeline
- Slip and slide segments in the Timeline

Adding and Patching Tracks

You can edit up to 8 audio tracks and up to 8 video tracks on Xpress DV.

Typically, you create a new sequence by splicing video and audio from your source tracks into the Timeline. For example, you might start a new sequence by splicing a clip with source tracks V1, A1, and A2 to the Timeline. The material is spliced to record tracks V1, A1, and A2. The sequence automatically creates the record tracks when you make that first edit. In fact, each new sequence displays V1, V2, and A1-A4 by default.

However, you may at some point need to add more tracks than are contained in your sequence. You need to explicitly add these tracks. For example, you can add tracks A5 and A6 to the sequence.

In addition, you may need to patch video or audio from tracks on the source to different tracks on the record. For example, after you add tracks A5 and A6 to the sequence, you can patch A1 from your source clip to A5 in the sequence and patch A2 in your source clip to A6 in your sequence.

Adding Tracks

Adding the Next Audio or Video Track

To add the next audio track:

■ With a sequence in the Timeline, choose New Audio Track from the Clip menu, right-click the Timeline window and choose New Audio Track (Windows), or press Control+U (Windows) or ⌘+U (Macintosh).

For example, if the sequence currently includes tracks A1-A4, the system adds track A5.

To add the next video track:

■ Repeat the above, substituting Video for Audio, and Y for U.

Adding a Specific Audio or Video Track

Sometimes you will want to add a specific audio or video track. For example, your sequence currently uses tracks A1-A2, but you want to put all audio effects on tracks A5 and A6.

To add a specific audio track:

1. While holding down the Alt (Windows) or Option (Macintosh) key, choose New Audio Track from the Clip menu or press Control+Alt+U (Windows) or ⌘+Option+U (Macintosh). A dialog box appears allowing you to select a specific track.

2. Select A (Audio) and the desired track from the two pop-up menus and click OK.

   An empty track is added to your Timeline.

To add a specific video track:

■ Repeat the above, substituting Video for Audio, and Y for U.

Patching Tracks

Patching tracks enables you to edit a source track onto a different track in the sequence. For example, you would patch source track A1 to record track A5 if the audio is on track A1 in the source clip, but you want to add it to track A5 in the Timeline.

To patch a track from a source clip to a different track in the sequence:

■ Press the source track panel and drag the arrow to the record track on which you want to make the edit.

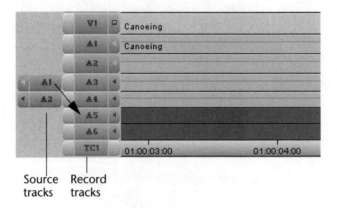

Source   Record
tracks   tracks

The source track you selected jumps next to the record track and is highlighted.

Editing Segments in the Timeline

You can reposition one or more segments in the Timeline using the Segment Mode buttons found below the Timeline.

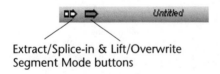

Extract/Splice-in & Lift/Overwrite
Segment Mode buttons

• Extract/Splice-in (yellow Segment Mode button) rearranges the order of segments within the Timeline.

• Lift/Overwrite (red Segment Mode button) repositions a segment in the Timeline, leaving black filler or silence at the original location, and placing the shot at the new location.

▲ Do not confuse these buttons with the Splice and Overwrite buttons.

▲ Segment Mode Editing mode ignores Sync Locks, so it is very easy to put your sequence out of sync when working in this mode.

Extracting and Splicing-in Segments

Extract/Splice-in can be used to move a selected segment forward or backward in the sequence. The Extract/Splice-in procedure extracts a segment, closes the gap, and splices in the segment at its new position.

The total duration of the sequence does not change when you use Extract/Splice-in segment editing.

To reposition one or more segments using Extract/Splice-in:

1. To prepare to Extract/Splice-in, do one of the following:

   • Click the yellow Extract/Splice-in Segment mode button to highlight the button. Then click a segment you want to edit.

   • While in Source/Record mode, lasso the area you want to reposition by drawing a lasso from *left to right* around the entire segment(s).

     Note that drawing a lasso right to left around segments in the Timeline while in Source/Record mode will automatically enable Slip and Slide mode, which will be covered later in the module.

     The cursor changes to a Segment pointer.

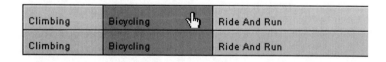

2. To include additional segments within the Segment mode edit, press the Shift key and click or lasso additional *adjacent* segments.

   Once a single segment is selected, you can Shift+lasso from left or right or right to left to add other segments. You will not be forced into Slip and Slide mode by lassoing from left to right.

3. Drag the segment horizontally and/or vertically to a new position. (If you selected multiple adjacent segments, you only need to drag one of the selected clips; the others will follow.)

Climbing	Bicycling	Ride And Run	
Climbing	Bicycling	Ride And Run	

 To snap a segment to the tail of a shot, Control+Alt+drag the segment.

 You cannot reposition a segment to any frame in the Timeline. You can only snap to another edit point (on any track), the blue Position indicator, or an IN or OUT mark.

The Avid system extracts the selected segment from its old position, closing the gap left by its removal, then splices the material back into the sequence at the new location.

The insertion point is located at the frame before the head of the segment you're dragging into position.

4. Click the Extract/Splice-in Segment mode button again to leave Segment mode and return to Source/Record mode.

Useful Application

Use Extract/Splice-in to rearrange shots in a sequence.

Lifting and Overwriting

If you use the Lift/Overwrite (red) Segment Mode button instead of the Extract/Splice-in button, the lifted segment replaces material at the new position, while leaving filler in its previous position.

The total duration of the sequence is unaffected unless you place the segment you're moving beyond the end of the sequence.

It's often better to use the Lift/Overwrite Segment Mode button when you move from track to track. If you don't, dragging to a different track will pull up all later segments on the track you're moving from, and push down all segments on the track you're moving to.

Useful Application

Use Lift/Overwrite to:

- Move sound effects on an audio track

- Move a title to a new location on the Timeline

- Move audio segments from one track to another to create an audio overlap

Removing Segments Using Segment Mode

In an earlier module, you learned how to extract and lift material from the sequence. You can also use Segment mode to remove clips from a sequence, either closing or retaining the gap that results.

To remove material from the Timeline using Segment mode:

1. Click one of the Segment Mode buttons at the bottom of Source/Record monitor.

    - Extract/Splice-in (yellow) will extract the selected segments.

    - Lift/Overwrite (red) will lift the selected segments.

2. Select a clip in the Timeline, and Shift-click additional clips on the same or other tracks. They do not have to be adjacent.

3. Press Delete to extract or lift the selected material, *depending on the Segment Mode button you selected.*

    If there is an effect or audio gain automation on any segment in your selection, this action will remove it and not the clip. Select the clip again and press Delete to remove the clip.

4. Click the Segment Mode button again to deselect it.

Useful Application

Use the Lift/Overwrite Segment Mode button (or the Lift button) to lift a shot from the sequence, holding its place with filler until you choose the replacement shot.

Slipping and Sliding Segments

In addition to Trimming and Segment Mode Editing, Avid Xpress DV has two more functions that allow you to alter the position or contents of various shots within your timeline: Slipping and Sliding. Slipping and sliding are forms of trimming, where two consecutive transitions are trimmed simultaneously.

Slip Mode: to change the contents of shot

Slip Left   Slip Right

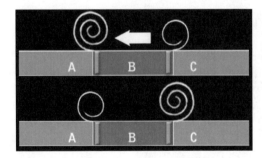
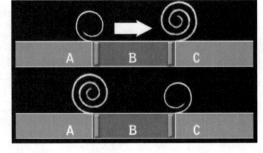

Slide Mode: to change the position of a shot

Slide Left

Slide Right

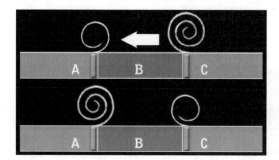 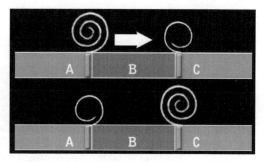

Slipping a Shot

You can slip a shot in your sequence, keeping its duration and its position in the Timeline the same, but changing its contents to earlier or later material in the master clip.

To slip a shot:

1. While in Source/Record mode, drag a lasso around the entire segment in the Timeline, from right to left.

   (Windows) Or, while in Trim mode, right-click in the Timeline window and choose Select Slip Trim from the menu.

Notice the four new pictures at the top of the monitor.

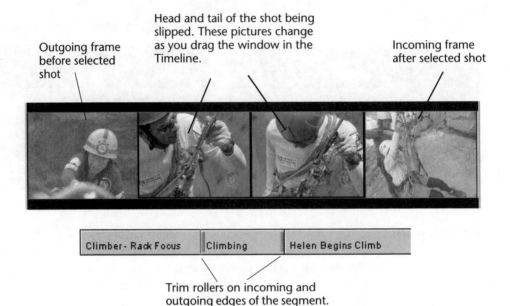

Outgoing frame before selected shot

Head and tail of the shot being slipped. These pictures change as you drag the window in the Timeline.

Incoming frame after selected shot

Climber - Rack Focus | Climbing | Helen Begins Climb

Trim rollers on incoming and outgoing edges of the segment.

The first picture is the outgoing frame before the selected shot; the last picture is the incoming frame after the selected shot. The middle two pictures are the head and tail of the shot you are slipping.

2. In the Timeline, press one of the selected heads or tails (it doesn't matter which), with the tail of the Trim mode cursor pointed toward the center of the segment you are sliding, then drag the selected material to the left or right.

Notice that the first and last pictures remain static as you drag, because you are not changing the position of the shot in the sequence. The middle two pictures (the first and last frames of the selected segment) change, because you are changing the content of the shot itself.

Dragging right reveals later material; dragging left reveals earlier material.

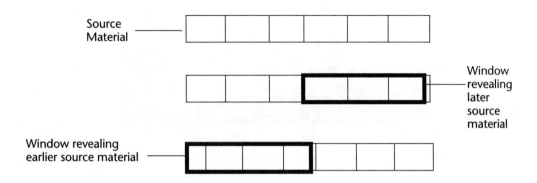

Source Material

Window revealing later source material

Window revealing earlier source material

Sliding a Shot

Sliding is similar to slipping, but instead of changing the shot itself, sliding trims the shots on either side. The end result is that your shot's position is changed (slid) in the sequence. In addition, the tail of the previous shot and the head of the following shot change.

To slide a shot:

1. While in Source/Record mode hold the Shift+Alt (Windows) or Option (Macintosh) key and drag a lasso from right to left around the material you want to slide.

    (Windows) Or, while in Trim mode, right-click in the Timeline window, and choose Select Slide Trim from the menu.

The same four pictures at the top of the monitor that we saw in Slip mode are also displayed.

In the Timeline, the Trim rollers are located on the outgoing and incoming frames preceding and following the segment.

Outgoing Frame 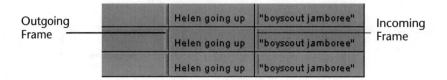 Incoming Frame

2. In the Timeline, press one of the selected heads or tails (it doesn't matter which), and drag left or right.

- Dragging to the right simultaneously extends the tail of the preceding shot, and reduces the head of the following shot, thus moving the segment to a later master timecode.

- Dragging to the left simultaneously reduces the tail of the preceding shot and extends the head of the following shot, thus moving the selected segment to an earlier master timecode.

Notice that the four pictures we had when we slipped a shot in the previous section update differently when we slide a segment. Because we are trimming the outgoing and incoming frames before and after the segment, it is these pictures that change as we drag. The middle two pictures, the first and last frames of the segment, remain static and unchanged.

Sliding vs. Segment Editing

The Slip and Slide display is very similar to the Segment Mode display. Sliding a clip is similar in many ways to performing a Segment Mode edit, but there are important differences between the two functions.

- Segment Mode Lift/Overwrite leaves a gap in the sequence at the original location of the clip that is moved.

- Segment Mode Extract/Splice inserts a clip at a new location. If the insertion point is not at an existing edit, the remaining frames of the shot are moved downstream.

- Sliding does not allow you to skip over other clips to an entirely new location in the sequence. Sliding is essentially a two-sided trim with a clip (or clips) in the middle.

Review Questions

1. If your Timeline displays tracks A1-A4, how would you display track A5? See "Adding and Patching Tracks" on page 7-2.

2. In Segment mode, how can you select multiple segments? See "Editing Segments in the Timeline" on page 7-4.

3. When Segment editing, what modifier key, if any, do you hold to snap the head of a segment to a transition? See "Editing Segments in the Timeline" on page 7-4.

4. Scenario: You are editing a three-shot sequence, and the first and third shots are perfect in terms of the IN and OUT points. The second shot, however, starts and ends too soon. Do you slip or slide the second shot? See "Slipping and Sliding Segments" on page 7-8.

5. What are the key differences between using Segment Mode Editing and using the Slide function? See "Sliding vs. Segment Editing" on page 7-12.

Exercise 7

Working in the Timeline

In this exercise, you continue to edit the advertising spot promoting the Canyonlands Outdoor Adventure School in Utah that you have been working on. The sequence will have extended voice-over narration, music, and some sync sound in the form of interviews with participants.

We provide you with two versions of the exercise; perform the one that best suits your abilities and work style. For a more guided exercise, see "Working in the Timeline (Guided)" on this page. For a less guided exercise, see "Working in the Timeline (Outlined)" on page 22.

Working in the Timeline (Guided)

For this exercise you continue to build the ECO Challenge sequence you created in the subclipping and storyboarding exercise.

You began editing this sequence by storyboard editing some climbing subclips. You will now add a narration and music track, and add additional video-only shots and a short interview segment. This exercise then focuses on how to manipulate shots in the sequence by rearranging and slipping them.

In the next exercises, you will continue to work on this sequence by adjusting audio levels and pan, and adding titles.

Because you have already practiced many of the tools that you need to cut this job, we provide less detailed instruction than in previous exercises. In some cases, however, it is necessary to follow specific instructions in order to demonstrate certain editing features.

Getting Started

1. In the **Avid Editing** project, open the **ECO Challenge** folder and the **ECO Sequences** bin.

2. If your **ECO Challenge** sequence is not loaded in the Timeline, please do so now.

3. Here is a transcription of the script you will use for the sequence.

ECO Challenge Narration

VOICE OVER

ARE YOU LOOKING FOR A CHALLENGE? DO YOU WANT TO TEST YOUR PHYSICAL AND MENTAL ENDURANCE TO THEIR LIMIT? THEN COME TO BEAUTIFUL SOUTHERN UTAH AND THE CANYONLANDS OUTDOOR ADVENTURE SCHOOL.

THE CANYONLANDS ADVENTURE SCHOOL OFFERS WEEK-LONG, INTENSIVE EXPEDITIONS WHERE YOU'LL MASTER THE SKILLS REQUIRED FOR RAPPELLING, HIKING, MOUNTAIN BIKING, WHITEWATER RAFTING, AND HORSEBACK RIDING.

THE CANYONLANDS OUTDOOR ADVENTURE SCHOOL: 1-800 OUT-DOOR.

Laying Down the Narration and Music

In this section you will lay down the narration and music tracks and continue building the video track.

Editing the Narration onto Track A2

1. Open the **Audio** bin and load the **Narration for ECO Challenge spot** clip into the Source monitor.

2. Play the clip and mark an IN where the narration starts and an OUT where the narration ends.

3. If your sequence has only one audio track, choose New Audio Track from the Clip menu to add the A2 audio track to the sequence.

4. Patch Source track A1 to Record track A2.

5. Make sure only source A1 and record A2 tracks are selected.

6. Place the Position indicator at the head of the sequence and clear IN and OUT marks, if present.

7. Click the red Overwrite button to edit the narration.

8. If a dialog box appears, choose the **ECO Sequences** bin to hold your sequence.

   Notice that the Timeline now has the narration on A2, and that the sequence now extends beyond the montage.

Editing the Music onto A3

Now you will add a music bed under the narration.

1. Play the **Music for ECO Challenge Spot** clip (which is in the **ECO Audio** bin) and mark an IN at the exact beginning of the music. (There is no need to mark an OUT at the end.)

2. Mark an IN in the beginning **of your sequence** and an OUT at the end.

3. If your sequence has only two audio tracks, choose New Audio Track from the Clip menu to add the A3 audio track to the sequence.

4. Patch Source track A2 to Record track A3.

5. Make sure only source A2 and record A3 tracks are selected.

6. Click the Overwrite button.

7. Play the sequence.

> The music cuts off at the end. We will fix that later.

Adding a Short Montage of Activities

Now, you'll build a short montage. Later you will slip some of the shots to change their content.

■ Using clips from the ECO Selects bin, build a series of video-only shots over this voice-over narration: "RAPPELLING, HIKING, MOUNTAIN BIKING, WHITEWATER RAFTING, AND HORSEBACK RIDING."

Consider the following as you build this montage:

• You can solo the narration track to isolate that audio.

• There are several ways you can add video-only shots. Which way will you use?

Fine-tuning the Sequence

In this section you will fine-tune the sequence by moving segments in the Timeline and slipping edits.

Moving Segments in the Timeline

Now experiment a little by swapping the order of any two clips in your opening climbing montage. If you think you might prefer your existing cut, how can you return to it after you swap the two clips? (There are at least two ways.)

1. Select the yellow Extract/Splice-in arrow at the bottom of the Timeline.

2. Shift-click the clip (on tracks V1 and A1) in the Timeline you want to swap to highlight it.

3. To snap the clip to the head of the other clip, drag the clip to the right or left. When the clip you're moving snaps to the insertion point, release the mouse.

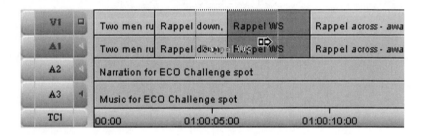

The order of your two clips is swapped.

4. Deselect the Extract/Splice-In button.

5. Play your sequence to view the result.

6. Swap any other shots in the montage.

Slipping a Shot in the Timeline

To prepare for this part of the exercise, we'll add part of the Ride and run clip.

1. In your sequence, park the Position indicator on the first frame of black after the opening climbing montage. Clear any IN and OUT marks.

2. Load the **Ride and run** clip from the **Selects** bin into the Source monitor.

3. Mark an IN and OUT to isolate the rider's dialog: "SUPER!
   COULDN'T BE BETTER! THIS IS SO AWESOME! THIS IS SO
   EXCITING!"

4. Set the track panel to record V1 and A1.

5. Click the Overwrite button.

6. Play the section.

We don't need to include all of the rider's exclamations. So let's slip the
shot a little later to omit the word, "Super!" Slipping it allows you to
keep the duration of the clip the same, and maintain the timing of the
edits downstream.

1. Enter Slip mode by dragging a lasso from upper right (starting **above**
   the Timeline) to lower left around tracks V1 and A1 of the **Ride and
   Run** clip.

   Make sure you lasso both V1 and A1 or you will go out of sync in
   the next step.

   *If you accidentally lasso your clips from left to right, you will end up in
   Segment mode. Click the highlighted Segment Mode button at the
   bottom of the Timeline to exit this mode and start again.*

   The system enters Slip mode where you can now view the first
   and last frames of the clip.

First frame   Last frame

2. Slip the clip to later material using the Trim buttons or the numeric
   keypad. (Slip approximately + 1/2 second for good results).

3. Press 5 to play the result.

4. Press 5 again to stop.

Practicing Slipping On Your Own

Here, you'll slip some of the shots in the short montage you created over the dialog, "rappelling, hiking, mountain biking, whitewater rafting, and horseback riding," to change their content. We provide suggestions, but feel free to make your own decisions about what to slip.

1. Slip several of the shots to change the content of the shot without changing its duration. Here are some suggestions:

    a. For the bikers shot, change from bikes coming toward the camera to bikes moving away (early in the clip), or vice versa.

    b. For the rafters, change from them successfully riding the raft to falling off, or vice versa.

    c. Slip a shot a little to improve the movement or pacing within the shot or the rhythm from shot to shot.

2. Play through your changes and make adjustments as desired.

Free-style Editing

You've now completed the structured part of this exercise. Spend the remaining time continuing to build the sequence making your own editorial decisions. In addition to adding shots into the sequence, practice moving segments in the Timeline, and slipping and sliding clips.

Also, as we mentioned earlier, the music ends abruptly. You can use Match Frame to see if there is a better end to the music (listen around 2 seconds after the current ending). (See the module, "Additional Editing Tools," for information about Match Frame.) Add this music to the end of the sequence and extend the video so the video and audio tracks end at the same time.

In later exercises, you will finish the audio by adjusting audio levels and pan, and by adding titles to the sequence.

Working in the Timeline (Outlined)

If you want to refer to the guided exercise for more information, see "Working in the Timeline (Guided)" on page 15.

Getting Started

1. In the Avid Editing project, open the **ECO Audio** bin in the **ECO Challenge** folder.

2. Edit the **Narration for ECO Challenge Spot** voice-over narration onto track A2 of the ECO Challenge sequence begun earlier. (For the printed narration, see "ECO Challenge Narration" on page 16.) (If necessary, add track A2 to your sequence, and then patch the audio from source A1 to record A2 track.)

3. Edit the **Music for ECO Challenge Spot** clip onto track A3.

4. Edit a video-only track over this voice-over, using clips in the **ECO Selects** bin: "RAPPELLING, HIKING, MOUNTAIN BIKING, WHITEWATER RAFTING, AND HORSEBACK RIDING."

Working in the Timeline

1. Rearrange, add, or remove shots or segments that play over the voice over and music. When you rearrange, add, and remove shots in the sequence, here are some things to think about doing:

   - Increase the continuity of movement between shots.

   - Increase the conflict of direction between shots. (For example, a shot with movement from left to right is followed by a shot with movement from right to left. Or a high angle shot is followed by a low angle shot.)

   - Replace natural audio in track A1. You can do this anywhere you don't see people's lips moving. Hint: Mark the clip you want to change in the timeline, make sure you select the correct tracks, and use an overwrite edit.

   - Improve pacing and rhythm

2. Move at least one shot earlier or later in the sequence.

3. Extract or lift at least one shot from the sequence using the Segment mode buttons. If you lift a shot, replace it with another.

4. Slip the content of a shot to improve the shot to shot movement.

5. Slide a shot to reposition it in the sequence.

You may use any of the following tools to further refine the sequence, but you should particularly practice the tools learned in the previous module.

- Extract or Lift to remove material from the sequence

- Overwrite to replace shots in the sequence

- Trim shots in the sequence

- Extract/Splice to rearrange shots in the sequence

- Lift/Overwrite to move shots but maintain other relationships in the sequence

- Slip to maintain the position of a shot in the sequence, but change its start and end point

- Slide to move a shot within the sequence

Module 8

Working with Audio

Most of the editing techniques used when editing the video track can also be used on the audio track. As described in previous modules, you can quickly:

- Cut and trim sound

- Create split edits

This module focuses on ways to optimize the audio quality by regulating the stereo balance of the speakers for each track and adjusting audio levels within a specific segment of a sequence.

Objectives

After you complete this module, you will be able to:

- Adjust audio level and pan

- Use Audio Gain Automation

Setting Level and Pan

Level and pan can be set in the Audio Mix tool. In addition, the Audio Gain Automation tool allows you to graphically manipulate levels and change levels in real time within a clip or segment.

The typical workflow for adjusting audio gain is the following:

1. Use the Audio Mix tool to adjust the overall volume of an entire clip or track.

2. (Optional) Use Audio Gain Automation recording to adjust gain in real time.

3. Add and manipulate audio gain keyframes to fine-tune the volume of different sections of the audio in the sequence.

Adjusting Level and Pan in the Audio Mix Tool

Use the Audio Mix tool to set the level and pan for a clip, sequence, or multiple clips within a sequence.

Changes made in the Audio Mix tool affect the entire clip in the Source monitor, or the segment on which your blue Position bar is parked in the sequence.

To set level and pan:

1. Do one of the following:

   • Load the clip into the Source monitor.

   • To set pan or level for a segment in a sequence, load the sequence into the Timeline and move to the segment you want to adjust.

   If you know an entire clip is too loud or soft, adjust the clip before editing it into the sequence, especially if you know you will use the clip repeatedly in the sequence.

2. (Option) If you are setting level in the sequence and want to display the level in the Timeline:

   a. Expand the audio track.

   b. Choose Audio Clip Gain from the Timeline Fast menu.

   A straight line appears in the selected audio track, showing the current volume level for that track in the Audio Mix tool.

Opening the Audio Mix Tool

There are two ways to open the Audio Mix tool.

First Method

■ Choose Audio Mix from the Tools menu.

The Audio Mix tool appears.

Second Method

The second method uses the Avid system's Audio Editing Toolset, one of its predesigned work environments.

1. Choose Audio Editing from the Toolset menu, or press Shift+F11.

   The Audio Editing Toolset appears.

2. By default, the Composer monitor is displayed, not the Source/Record monitor. To display the Source/Record monitor, hold the mouse over the left edge of the Composer monitor. When the cursor becomes a double-sided arrow, click and drag the left edge to the left. When you release the mouse, the Source/Record monitor is displayed. (If it isn't, repeat and drag farther to the left.)

3. Rearrange, open, or close Audio tools to customize the display as you wish.

4. Choose Save Current from the Toolset menu.

   Any time you return to the Audio Editing toolset this arrangement appears.

5. To remove the customization, choose Restore Current to Default from the Toolset menu.

6. To return to the toolset for editing, choose Source/Record Editing from the Toolset menu.

Working with the Audio Mix Tool

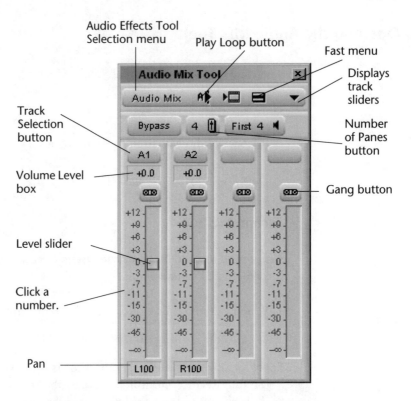

Audio Effects Tool
Selection menu

Play Loop button

Fast menu

Displays track sliders

Track Selection button

Number of Panes button

Volume Level box

Gang button

Level slider

Click a number.

Pan

The Audio Mix window is divided into four or eight panes. It can only display tracks that exist in the sequence, or tracks that were digitized with the source clip.

1. Click the Number of Panes button to switch between displaying four or eight tracks. (If you display four tracks, you can display the first four or second four tracks.)

2. Click the Track Selection button for the audio track to be adjusted.

3. (Option) To link (gang) tracks together so they are adjusted in tandem, click the Gang buttons on the desired tracks.

4. Click the Play Loop button. The system repeatedly loops through the selected area as follows:

   • If you have IN and OUT marks on your sequence, it loops over the selected area.

   • If there are no IN or OUT marks, it loops over the smallest audio clip on a selected track, identified by the Position indicator.

   If you adjust the level while playing, the new level will go into affect in the next go-around.

To adjust level for a track:

■ Move the sliders up or down, type a number in the Volume Level box, or click a number next to the slide panel.

To type a number in the Volume Level box, click in the Volume Level box and type a number (negative number to decrease the level) in the numeric keypad.

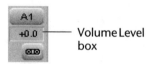 —— Volume Level box

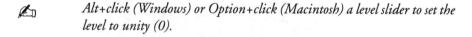 *Alt+click (Windows) or Option+click (Macintosh) a level slider to set the level to unity (0).*

To adjust pan for a track:

■ Click and hold the Pan value display to open a pop-up slider, and move the slider left or right.

Alt+click (Windows) or Option+click (Macintosh) a pan slider to set the pan to MID.

Setting Global Pan and Level

The Global Pan and Level options apply the current pan or level settings to all clips on entire track(s) in a sequence. To set this option:

1. Clear any IN or OUT marks from the Timeline.

2. (Option) If you want to modify multiple tracks, click the Gang button for each track you want to modify.

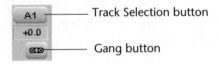

Track Selection button

Gang button

3. Adjust the pan or level for the track in the Audio Mix tool.

4. Click the Track Selection button(s) for the track(s) you want to modify.

5. Press the Audio Mix Fast menu button for the desired track and choose Set Pan (or Level) on Track - Global. (If the menu is grayed out, click the Track Selection button(s) and try again.)

Pan or level will be adjusted for the entire track or multiple ganged tracks.

Setting Pan and Level Using Marks

You can set level and pan for clips contained within marked IN and OUT points, or from the beginning of a clip with an IN point to the end of the sequence.

To set this option for clips contained within IN and OUT points:

1. Mark an IN and OUT in the sequence around the clip or clips you want to affect.

   Pan and level will be set throughout the entire segment, not just the portion of the segment within the IN and OUT marks.

2. Make sure the Position indicator is within the IN and OUT marks and within an audio clip (not filler) on the track(s) you are adjusting.

3. (Option) If you want to modify multiple tracks, click the Gang button for each track you want to modify.

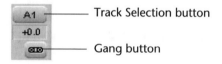
Track Selection button

Gang button

4. Adjust the pan or level for the track in the Audio Mix tool.

5. Click the Track Selection button(s) for the track(s) you want to modify.

6. Press the Audio Mix fast menu and choose Set Pan (or Level)-In/Out. (If the menu is grayed out, click the Track Selection button and try again.)

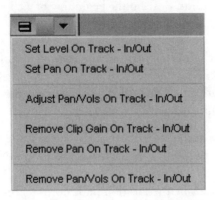

Set Level On Track - In/Out
Set Pan On Track - In/Out

Adjust Pan/Vols On Track - In/Out

Remove Clip Gain On Track - In/Out
Remove Pan On Track - In/Out

Remove Pan/Vols On Track - In/Out

The system sets the level or pan from the beginning of the segment with the IN mark to the end of the clip with the OUT mark.

Adjusting Audio Gain with Keyframes

Audio Gain Automation (also called audio rubberbanding) allows you to change the volume of a segment by adding and manipulating gain keyframes (break points) in the Timeline.

When you add a keyframe, the system adds the point at the level currently set for that track in the Audio Mix tool. Audio gain keyframes are **additive** to the values set in the Audio Mix tool. This allows you to adjust the values separately.

Preparing the Timeline

To prepare the tracks to add and manipulate keyframes:

1. In the Timeline, select the audio track(s) you want to adjust. Also, select the speaker monitors for the tracks you want to hear.

2. Expand the audio track(s) you want to adjust.

3. Choose Audio Auto Gain from the Timeline Fast menu.

   A straight line appears in the selected audio track, showing the current gain level for that track in the Automation Gain tool.

4. To view the clip gain values in the Timeline at the same time, choose Audio Clip Gain from the Timeline Fast menu.

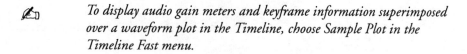 *To display audio gain meters and keyframe information superimposed over a waveform plot in the Timeline, choose Sample Plot in the Timeline Fast menu.*

Adding Keyframes

To add a keyframe to the sequence:

1. Place the Position indicator where you want to add the keyframe in the sequence.

2. Select the track(s) where you want to add the keyframe(s).

3. Click the Add Keyframe button in the Tool Palette.

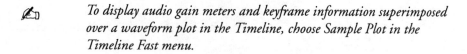 *The Add Keyframe button is mapped to the keyboard on the N key. You can also map the button to another key; the button is on the FX tab of the Command palette.*

Adjusting Keyframes

Use the following methods to adjust the gain on a selected track or tracks:

1. To raise or lower the level, do one of the following:

- Click and drag a keyframe up or down to increase or decrease the gain at that point. If there is a keyframe at the same position on another enabled track, it moves also.

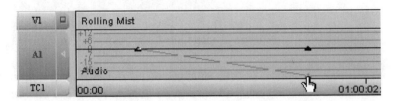

If the Automation Gain window is open, you see that the corresponding volume slider moves.

- To snap to the decibel lines, hold the Control (Windows) or ⌘ (Macintosh) key while you drag the keyframe.

- If the Automation Gain window is open, you can click in the Volume Level box and type a number (negative number to decrease the level) in the numeric keypad.

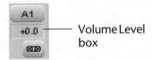 Volume Level box

2. To change the start or end of a ramp, Alt+click (Windows) or Option+click (Macintosh) a keyframe and drag it left or right. This moves the keyframe horizontally earlier or later in the Timeline.

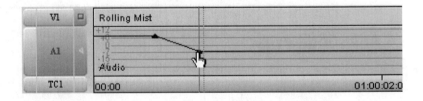

You cannot move one keyframe on top of another or past another.

Deleting Keyframes

To delete a single keyframe:

1. Move the cursor over the keyframe until the cursor turns into the pointing hand. (Make sure the Position indicator is not parked on the keyframe.)

2. Press the Delete key.

   If there are identical keyframes in other active tracks the system deletes them also.

To delete groups of keyframes:

1. Do one of the following:

   • Mark an IN and OUT surrounding the area.

   • Mark the entire segment with the Mark Clip button (T key).

2. Select the appropriate audio tracks.

3. Move the cursor over one of the keyframes until the cursor turns into a pointing hand.

4. Press the Delete key.

   All the keyframes are deleted.

Typical Scenarios for Adjusting Gain with Keyframes

These are typical scenarios for adjusting the gain on a selected track or tracks:

• **To adjust gain evenly throughout a segment, on all enabled tracks:**

   a. Add a single keyframe in the segment.

   b. Click a keyframe and drag it up or down to increase or decrease the gain within the entire segment.

• **To create a gradual increase or decrease within a segment, on all enabled tracks:**

a. Add two keyframes in the Timeline: one at the start of the change in level and the other at the end.

b. Click a keyframe and drag it up or down to increase or decrease the gain at that point.

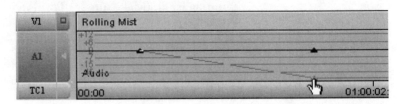

- **To adjust the gain in a marked portion of the Timeline, on all enabled tracks:**

  a. Add four keyframes in the Timeline:

     - Just before the change in level begins

     - Just after the change in level begins

     - Just before the change in level ends

     - Just after the change in level ends

  b. Add an IN mark between keyframes 1 and 2, and an OUT mark between keyframes 3 and 4.

  c. Drag keyframe 2 or 3 up or down.

     Notice how the keyframes outside the IN/OUT marks do not move.

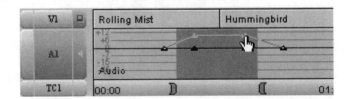

Automation Gain Real-Time Recording

You can use Audio Gain Automation recording to adjust gain in real time. If you want to use this feature, you will most likely perform this procedure *after* setting overall levels in the Audio Mix tool and *before* adjusting keyframes, as described in the previous section.

1. (Option) Prepare the Timeline as in "Preparing the Timeline" on page 8-8.

    If you adjust audio gain on a track in your sequence and do not display any volume information, a little pink triangle appears in each clip to which audio gain adjustments have been made.

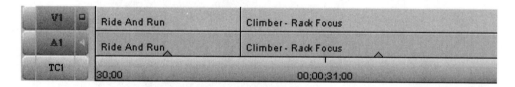

2. Mark IN and OUT points on the area you want to adjust. If you don't set IN and OUT marks, you can adjust the entire sequence.

3. Choose Automation Gain from the Tools menu.

The Automation Gain Tool appears.

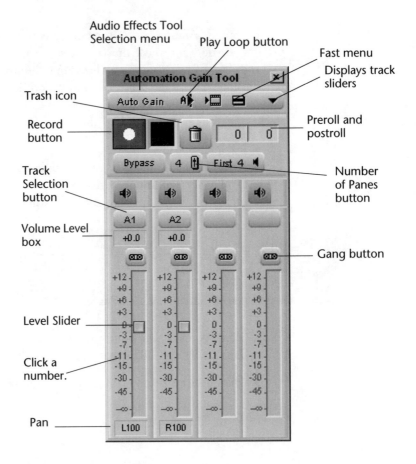

4. (Option) Type a number in the Preroll and Postroll boxes to play frames before and after the automation gain adjustments. For example, type 2 for two seconds.

5. Click the Track Selection button(s) for the audio track(s) to be adjusted.

6. (Option) To link (gang) tracks together so they are adjusted in tandem, click the Gang buttons on the desired tracks.

7. Click the Record button or press the B key to start recording your actions.

8. Adjust the level sliders as you listen.

9. If you want to stop recording, click the Record button again.

10. If you want to abort the process and try again, click the Trash icon.

During Audio Gain recording, the system adds volume keyframes to the audio in the Timeline. Because it records every movement of the sliders, there are usually more keyframes than you need.

To decrease the number of keyframes:

1. Click the Track Selection button to enable the Automation Gain Fast menu.

2. Choose Filter Automation Gain on Track In/Out from the Automation Gain Fast menu.

   The system removes approximately 10 per cent of the keyframes while maintaining the overall shape of the curves.

3. Repeat the previous step until you have decreased the number of keyframes to an acceptable level.

   You should remove as many excess keyframes as possible while still maintaining the desired volume changes.

Now you can adjust keyframes manually to fine tune the levels.

Deleting All Keyframes

To clear all keyframes, thereby undoing the changes in levels made in Audio Gain Automation:

1. Remove any IN/OUT points on the track.

2. In the Automation Gain Tool, choose Remove Automation Gain on Track from the Automation Gain Fast menu.

Review Questions

1. Where in the Audio Mix tool would you go to apply a level to an entire track? See "Setting Global Pan and Level" on page 8-6.

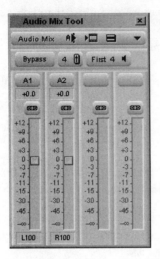

2. How would you start ramping up the music a little earlier? See "Adjusting Keyframes" on page 8-9.

3. You want to raise the audio level for the portion between point A and point B, but you want the level before A and after B to remain the same. The levels will gradually increase and then gradually diminish. How would you do that? See "Adjusting Keyframes" on page 8-9.

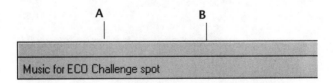

Exercise 8

Fine-Tuning Audio

Now that you have fine-tuned the structure of the ECO Challenge advertising spot, it's time to work on the audio. You will adjust levels for entire clips and for portions of clips.

We provide you with two versions of the exercise; perform the one that best suits your abilities and work style. For a more guided exercise, see "Fine-Tuning Audio (Guided)" on this page. For a less guided exercise, see "Fine-Tuning Audio (Outlined)" on page 26.

Fine-Tuning Audio (Guided)

In this exercise, you continue the work begun in previous exercises.

Getting Started

1. In the **Avid Editing** project, open the **ECO Challenge** folder and the **ECO Sequences** bin.

2. Duplicate the sequence you worked on in the previous exercise, and name the duplicate.

3. Load the duplicated sequence into the Timeline.

Using the Audio Editing Toolset

1. Choose Audio Editing from the Toolset menu, or press Shift+F11.

   Let's customize the display.

2. To display the Source/Record monitor, hold the mouse over the left edge of the Composer monitor. When the cursor becomes a double-sided arrow, click and drag the left edge to the left. When you release the mouse, the Source/Record monitor is displayed. (If it isn't, repeat and drag farther to the left.)

3. Adjust the interface so that the only Audio tool that's displayed is Audio Mix and place it where you want it. If the Audio Mix tool is not displayed, choose Audio Mix from the Tools menu.

4. Choose Save Current from the Toolset menu.

Any time you return to the Audio Editing toolset this arrangement appears.

 When you want to return to the toolset for editing, choose Source/Record Editing from the Toolset menu.

Centering Pan

If you are sharing your system with someone, it is sometimes difficult to hear one of the speakers. You might want to center pan all of the audio tracks. Let's do that now.

To center pan all audio tracks using the Audio Mix tool:

1. Clear any IN or OUT marks from the Timeline.

2. In the Audio Mix tool, click the Gang button for tracks A1, A2, and A3.

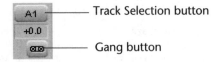

3. Press the Alt (Windows) or Option (Macintosh) key and click in the Pan Adjustment box for one of the tracks. All boxes now display the letters, "MID."

4. Click the Track Selection buttons for tracks A1, A2, and A3.

5. Press the Audio Mix Fast menu button and choose Set Pan on Track - Global.

Pan will be adjusted to the midpoint for the ganged tracks.

Adjusting Audio Levels

In this part of the exercise, you will adjust audio levels using Audio Mix and add and manipulate keyframes.

Adjusting Audio Levels in the Audio Mix Tool

First, adjust the audio playback level of the narration on A2.

1. Play the sequence and listen first to the narration in relation to the music. It's too soft. We'll use the Audio Mix tool to increase the level for the entire narration track.

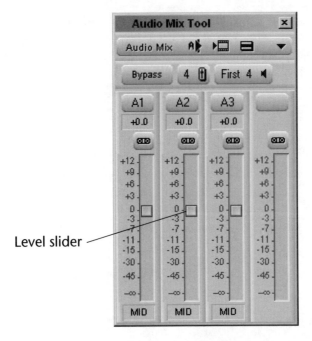

Level slider

2. Drag the vertical slider for track A2 up to raise its audio level. The new level is applied to the entire track.

3. Listen to part of the sequence. Continue to modify the level until you like the result.

Now let's raise the overall level of the rider's comment to the camera in the Ride and run clip. (The music will still be too loud; you'll adjust that next.)

1. Place your blue Position indicator in the **Ride and Run** clip.

2. In the Audio Mix tool, drag the A1 slider up a few decibels.

3. If you can't hear well over the music track, what can you do? (If you said, "Solo the A1 track," you're right!)

4. Play the result, and adjust as necessary.

Adjusting Levels Using Audio Gain Automation

One key task in an audio mix is to adjust the levels of the dialog in relation to music. In the ECO Challenge sequence, the music overwhelms the Ride and Run sync audio. Let's adjust the audio level for just that segment of the music (we'll soon get to the rest of the music track). We will add and adjust audio gain keyframes to accomplish this task.

First, set up the Timeline to prepare for working with Audio Gain Automation keyframes.

Setting Up the Timeline

To set up the Timeline:

1. Choose Audio Auto Gain from the Timeline Fast menu.

2. To expand the music track, click anywhere in the Timeline window. Then press the Control (Windows) or Option (Macintosh) key (just below the A3 track selector). When the cursor changes to a double-sided arrow, press and drag down the bottom boundary of the A3 track selector.

   How else could you expand track A3? Why might this second way not be the best method for this situation?

Adjusting Level for a Section of the Music Track

Now you can adjust the level of the music in relation to the Ride and Run clip.

1. Play the music under the **Ride and Run** clip. It's too loud. Let's lower it.

2. Select only the A3 record track selector; deselect other tracks.

3. For each of the following keyframes, place the Position indicator where you want to add the keyframe in the sequence and click the Add Keyframe button (in the Tool Palette), or press the N key.

- Keyframe 1: Just before the Ride and run clip begins

- Keyframe 2: Just after the Ride and run clip begins

- Keyframe 3: Just before the Ride and run clip ends

- Keyframe 4: Just after the Ride and run clip ends

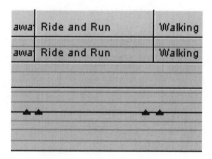

4. Add an IN mark between keyframes 1 and 2, and an OUT mark between keyframes 3 and 4.

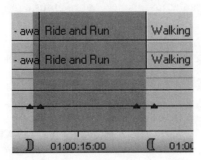

5. Drag keyframe 2 or 3 down to lower the level. To snap to the decibel lines, hold the Control key (Windows) or ⌘ key (Macintosh) as you drag the keyframe.

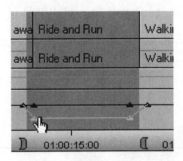

6. Listen to the segment and adjust as necessary.

Working on Your Own

You've now completed the structured part of this exercise. Spend the remaining time going over the audio levels and making further adjustments using the Audio Mix and Audio Gain Automation tools, and by adding and manipulating keyframes.

In a later module, you will learn how to create titles, and then you will have the opportunity to complete this spot.

Fine-Tuning Audio (Outlined)

If you want to refer to the guided exercise for more information, see "Fine-Tuning Audio (Guided)" on page 17.

Getting Started

1. In the **Avid Editing** project, duplicate the **ECO Challenge** sequence you worked on in the previous exercise, name the duplicate, and load it into the Timeline.

2. Display the Audio Editing Toolset and customize it so Audio Mix is the only audio tool displayed and so that both the Source and Record monitors are displayed (drag the left edge of the Composer monitor to the left). Save this customized version.

Optimizing Audio

First you want to prepare for using the Audio Mix tool and Audio Gain Automation keyframes by doing the following:

1. In the Timeline, expand the audio tracks and display Audio Clip Gain and Audio Auto Gain.

2. Raise or lower the levels for entire clips or tracks using the Audio Mix tool.

3. Add and manipulate keyframes or use the Record function in the Audio Gain Automation tool to dip and swell the music, so the music plays better with the rest of the audio in your sequence. (If you use the Record function, be sure to adjust keyframes afterward.) For example, you might:

   • Lower the level for the music that plays under the voice-over narration

   • Exaggerate a swelling of the music by raising the level

   • Dip the music to hear the audio on tracks A1 and A2 more clearly

4. Add and manipulate keyframes to adjust the narration, sync audio, and music.

5. Change the Pan for the music and/or narration track.

Module 9

Input

When you use Avid Xpress DV to edit material, you are not working with the actual physical source tapes. Instead, you are working with recorded clips and media files that contain the audio and video information captured from the source tapes.

This module describes and demonstrates the process of logging and recording material.

Objectives

After you complete this module, you will be able to:

- Set record options
- Set audio levels
- Record individual clips
- Log and batch record clips

Setting the Record Options

To set your record options and begin recording, you must first:

1. Open the bin where you want to store your clips.

2. With that bin highlighted, choose Record from the Tools menu.

   You can also type Control+7.

   ✍ *If you like, you can also use the Recording Toolset, by choosing Recording from the Toolset menu. The Composer monitor is displayed for that Toolset, but that should be fine.*

The screen displays the Record tool.

Record button

Click to switch
between recording
and logging.

Deck
button

Audio tool

Click to
activate tracks
to record.

Press to
choose
your target
bin.

Single/Dual
Drive Toggle

Resolution
Pop-up

Press to
select the
target
drive(s).

Deck pop-up
menu

Click here to
choose a new
tape.

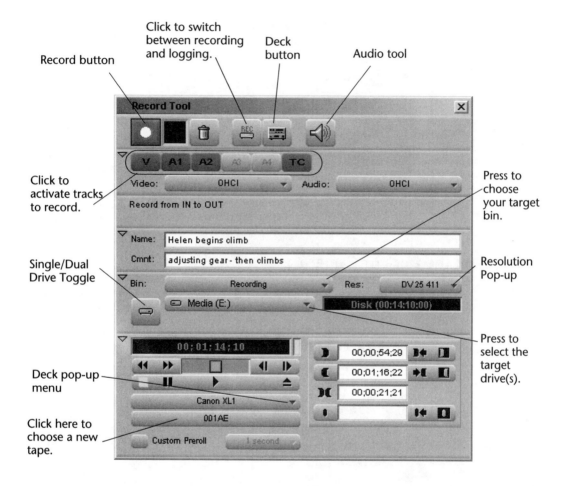

Working in the Record Tool

The Record tool provides all the controls you need to capture your footage in digital form. To set up the tool, you will select:

- Source deck

- Source tape name

- Tracks to record

- Video and audio formats

- Target bin for storing the clips

- Target drives for storing the recorded media

Selecting the Deck or Camera

1. Physically connect the deck or camera you will use.

2. If no deck or camera appears in the Record tool's Deck window, choose Check Decks from the Deck pop-up menu. This works if the Avid system knows that the deck exists, but the deck was not on or connected when you entered Record mode.

3. If the deck or camera still does not appear in the Deck window, choose Auto-configure from the Deck pop-up menu. The system will automatically configure the correct deck or camera and display it in the Deck window.

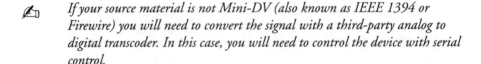 *If your source material is not Mini-DV (also known as IEEE 1394 or Firewire) you will need to convert the signal with a third-party analog to digital transcoder. In this case, you will need to control the device with serial control.*

Identifying the Source Tape

To specify the source tape name:

1. Insert a tape into the play deck.

   If the tape deck is in Remote mode, the Select Tape dialog box appears.

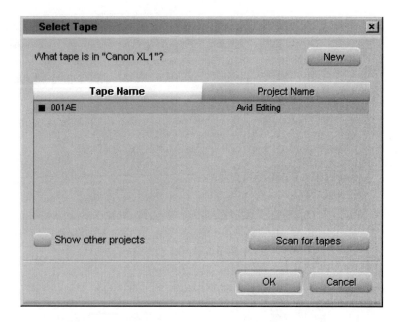

2. If the name of your tape shows up in the list, move the mouse cursor over the tape icon next to the tape name. Double-click when the cursor becomes a hand. Proceed to Step 4.

3. If your tape isn't in the list:

   a. Click New, or press Control+N (Windows) or ⌘+N (Macintosh).

      A new tape name line appears at the bottom of the list.

   b. Type the tape name and press Enter or Return.

      Use a unique name for each new tape (and write the same name on the physical tape and on the tape box). The flexibility of the

Avid Xpress DV editing system relies in part on the system's ability to correctly associate clips with the correct physical tapes. The system cannot distinguish between two tapes with the same name.

Tape naming schemes should reflect the finishing plan for the project. A program that will be finished in an Avid online has considerable tolerance in the length and format of tape names.

Projects that will be finished from an EDL in a linear online session should be assigned tape names of no more than six characters, numbers leading, with no punctuation or spaces, for example, 001AES. If you plan to create an EDL, check with your online house if you are unsure about how to name your tape.

4. Click OK.

Selecting Active Tracks

The Record tool captures information from the active tracks. Avid Xpress DV automatically activates the tracks that were active in the previous session.

You can change these settings by clicking tracks to activate or deactivate them.

■ Select the desired tracks, for example V, A1, A2, and TC.

▲ **Make sure to record only the tracks you need; recording unneeded tracks consumes valuable drive space.**

Setting the Video and Audio Input Formats

The Video and Audio pop-up menus in the Record tool show you the current settings for the video and audio input formats. You can change the Audio settings by selecting the pop-up menu and choosing a different option.

- Video input: OHCI.

- Audio input: OHCI (the default), Midi, CD Audio, Line in, and Microphone. These options may vary depending on your platform.

Choosing the Video Resolution

Avid Xpress DV offers the following two-field resolutions:

- DV-25 4:1:1

- DV-25 4:2:0 (PAL only)

Selecting the Target Bin

Any bin that is open can be selected from the Target Bin pop-up menu.

- To choose an open bin, click the Target Bin pop-up menu and choose the bin in which you want your captured material to be organized.

If the bin you want to record to is not in the Target Bin pop up list do one of the following:

- To open a previously created bin, choose the bin from the Project window, choose Open Bin from the File menu, or press Control+O (Windows) or ⌘+O (Macintosh).

- To create a new bin, choose New Bin from the File menu, or press Control+N (Windows) or ⌘+N (Macintosh).

Selecting the Target Drive(s)

The Record tool displays information about the target drives where your recorded video and audio material is to be stored. In addition to the name of the target drives, the tool also displays an estimate of how much time is available on that drive to store new material.

 The estimate is based on the number of tracks to be stored on the drive, and the free space available on the target drive.

You must decide where to store your recorded material. To select your target drive(s):

1. If you have not done so, select the desired tracks.

2. Make sure the Single/Dual Drive Mode button shows one drive. If it doesn't, click it once.

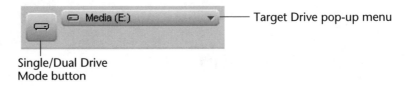

Target Drive pop-up menu

Single/Dual Drive
Mode button

3. Choose a drive from the Target Drive pop-up menu.

   The drive with the most available free space appears in bold type.

   The Time Remaining indicator displays an estimate of the amount of storage left on the drive based on your capture settings, number of tracks, and capacity of the target disk.

 If you are recording complex material, the Time Remaining indicator decreases more rapidly than with simple material.

 If you choose the two drive icon, make sure you choose two separate physical drives, not two partitions on the same drive.

Setting Audio Levels

Before recording, you should choose the audio rate setting and use the Audio tool to prepare audio levels. The process for preparing audio levels involves two steps:

- Step 1: Choose the audio rate setting.

- Step 2: Set the audio input levels.

Choosing the Audio Rate Setting

An audio sample rate of 48 kHz gives marginally better quality than 44.1 kHz, which offers somewhat higher quality than audio captured at 32 kHz. CD audio is 44.1 kHz, and DAT audio is 48 kHz.

The higher the sample rate, the more disk space is required to store the audio. However, the difference in disk space used for the various sample rates is not significant and should not influence your choice of sample rates.

To choose the audio sample rate setting:

1. Double-click the Audio Project setting in your Project window.

   The setting opens.

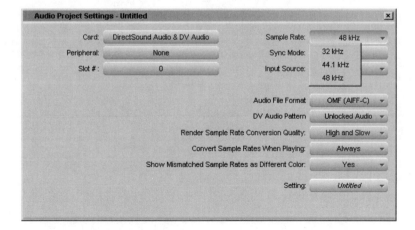

2. Choose 32, 44.1, or 48 kHz from the Sample Rate pop-up menu. (The default sample rate for Xpress DV is 48 kHz.)

You can play different audio sample rates within a sequence only if the "Convert Sample Rates When Playing" is set to Always. This will perform a sample rate conversion of your audio on the fly to match it to the sample rate chosen in the Audio Project Settings. This conversion is useful for offline editing, but may not be suitable for the final version of your sequence.

If you set the "Convert Sample Rates When Playing" option to Never, then audio in your Timeline that does not match the sample rate chosen in the Audio Project Setting will play back as silence.

3. Close the Audio Project settings.

Setting the Audio Input Level

Avid Xpress DV allows you to adjust the input level of audio devices such as CD-ROMs or a microphone. However, digital material coming from Firewire cannot be adjusted.

1. Open the Audio tool by clicking the Audio Tool icon in the Record Tool window, by choosing Audio Tool from the Tools menu, or by pressing Control+1 (Windows) or ⌘+1 (Macintosh).

 Audio Tool icon

2. To display the Input Level Controls, click the Microphone icon.

Microphone
icon

The screen displays the Input Level Control panel.

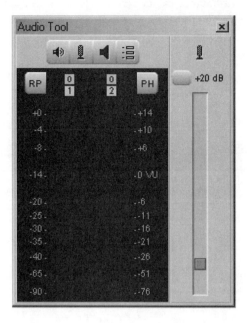

3. Play the tone or other audio from your source tape, DAT, CD, or other source.

4. Watch the Audio Tool LED display. If your source tape has audio tone at the head of it, set the tone to -14* on the digital meter by dragging the input level control. If you don't have tone, play a portion of the audio; the level should peak around -4 to avoid clipping and distortion.

The scale on the right corresponds to your VU meter. The scale on the left corresponds to digital audio. By default, 0 on the VU meter is set to correspond to -14 on the digital meter.

*You can adjust the reference level to match other systems in your facility. (On some systems, 0 on the VU meter is set to correspond to -20 on the digital meter.) To change the reference level, click the Peak Hold (PH) button on the right side of the Audio Tool and choose Set Reference Level from the menu that appears. Type a new reference level and click OK.

▲ Notice that there is only one slider for adjusting level. If an imbalance exists between two audio tracks or the scale doesn't give you a large enough range of adjustment, you should adjust them on the camera or playback deck.

5. Close the Audio tool, or leave it open to check audio levels while recording.

Recording

Once you have set all your recording parameters, you can record your clips. But first, a brief discussion of Timecode.

The Importance of Timecode

Timecode helps to keep track of and count individual frames of video. Each video frame is assigned a timecode number in terms of hours, minutes, seconds, and frames. For example, 01:03:45:15 is read as 1 hour, 3 minutes, 45 seconds, and 15 frames.

The Avid system uses the timecode from your video cassette to navigate to various video frames. (Most video cassettes have Timecode, including Beta SP, Digi-Beta, and MiniDV; the exception is VHS.) Timecode is also required for the Avid system to perform a Batch Record. We will discuss Batch Record later in this module.

Timecode is recorded onto the video cassette by most consumer and prosumer cameras. In general, after a camera is initially powered on it will start recording at a specific start timecode. For example, most DV cameras start recording at 00:00:00:00.

To save on battery power you might turn off the camera several times over the course of shooting. However, if the camera is powered off in the middle of shooting and then powered back on again, the default recording start timecode might be reset.

When the timecode is reset in the middle of the cassette the result is a discontinuity in timecode, called a timecode break.

Because these timecode breaks can prevent the Avid Xpress DV system from being able to accurately seek video frames and Batch Record, you should avoid as many timecode breaks as possible while shooting your footage.

Here are two techniques that might help:

- Pause the camera instead of stopping it. Pausing does not usually create a timecode break.

- If you have stopped the camera, you might prevent broken Timecode by rolling the video back a few seconds before starting to record again.

Recording from IN to OUT

This method enables you to play the tape and mark an IN and OUT before recording.

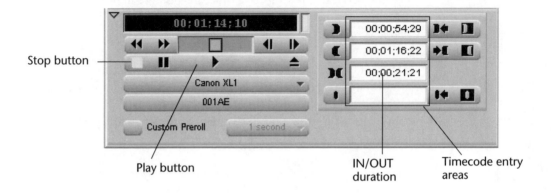

Stop button

Play button

IN/OUT duration

Timecode entry areas

To record from IN to OUT:

1. Check that you did the following:

   a. Open the destination bin.

   b. Make sure that your camera is on, or that your deck is in Remote mode.

   c. Insert a tape and name it in the Tape Name dialog box.

   d. Check the Record tool settings explained earlier in the module.

2. Enter the IN and OUT points for the clip you want to record using either of the following methods.

   - Use the Mark IN and OUT buttons in the Deck Controller tool or the Mark IN/OUT (I, O) keys:

   a. Using the deck controls in the Record tool, cue your source tape to the point where you want to start the clip.

b. Click the mark IN icon.

c. Cue your source tape to the point where you want to end the clip.

d. Click the mark OUT icon.

e. Click the Pause button to stop the tape.

or

- Type the timecodes for the clip's IN and OUT points.

 Always set your IN and OUT points loose, so you have extra material for trimming and transition effects.

3. Click the large red Record button.

The Record tool automatically rewinds the tape to a point before the IN point of the clip.

The bar next to the Record button flashes red, indicating that the Avid system is recording your material.

When the tape reaches the clip's OUT point, recording stops, and the clip appears in the bin.

4. Type a new name for the clip and press Enter or Return.

Typing a Clip Name and Comments While Recording

You can type in a clip name and other information while the material is being recorded.

The information that you type does not appear in the bin until you have completed recording.

To type in a name and any comments you want while the clip is being recorded:

1. Once recording has begun, type a name for the clip in the Name entry box.

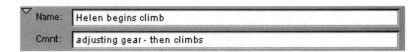

2. Press Tab and type your comments in the Comments entry box.

3. Press Enter or Return.

   When recording stops, the new name and Comments column appear in the bin.

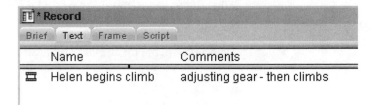

Recording on the Fly

If you do not know the IN or OUT points of your clips, you can record on the fly.

To record on the fly:

1. Check the Record tool settings explained earlier in the module.

2. Clear any marks in the Record tool's deck controls.

3. Use the deck controls in the Record tool to get near the material you want to record, and then click the Play button.

4. To begin recording, click the red Record button.

   The red square adjacent to the Record button flashes on and off.

Stopping Recording

To stop recording:

1. Click the red Record button again, or press the Escape key.

   The clip appears in the bin.

2. Click the Stop button in the Deck Control tool to stop the tape.

3. If you haven't already done so, name the clip by highlighting it in black in the bin and typing a new name.

Logging and Batch Recording

Many editors prefer to log all their clips (shots) first, and then use the Batch Record function to capture their material automatically. This is often considered the most efficient method.

Naming Bins

When you begin mounting a project on an Avid system by logging or recording footage, you must create a bin(s) in which the system will store the clips. You should also name the bins. Your choice of bin names will affect the editing process. The simplest scheme is to name the initial bins you create by tape name, in other words, a separate "source bin" for each source tape. For example, you would record all the clips from tape 001 into a bin titled 001.

This strategy will be helpful in two ways:

- The bin becomes a database for a specific tape. A printout of the bin can serve as a useful archiving tool.

- Any scenes that were not logged and recorded when the project was initially mounted will be easier to find because of visual associations with the clips in the bin bearing that tape's name.

Logging to a Bin from a Source Tape

You can use Avid Xpress DV to control a source deck, log shots (clips) from your source tapes, and record clip data (without associated media) directly into a bin.

To log to a bin from a source tape:

1. Open the bin where you want to store the clips.

2. Choose Record from the Tools menu.

3. Click the Record/Log button until you see the Log mode icon.

Record mode   Log mode

The system switches to Log mode.

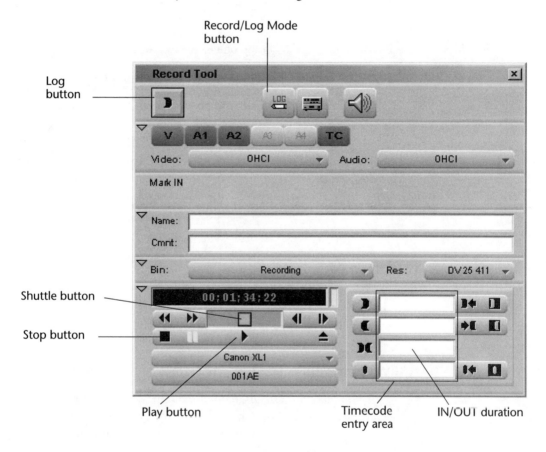

4. Play or shuttle to the point where you want to mark an IN for the start of the clip.

5. Mark an IN by doing one of the following:

   • Press the IN (I) key on the keyboard or press F4.

   • Click the IN mark and pencil icon in the Log button.

   • Type the timecode for the IN point.

The timecode for the IN point is displayed, the icon in the Record button changes to an OUT mark and a pencil, and the bar in the middle of the window displays a message ("Mark OUT"), telling you that the system is waiting for an OUT point to be established.

6. Shuttle or play to the place where you want to mark the OUT point of the clip.

7. Mark an OUT by doing one of the following:

   • Press the OUT (O) key on the keyboard or press F4.

   • Click the OUT mark and pencil icon in the Log button.

   • Type the timecode for the OUT point.

   The Log/Mark OUT button changes to the Log button, and the deck pauses.

8. (Option) Enter a clip name, then press Tab and enter a comment.

9. Click the pencil icon in the Log button or press F4.

   The clip is logged into the bin. The default clip name is the bin name plus a number.

10. The tape pauses for a few seconds, then continues to play.

   If you have not already named the clip, notice that the default clip name is the bin name followed by a number. You can use this pause to type in a new name (and comments) for the logged clip, and press Enter or Return.

   If you select Pause Deck While Logging in the Record settings, the system will automatically pause when the deck reaches the OUT point and then resume play when you press Enter or Return after entering the name (and comments).

   You can also click the Pause button (or press the Space bar) and rename your clip.

11. Repeat these steps until you have logged all your clips.

12. Stop the tape.

 If you're using more than one tape, be sure to create a new tape in Avid Xpress DV for each physical tape and give each one a unique name.

Batch Recording Logged Clips

After you have logged a group of clips, you record them automatically using the Avid system's Batch Record capabilities.

To batch record your clips:

1. Click the Record/Log mode button once in the Record tool to return to Record mode.

   The red Record button appears.

Record button

2. Activate the bin with the clips you want to record.

3. Select the clips you want to record.

4. Choose Batch Record from the Bin menu.

 If the bin with the logged clips is not active, Batch Record is dimmed in the menu.

   A dialog box appears.

5. Confirm that the "Offline media only" option is selected. When this option is checked, all selected clips that are offline will be recorded.

   When this option isn't checked and some of the selected clips have media files, the system deletes the media files and re-digitizes new media files.

6. Click OK.

7. If you have not inserted a tape into the tape deck, a dialog box will prompt you to do so.

   a. Once the tape is inserted, click Mounted to indicate to the system that the correct tape is loaded and ready for recording.

      A confirmation dialog box opens.

   b. Click OK to confirm the tape and deck entries.

   ▲ **If you insert the wrong tape and Avid Xpress DV finds the required timecode, it will record from this tape.**

   The system digitizes each clip from the tape, in Start Timecode order. If another source tape is needed, the system prompts you for the tape.

   At the end of the batch recording process, a dialog box notifies you that the process is complete.

   ✍ *You can stop the Batch Record process at any time by clicking the Trash icon in the Record tool.*

Recording from a Non-timecode Source

Sometimes you have to record from a source such as VHS, DAT, or CD that does not have timecode. Or you may choose to record without timecode simply to acquire video across a timecode break. In these cases, Avid Xpress DV will generate timecode based on time of day. The Time of Day timecode is arbitrary; it does not actually match up to individual frames on the tape and thus cannot be used to batch record or create an EDL. The flexibility of the Avid system depends on its ability to reference any frame in the clip to its original source tape using timecode.

Recording from a non-timecode source requires that you record on the fly. When recording a non-timecode source, you can adjust audio input levels, and enter names and comments as usual.

▲ **In order to record from a non-DV source you can use a signal transcoder to convert the analog signal to a DV signal.**

▲ **The timecode generated when recording from a non-timecode source cannot be used for rerecording or in an EDL because the source never had "real" timecode.**

To record a non-timecode source:

1. Click the Deck icon in the Record tool.

 — Deck icon

The system places a red circle with a line through it over the deck icon to indicate that a deck will not be used in the following procedure.

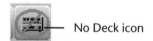 — No Deck icon

The system also removes the Timecode (TC) button from the Track Selector panel as well as the deck control interface buttons.

2. Click once in the Tape Name box.

The Select Tape dialog box appears.

3. Do one of the following:

• Choose an existing tape name.

• Click New and enter a new source tape name and press Enter or Return.

4. Click OK to return to the Record tool.

5. Play the non-timecode source.

6. Click the red Record button to start recording on-the-fly.

7. Press the Record button again to stop recording.

Your clip appears in the bin and can immediately be used for editing.

8. Stop playback of your non-timecode source.

9. Click the Deck icon until it returns to the normal **recording** mode.

—Deck icon

✐ *If you plan to finish your work using an EDL, make sure to bring a digital cut to the online session so you can manually match the segments in the sequence which do not have timecode.*

✐ *If you used non-timecode sources for your audio, such as DAT or CD, and you are planning on using your EDL to finish your work, consider using the audio output as your finished audio track. Remember, Avid Xpress DV can output CD-quality (44.1 kHz) and DAT- or DVD-quality (48 kHz) audio. This will save you from having to rebuild the audio tracks.*

Review Questions

1. Label the following items in the Record tool:

   a. The button you click when you are ready to record a clip

   b. The button you click to toggle between logging and recording

   c. The button to display the Audio tool

   d. The button you deselect if you are recording a non-timecode source

   e. The button you click to set a Mark OUT point for a clip

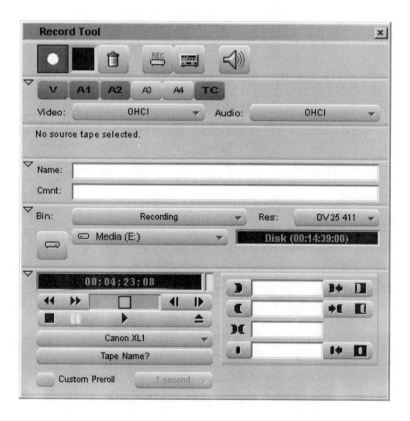

Exercise 9

Inputting Video

Until you actually record for yourself, it may seem like the most mystical part of nonlinear editing. The following exercise takes you through the logging and recording process step-by-step, to help you feel comfortable with all the buttons and tools used in this process. Remember, one of the most important aspects of recording is being organized.

We do not provide you with a tape. Locate a MiniDV tape with footage you can record to go through this exercise.

We provide you with two versions of the exercise; perform the one that best suits your abilities and work style. For a more guided exercise, see "Inputting Video (Guided)" on this page. For a less guided exercise, see "Inputting Video (Outlined)" on page 34.

Inputting Video (Guided)

Getting Started

To get started:

1. Do one of the following, based on the status of the Avid system:

   - If you have quit the Avid application, launch it now.

   - If the Project Selection dialog box is displayed, go to step 2.

   - If you are in a project, close it to return to the Project Selection dialog box.

2. Create a new project by clicking New Project in the Project Selection dialog box, and name it Record.

3. In the New Project dialog box, type a new project name, and choose NTSC or PAL.

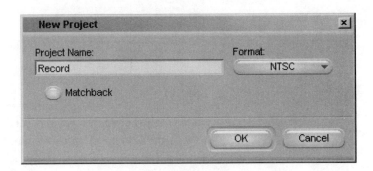

4. Click OK.

Now we'll get ready to record by creating a new bin.

1. Create a new bin which will hold your recorded clips, and name it **New Clips.**

2. With that bin highlighted, choose Record from the Tools menu.

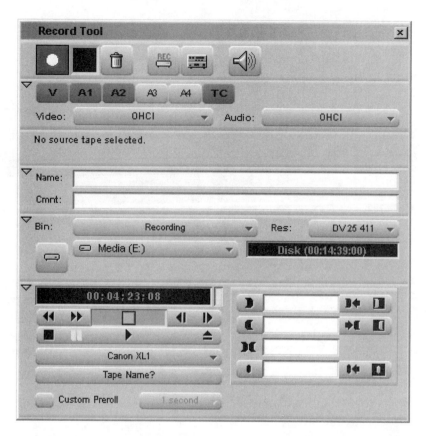

3. Insert the tape into the deck.

A New Tape appears in the Select Tape dialog box.

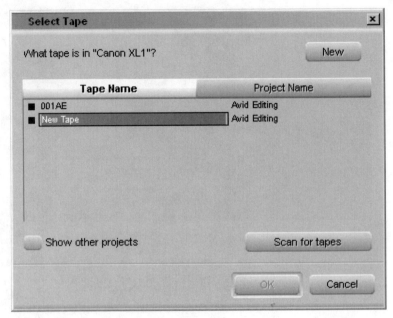

4. Type the name of the tape (the same name that's on the tape cassette) and press Enter or Return.

5. Click OK.

Selecting Tracks and Target Disks

In this exercise you will record video and one or two channels of audio.

1. In the top of the Record tool, click the desired tracks: V, A1, A2. Make sure the TC track is selected. (If only one audio track was recorded on your tape, don't click A2.)

To ensure that recorded video and audio material is sent to the same target disk:

2. Click the Single Drive/Dual Drive button until it displays a single drive.

3. Press the Target Drive pop-up and choose your target disk from the menu of available disks.

Recording

To record:

1. Locate the first shot on the tape.

2. Mark an IN by clicking the Mark IN button.

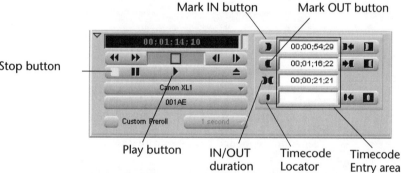

Mark IN button   Mark OUT button

Stop button

Play button   IN/OUT duration   Timecode Locator   Timecode Entry area

3. Play the tape, and click the Mark OUT button at the end of the shot.

4. Pause the tape by clicking the Pause button.

5. Click the large red Record button to record the material and simultaneously make a master clip.

Once the system is finished recording, notice that a master clip icon appears in your bin, and the tape is paused.

6. Name your clip.

Logging and Batch Recording

Now you'll log several clips. Avid Xpress DV will record the clips' INs and OUTs but will not record them until you specify.

To log the clips:

1. Click the Record/Log mode button.

    Record mode

   The system switches to Log mode.

    Log mode

2. Forward the tape to the next shot.

3. Mark an IN and OUT to select this shot (or a portion of it). (For the sake of time and drive space, limit your clip to maximum 5 seconds.)

4. Click on the pencil icon to create a master clip.

   A new clip is created, and is ready for naming.

5. Type a new name and press Enter on the numeric keypad.

6. Log two more clips. For each one, mark an IN and OUT, then click the Log pencil and name the clip.

7. When you finish, click the Record/Log mode button once in the Record tool to return to Record mode.

8. Click in the Bin window that contains the logged clips to make it active.

9. Choose Select All from the Edit menu to highlight all the clips in the bin.

Although you have already recorded a clip, you can select all and then choose to record only those clips for which there is no media. This is very useful when you have a large bin full of recorded and unrecorded clips and don't want to have to shift-select only the clips that need to be recorded.

10. Choose Batch Record from the Bin menu. Make sure the option "Offline media only" is selected and click OK.

    The clips will now be recorded in real-time in the order they appear on the tape.

11. Click OK when the batch record is complete.

12. Close the Record tool.

13. Play the clips.

Inputting Video (Outlined)

We do not provide you with a tape. Locate a MiniDV tape to go through this exercise.

Getting Started

1. Connect the tape deck to the Avid system.

2. Launch the Avid system and create a new project.

3. Create a bin to hold the recorded clips, and name it.

4. Open the Record tool.

5. Insert the tape into the deck and select the correct tape name, if it exists, or create a new one (give it the same name that's on the cassette). Be sure to follow proper naming conventions.

Recording

1. In the Record tool, mark an IN and OUT for the first shot on the tape.

2. Record and name the clip.

Logging and Batch Recording

1. In Log mode of the Record tool, log each of the next three shots on the tape.

2. Select all the clips in the bin and batch record them. (What should you do to avoid recapturing any clips already recorded in that bin?)

3. Play the clips to make sure they were properly recorded.

Module 10

Preparing Your Bin for Editing

The best time to begin organizing your clips and bins is during the logging process. You can add detailed comments about each clip to identify the shot you need, or create new bins to keep all clips that meet a specific criterion together, for example, all the close-ups in the CU bin.

Objectives

After completing this module, you will be able to:

- Show headings in Text view

- Add a custom column to a bin

- Sort and sift bins

- Move clips between bins

Text View

Preparing your bin for editing is best done in Text view. A new bin displays only the clip icon and the clip name for new clips.

To add statistical headings to your current view:

1. Choose Headings from the Bin menu.

   A window appears displaying all of the available headings, with the ones already displayed in your bin highlighted.

2. To add a heading, Control+click (Windows) or click (Macintosh) on the heading in the list.

3. To remove a heading that is already selected, Control+click (Windows) or click (Macintosh) on it in the list.

4. Click OK.

Adding a Custom Column to a Bin

In addition to the standard headings that can be displayed in Text view, you can add your own custom column headings to describe information about clips and sequences. For example, you might want to add any of the following custom column headings:

- Shot Size: Each clip's shot size (wide shot, medium shot, close-up, extreme close-up, and so on).

- Quality: Asterisks for good (*), better (**), and best (***) quality.

- Good: Each entry is either Yes or No.

- Description: Content of the shot.

- Dialog: First few words of each dialog clip

Once you create a custom column and enter data for each clip, you can sort and sift the column.

To add a new column:

1. Put the bin into Text view.

2. Click an empty area to the right of all of the headings.

   You can also move any existing column to the right or left (by dragging the column heading) to create an empty area.

3. Type the column heading you want. Column headings must contain fewer than 14 characters, including spaces.

4. Press Enter (Windows) or Return (Macintosh).

   This puts the pointer in the data box, beside the first clip in the bin.

5. Type the information and press Enter/Return to move to the next line.

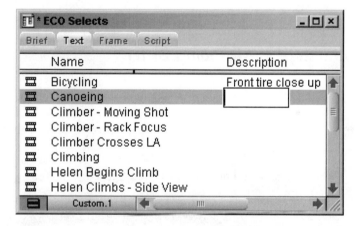

6. Create any additional columns and enter information.

   Devise a good naming plan. For example, label all close-ups "CU." Otherwise you will not be able to sort or sift the column in any meaningful way.

7. Choose Align Columns in the Bin Fast menu, or press Control+T (Windows) or ⌘+T (Macintosh) if you need to straighten out the rows.

Sorting and Sifting Clips

Sorting and sifting clips are valuable tools for organizing your footage. You can either sort or sift clips in a bin to find a specific clip or to see clips that meet specific criteria:

- *Sorting clips* arranges clips in alphanumeric order (initial numbers come before initial letters).

  For example, sort the Scene column, in ascending order, and you will create a list of all clips of Scene 1, followed by all clips of Scene 2, and so on. You might sort by Timecode to obtain the order in which the clips appear in your source tapes.

- *Sifting clips* shows only clips that meet specific criteria.

  For example, sift the Name column for the name of a character, or sift a custom column called Shot Size for "CU" to obtain a list of all close-ups.

Sorting Clips in Ascending Order

To sort clips in ascending order:

1. In Text view, click the heading of the column that you want to use as the criterion.

   The column is highlighted.

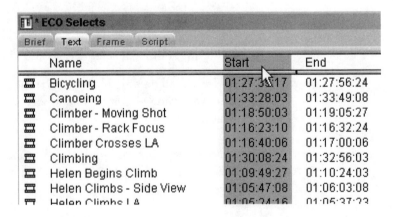

2. If you do not see the heading you want, choose Headings from the Bin menu and select desired headings.

To show only the columns you need to see, you can rearrange columns in Text view any time by dragging the headings to the right or left.

3. Choose Sort from the Bin menu, or press Control+E (Windows) or ⌘+E (Macintosh) or right-click the Column heading and choose Sort on Column, Ascending (Windows).

The objects in the bin are sorted.

4. To sort clips in descending order, hold down the Alt (Windows) or Option (Macintosh) key while you choose Sort Reversed from the Bin menu. Or press Alt+Control+E (Windows) or Option+⌘+E (Macintosh) or right-click the Column heading and choose Sort on Column, Descending (Windows).

If the Sort command is dimmed in the menu, it means that you have not selected a column.

To reapply the last sort, choose Sort Again from the Bin menu with no column selected. This is especially useful after new clips are added to a sorted bin.

Sorting Multiple Columns

You can sort multiple columns in a bin at once. The left-most column in Text view is the primary criterion for the sorting operation. You can rearrange the columns in the bin, by dragging a column heading to the right or left, in order to establish which column is primary. For example, if you want to arrange your clips according to Start Timecode within Quality, arrange the columns this way:

Name	Quality	Start
Starting Line	*	01:20:40:28
Helen Climbs LA	**	01:05:24:16
Helen Climbs - Side View	**	01:05:47:08
Helen Looks Up	**	01:11:24:23
Climber Crosses LA	**	01:16:40:06
Ride And Run	**	01:25:32:26
Bicycling	**	01:27:39:17
Climbing	**	01:30:08:24
Canoeing	**	01:33:28:03
Rafting All	**	01:36:51:04
Interview "No Sleep"	**	01:42:09:06
Interview "Boyscout Jamboree"	***	01:03:45:12

(ECO Selects — Brief / Text / Frame / Script)

Useful Application

You can keep your most recent sequence at the top of the bin by giving the name an initial character of "!" (exclamation point). You can keep your old sequences at the bottom of the bin by giving the names an initial character of "z". Then sort the Name column in ascending order.

Sifting Clips

Sifting clips allows you to show only those clips that meet certain criteria. For example, you might want to sift the clips in your bin to show only the clips that contain "CU" in the Name column. You can also use the sift function to perform more complex sifts.

To sift clips:

1. Choose Custom Sift from the Bin menu.

    The Sift dialog box opens.

2. Choose among the following operations in the Criterion shadow box.

- Contains
- Begins with
- Matches exactly

3. Click in the Text to Find box, and enter the text that you want the system to find.

4. Choose the column that you want to search from the Column or Range to Search shadow box.

   A menu lists the headings in the current bin view. You can also select Any to search all the columns, including those not currently displayed.

5. Repeat the procedure for other search criteria.

6. If you're not sure that you have set up the dialog box correctly, click Apply. The results of the sift appear in the bin, and the Sift dialog box remains open.

7. Revise the search criteria, if necessary.

8. When you are satisfied with your results, click OK.

   The clips that meet your criteria appear in the bin, with the word "Sifted" added to the bin name.

Clips sifted for Helen in the Name column

Sifting Multiple Criteria

You can sift more than one criteria, using one of the following methods.

- OR (inclusive) sift: sifts more than one criterion (in one or more columns), where a clip must meet *only one* criterion to appear in the sifted bin

  For example, you might want to sift for clips that contain either "CU" or "MS" in the Shot Size column.

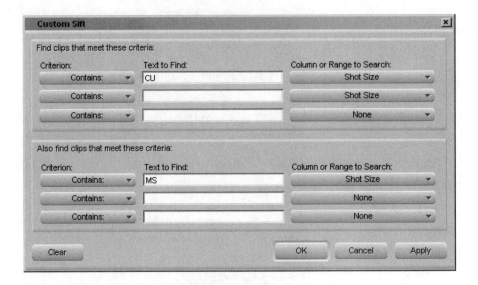

Here are the results.

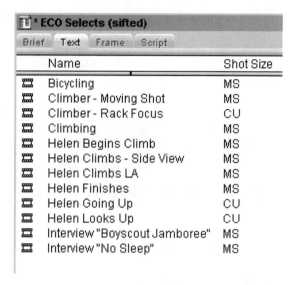

- AND (exclusive) sift: sifts more than one criterion (in one or more columns), where a clip must meet *all* criteria to appear in the sifted bin

For example, you might want to sift for clips that contain both "Helen" in the Name column and "MS" in the Shot Size column.

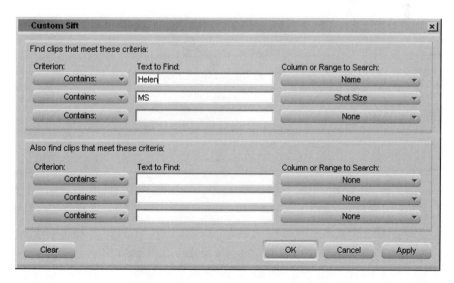

Here are the results.

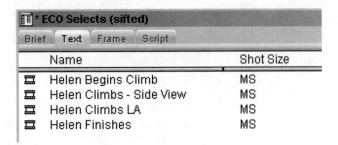

Showing Sifted and Unsifted Views of the Bin

After you have sifted the clips in a bin, you can display the bin in a sifted state or in an unsifted state.

- To view the entire bin, choose Show Unsifted from the Bin menu.

- To view the sifted bin, choose Show Sifted from the Bin menu.

✍ *The check mark in the menu indicates the current state of the bin.*

✍ *Unsifted and sifted are dimmed in the menu if a Sift has not been set up.*

Moving Clips Between Bins

Once you have sifted clips in a bin, you can move or copy them into a new bin. For example, if you sift for all clips with Helen in the Name column, you can move or copy all the clips with Helen into a single bin. Note the distinction between moving and copying clips:

- *Moving* a clip removes it from Bin A and places it in Bin B.

- *Copying* a clip leaves it in Bin A and places a copy of it in Bin B.

Here are some common applications:

- You might want to copy sifted clips to a new bin.

- If you digitized clips into a bin based on tape name, you might want to copy clips to new bins based on content. The clips remain in the bin bearing the tape name, and also reside in content bins.

- You can create new bins as the edit progresses. In this way, you can organize the entire body of clips available to the edit in an understandable, project-specific way.

To move or copy clips and sequences to a new bin:

1. Create a new bin.

   Give the bin a name that describes the clips it will contain. For example, if you move all close-ups to a new bin, name the bin *CU Clips*.

2. Position the bins so that you can see both of them at the same time. You may need to resize the bins to do this.

3. In the original bin, select the clips that you want to move.

4. Do one of the following:

   a. Drag the clips to the destination bin to move them.

   b. Alt+drag (Windows) or Option+drag (Macintosh) the clips to the destination bin to copy them.

   The clips are now contained in the new bin and may or may not reside in the original bin.

Duplicating Versus Alt/Option-Dragging Clips

There is a difference between duplicating (Control+D or ⌘+D) and Alt/Option-dragging clips to a bin.

- Duplicating creates a different clip pointing to the same media.

  For example, if you mark an IN in one clip, the IN mark is not automatically added to the duplicate clip.

- If you Alt/Option+drag a clip, it creates an exact copy of the clip.

  For example, if you mark an IN in one clip, it automatically appears in the other.

Review Questions

1. How can you find the Start Timecode of your clips? See "Text View" on page 10-2.

2. How do you add a custom column to a bin in Text view? See "Adding a Custom Column to a Bin" on page 10-2.

3. Fill in the Sift dialog box to perform the following sift:

Display the clips of Helen (in the Name column) in Disk 2A. See "Sifting Clips" on page 10-6.

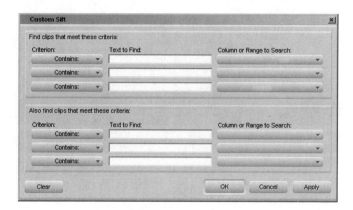

4. You want to rerecord audio clips for tape 002 that were originally recorded at 44.1 kHz at 48 kHz. Fill in the Sift dialog box to display only the clips that need to be rerecorded.

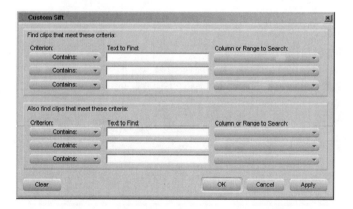

5. Fill in the Sift dialog box to display the clips which contain "Sc1," "Sc2," or "Sc3" in the Name column.

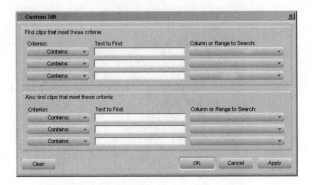

6. What is the difference between duplicating a clip and Alt+dragging (Windows) or Option+dragging (Macintosh) a clip to a new bin? See "Moving Clips Between Bins" on page 10-11.

Module 11

Creating Titles

The Title tool is a powerful yet easy-to-use program that is accessed from within Avid Xpress DV, and creates high quality titles and graphics. This module introduces the basic concepts of using the Title tool. To learn more about creating titles, see the *Avid Xpress DV Effects Reference Guide*.

Objectives

After you complete this module, you will be able to:

• Create a title in Title tool

Getting Started

To get started:

1. In the sequence, place the Position indicator within the shot where you want your title to appear. This frame will be visible in the Title tool as a background. This frame is for reference only; it is not part of your title.

2. In Source/Record mode, choose New Title from the Clip menu.

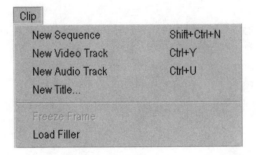

The Title Tool opens with the video frame currently displayed in the sequence as a reference. (If there is no sequence in the Timeline, the Title tool opens with a black background.)

Working with the Title Tool

The Title tool creates pages of text and graphics that can be saved over a color background or keyed over video. When titles are created for keying over video, they carry transparency information (in the Alpha channel) which makes the pixels around the text or shapes transparent to the underlying video.

Objects created in the Title tool are anti-aliased so that the edges are smooth over any background. You must render titles created in the Title tool to output them.

Each title you create is saved in a bin and can be edited into a sequence using standard editing procedures.

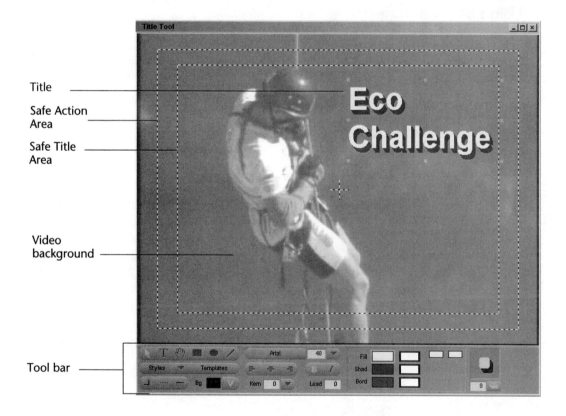

Title

Safe Action
Area

Safe Title
Area

Video
background

Tool bar

Using Safe Title and Action Guidelines

By default, the system displays two outlined boxes in the Title tool window to use as guidelines.

- Safe Title area is the inner box. All text for television broadcast should remain within this inner box.

- Safe Action area is the outer box. This is the area for video display.

These guidelines are self-adjusting for PAL and NTSC projects.

■ If Safe Title and Safe Action area guidelines are not displayed, choose Safe Title Area/Global Grid from the Object menu.

Using Safe Colors

If you plan to use your title for television broadcast, you should make sure Safe Colors is on. This command displays only low saturation colors for use in text, objects, and background. Colors with low saturation look best when combined with video. By default, Safe Colors is turned on.

■ If Safe Colors is not on, choose Safe Colors from the Object menu.

Understanding the Tool Bar

At the bottom of the Title tool window are tools and menus you can use for creating and editing text and objects. They work much like similar tools in other draw and paint programs.

After you use a tool, the system reverts to the Selection tool, and the cursor becomes an arrow. To prevent a tool from automatically reverting to the Selection tool, double-click the tool's icon.

The following illustration identifies the different sections of the tool bar.

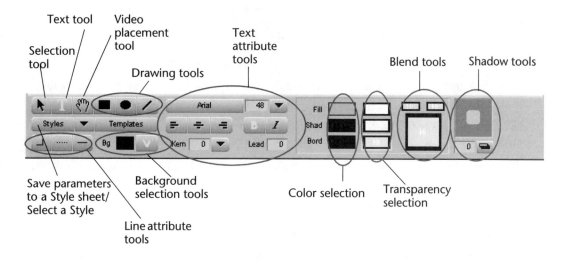

Table 9 briefly describes each section of the tool bar:

Table 9: Tool Bar Elements

Tool	Description
Selection tool	Changes the cursor from the text I-beam to an arrow and allows you to select text or objects for operations such as moving and color modification.
Text tool	Changes the cursor to an I-beam and allows you to enter text.
Video placement tool	Changes the cursor to a hand and allows you to scroll the entire video clip in the Title tool window within the frame.
Drawing tools	Allow you to draw boxes, circles, ovals, and lines.
Style sheet	Allows you to set up basic title and drawing parameters that you can use throughout your work.
Display/select Styles	Displays examples of the styles you defined and allows you to select one.
Line attributes	Allow you to change the corners of boxes, line and border thickness, and arrowhead styles.
Background selection tools	Allow you to switch between a video and opaque background. Also allow you to change the color of opaque backgrounds.
Text attribute tools	Allow you to set various text attributes such as font, font size, kerning, and leading.
Color selection	Allows you to change the color of text and objects.
Transparency selection	Allows you to change the transparency levels of text and objects.
Color and Transparency blend	When a color blend or transparency is associated with a style or object, this area displays the current values.
Shadow tools	Allow you to create drop shadows and depth shadows for text and objects.

Creating the Text for a Title

When the Title tool opens, the Text tool is automatically selected, and the cursor becomes an I-beam.

1. If not selected, select the Text tool (T). The cursor becomes an I-beam.

Selection tool Text tool

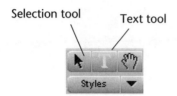

The Text tool remains selected until another tool is selected.

2. Click anywhere in the frame where you want to add text.

A blinking insertion point appears.

3. Type the text.

Repositioning Text

1. Click the Selection tool on the tool bar.

 You can Alt+click (Windows) or Option+click (Macintosh) anywhere in the Title tool window to switch between the Selection tool and the Text tool.

2. Click on the text. A box with six handles appears.

3. Click and drag inside the text box (but not the handles) to reposition the box.

 If you drag the handles, you readjust the size of the frame.

Formatting Text

You use the Text Attributes section of the Tool bar to adjust font, font size, text style, text justification, and kerning and leading.

Text attributes

Selecting a Font

When creating a title, you can use any of the fonts available in your Fonts folder, found in Control Panels (Windows) or the System folder (Macintosh). To select a new font for your text:

1. With the text selected (using the Text or Selection tool), click the Font Selection menu to display the available fonts.

Font Selection menu   Currently selected point size

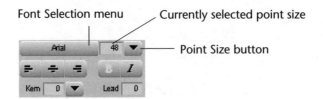

Point Size button

2. Choose a font from the menu.

   The system displays the name in the Font selection box and uses the font for text until you change it during the editing session.

Selecting Point Size

The point size controls the size of the selected text. A *point* is a typographical unit of measure. There are 12 points to the pica. As a rule of thumb, there are approximately 72 points/inch (but in fact a 72-point font will rarely be exactly an inch high).

1. With the text selected, click and hold the Point Size button.

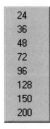

2. Choose a standard point size from the menu, or enter a point size between 6 and 500 into the Point Size window and press Enter on the numeric keypad.

   You can also select the point size number and use the Up and Down arrow keys to change the value incrementally.

Selecting Text Style

To change the text style:

With the text selected, click the Bold or Italics button.

Bold and Italic buttons

Text Justification

Text justification controls the alignment of all text within a text element.

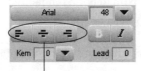

Text Justification buttons

You can use the text justification buttons in the Title tool to align the text.

- Click the left Text justification button to left justify text within the text box.

- Click the center button to center text as you type within the text box.

- Click the right button to right justify the text as you type.

You can also choose any of the options in the Alignment menu to align the text.

To center the text within the screen, you can also type the text, click the Selection button, drag the handles to the right and left edges of the safe title area, and click the center justification button.

Kerning and Leading

Text Kerning

Kerning controls the amount of space between characters. You can expand or condense the character spacing to make text more readable or to create special effects, such as dramatically expanded spacing in a title. The most common way to adjust kerning is to manually kern individual character pairs.

 If you mix italic and plain versions of a font in a title, you might want to adjust the spacing between characters.

To adjust text kerning:

1. Select the Text tool.

Text tool

2. Click between a character pair, or select a group of characters by clicking and dragging the mouse over it.

3. Press the Alt (Windows) or Option (Macintosh) key and use the left or right arrow keys to increase or decrease the spacing.

Leading Adjustment

Leading adjusts the spacing between lines in a title. Leading is measured in points, from baseline to baseline of the lines of text. It is applied uniformly to all lines in a text box. The Title tool uses the leading that is built into the font as the default.

You might want to add leading for sans serif, tall, or boldface fonts, and for fonts with a strong vertical emphasis.

— Leading Adjustment selection box

To adjust text leading:

1. Select the lines of text. All of the lines of text should be in one text box.

2. Click in the Leading Adjustment selection box.

3. To increase or decrease the leading values, do one of the following:

   - Enter a number for the desired leading value and press Return. Positive leading values add space between lines; negative values decrease space.

   - Use the up or down arrow keys.

Leading Between Selected Lines in a Block

By default, leading within the Title Tool applies to all lines in a block. However, you often need to add extra leading between certain lines within a block. For example, you need a certain amount of leading between a person's name and his title but more leading between one name and title and the next name and title.

Remember that leading is based upon the point size of the text within that line. A leading value of –20 that might be acceptable for text at 64 points is often far too close for text at 24 points.

To add extra "leading" between two lines, simply add a blank line, select the entire blank line, and change the point size of the text within the line (including the carriage return). You aren't actually modifying leading, but adding an adjustable vertical space between two lines of type.

To add space between two lines in a block:

1. Place the cursor at the end of the line where you want to add space.

2. Press Enter or Return to add a carriage return.

3. Place your cursor at the head of the new line of type and drag downward until the entire new line is highlighted.

4. Change the type size to a smaller or larger amount until you have the desired space.

To apply the same space again at a new location, simply copy the line while it is selected and use paste to insert it where needed.

Accessing Special Characters

Windows

Special characters including language and diacritical marks can be accessed by holding the Alt key down and typing a key code on the numeric keypad. The accessory Character Map provides a map of the additional characters. You can access it by choosing Start Menu > Programs > Accessories > System Tools > Character Map.

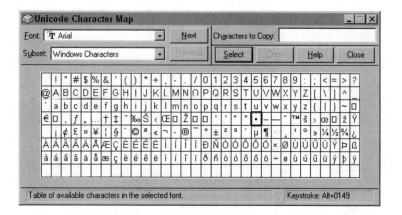

Macintosh

Additional characters including language and diacritical marks can be accessed by holding down the Option key and typing a key combination. The desk accessory Key Caps provides a map of the additional characters. You can access it by choosing Apple Menu > Key Caps.

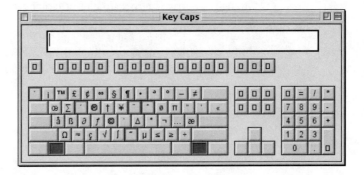

The key codes for common special characters are identical for every roman font on the system. You can also use Character Map or Key Caps to discover the key codes for symbol and dingbat fonts.

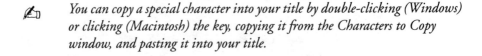 *You can copy a special character into your title by double-clicking (Windows) or clicking (Macintosh) the key, copying it from the Characters to Copy window, and pasting it into your title.*

Commonly Used Special Characters

Special characters are accessed via the same key codes regardless of the font used. The following table provides the Windows and Macintosh keyboard shortcuts for commonly used special characters:

Table 10: Commonly Used Special Characters

Character	Windows Key Code	Macintosh Key Code
• (Bullet)	Alt+0149	Option+8
' (Proper Apostrophe)	Alt+0146	Option+Shift+]
" (Open Quotes)	Alt+0147	Option+[
" (Close Quotes)	Alt+0148	Option+Shift+]
– (Dash / Endash)	Alt+0150	Option+ - (Hyphen)
— (Long Dash / Emdash)	Alt+0151	Option+Shift+ - (Hyphen)
™ (Trademark)	Alt+0153	Option+2
© (Copyright)	Alt+0169	Option+G
® (Registered)	Alt+0174	Option+R
¼ (One Quarter)	Alt+0188	Not Available
½ (One Half)	Alt+0189	Not Available
é	Alt+0233	Option+e, then e
ñ	Alt+0241	Option+n, then n

Applying Shadows and Borders

This section covers drop and depth shadows, soft shadows and glows, and borders.

Applying Drop or Depth Shadows to Text

Adding a drop shadow to a title gives the perception of depth, as though the title were lying on a different plane than the video beneath. You can apply drop or depth shadows to text, and select their width, direction, and transparency.

The following illustration shows an example of drop and depth shadows:

Drop shadow
Depth shadow

To add a drop or depth shadow:

1. Select the text.

2. Toggle the Drop and Depth Shadow button to select a drop or depth shadow.

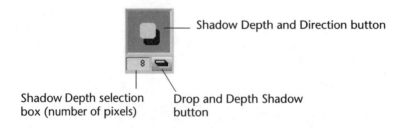

Shadow Depth and Direction button

Shadow Depth selection box (number of pixels)

Drop and Depth Shadow button

3. Choose one of the following methods to create a shadow:

- Click the Shadow Depth and Direction button and drag the cursor around to position the shadow in whatever direction you like.

- Type a value in the Shadow Depth selection box and press Enter or Return.

- Select the value and use the Up and Down arrow keys to change the value.

Adding Soft Shadows and Glows

Softening a shadow

To make the shadow seem more realistic, you can soften the edges of the shadow to your liking.

To soften a shadow:

1. Drag the Shadow Depth and Direction button in the direction you want the shadow to be cast.

2. Choose Soften Shadow from the Object menu or press Shift+Control+H (Windows) or Shift+⌘+H (Macintosh).

3. Enter the desired softness level. (Values range from 4 to 40.)

4. To preview the softness, click Apply.

5. Click OK when you are satisfied with the look.

Adding a Glow

Another popular effect for a title is a glow, in which a soft color radiates from the letters of your title, as though the letters were lit from behind. This effect is a simple variation of the drop shadow.

To create a glow effect:

■ Set Shadow Softness to a non-zero value and Shadow Depth to zero.

To create titles that have neither softened shadows nor glows, set Shadow Softness to zero.

Applying Borders to the Text

To apply a border to a text string:

1. Select the text.

2. Click the Solid Line button (the middle Line Attribute button in the lower left corner of the Tool bar) and choose a line width.

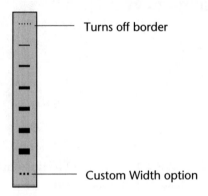

Turns off border

Custom Width option

3. Choose from the standard width selections or choose the Custom Width option to open a dialog box and enter a custom width.

4. If you choose the Custom Width option, in the dialog box type a whole number in pixels to specify a custom width. The minimum width for a text border is 1; the maximum width is 200.

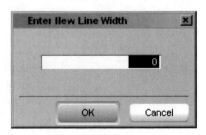

Choosing Colors

You can select the color for text, shadows, and borders.

The following illustration shows the boxes associated with color:

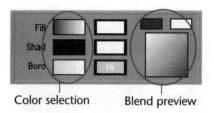

Color selection   Blend preview

- The Color selection boxes control the fill (Fill), shadow (Shad), and border (Bord) color selection.

- The Blend preview boxes appear when you select the fill or border color selection box.

If you select a color selection box, the top windows show the two colors that are used to create the blend. The bottom window shows the blended color and allows you to control the direction of the blend.

Adjusting the Color

You can select a color from the Title Tool Color Picker, use an eyedropper to select a color from any open application on your computer, or you can use the Windows/Macintosh Color dialog box to select a color. All of these features are available through the Title Tool Color Picker:

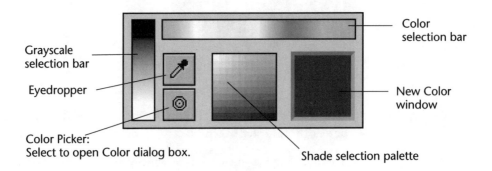

Color selection bar

Grayscale selection bar

Eyedropper

New Color window

Color Picker:
Select to open Color dialog box.

Shade selection palette

Selecting a Color from the Title Tool Color Picker

1. Select the text.

2. Click and hold one of the Color Selection boxes on the Title tool bar: fill (the text itself), shadow, or border (text outline). Keep holding, and drag the Title Tool Color Picker to the side, so that the window stays open.

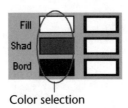

Color selection

3. To choose a color:

   a. Click or drag the cursor along the Color selection bar to the color you want.

   b. Click or drag the cursor in the Shade selection palette to choose a shade. The New Color window displays the shade.

c. Change the color and shade until you achieve the results you want.

To choose a grayscale value, choose a value from the grayscale selection bar.

4. Close the Title Tool Color Picker.

The color is applied to the selected object.

To use the Eyedropper

1. Select the text.

2. Click and hold one of the Color Selection buttons on the Title tool bar.

3. Drag the mouse to the eyedropper, and release the mouse button.

The cursor becomes an eyedropper.

4. Click the eyedropper on the color you want to pick up from the window or from any open application on your screen. The tip of the eyedropper should be on the color you want.

The color is applied to the selected object.

Blending Two Colors in an Object

☞ *You can blend the fill and border but you cannot blend a shadow.*

You can blend two colors in the text and specify the direction of the blend.

To blend two colors

1. Select the text.

2. Click the Color Selection button for either fill or border.

   The blend color selection boxes appear.

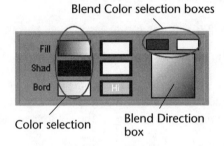

Blend Color selection boxes

Color selection

Blend Direction box

3. Click the right or left Blend Color selection box and choose a color using the Title Tool Color Picker.

4. Click on the other Blend Color selection box and choose the second color for your blend.

   The Blend Direction box appears below the two Color selection boxes. This box displays the blend and allows you to specify the direction of the blend (for example, left to right).

5. Click the Blend Direction box; hold the mouse button down and drag the cursor clockwise or counterclockwise to achieve the effect you want.

   As you rotate the pointer, the position of the two colors rotates as well. The change takes effect as soon as you release the mouse button.

Adjusting the Transparency

After you select a color, you can select the color transparency. The following illustration shows the tools used to create transparencies.

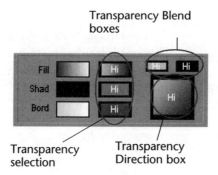

1. To select a color transparency, click the appropriate transparency button, depending on whether the transparency will apply to the text, or adjust a shadow or outline around the selected text.

   The Transparency Selection box contains an opaque white by default. As you reduce the level of transparency, the word "Hi" becomes more visible. Opaque white creates a fully opaque object or portion of an object. When the word "Hi" is completely visible over a solid black background the object or portion of the object becomes fully transparent.

2. Move the slider until you attain the transparency you desire. As you move the sliders, the system immediately applies the transparency to your selection.

3. The Transparency Blend boxes appear.

4. You can create a transparency blend and then apply direction just as you did for blending two colors in the previous section.

You might find it useful to turn off the shadow for an object while experimenting with transparency. Set the shadow value to 0 in the Shadow Depth window.

Using Title Templates

Title Templates are reusable title layouts. A good use of a title layout would be for a set of lower thirds titles you want to use to "ID" people in a show. Title Templates can be designed by the graphics department and be used by every editor on the system.

Creating Title Templates

1. In the Title Tool, create the layout of your title.

   Create every element in the title, including any text boxes.

2. Adjust the width of all text boxes to the maximum width that will be needed.

   If you don't do this and you want to type text that extends beyond the boundary of the text box, the text won't fit.

3. Click the Templates button at the bottom of the Title Tool.

4. Select Save Template from the menu that appears.

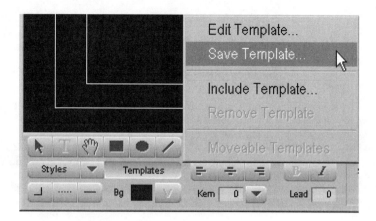

The Save Template As dialog box opens.

5. Type a name for your title template and click Save.

▲ **(Windows) Append the extension .pct to the end of the template name to make it easier to access.**

The template is saved in the Settings > Title_Templates folder.

Applying Title Templates

1. Click the Templates button and select Include Template.

The Open dialog box appears.

2. Select the template you wish to use and click Open.

The template appears in the Title Tool.

3. If the template loaded is not the one required, click the Template button and select the template from the Remove Template submenu.

4. Edit the type in one of the template's text boxes as required.

Only the text in a template text box can be edited. The box itself and any graphic blocks in the template cannot be individually resized or moved.

Moving and Editing Templates

By default title templates cannot be directly edited or moved. However, two options to move and edit a template are provided.

To be able to move a template within the screen:

1. Chose Moveable Templates from the Template menu.

2. Click the Selection tool.

3. Click on the template and drag it to its new location.

   The entire template moves as a block. It is not possible to move a single element within the template.

To edit a template:

1. Choose Edit Template from the Template menu.

   The Open dialog box appears.

2. Select the template you wish to edit and click Open.

3. Make any edits necessary.

4. Choose Save Template from the Template menu.

   A Save dialog box appears.

5. Type a name for your title template and click Save.

Managing Title Templates

Title templates are stored in by default in the Title_Templates folder located in the Settings folder in the Avid Xpress DV folder. Title templates can also be stored in or copied to any folder including shared directories on a Unity file system.

Saving, Fading, and Revising Titles

Saving the Title

When creating a new title, you should save the title soon after you begin working on it, for safety.

To save a title:

1. (Option) Create a bin for your titles and open it.

2. Choose Save from the File menu.

   The Save Title dialog box appears.

3. In the dialog box:

   • Name the title.

   • Select a destination bin.

   • Choose a target drive for the associated media files.

4. Click Save or click Fast Save if you don't want to render the title yet.

5. You are returned to the title page and can continue working on this title, or you can quit the Title tool by choosing Close from the File menu.

When you quit Title tool, a two-minute title is placed into your target bin, and the media is stored on the drive you specified.

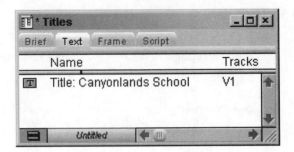

Editing the Title into the Sequence

To key the title over video:

1. If necessary, edit your background video onto track V1.

2. To add V2 track to your sequence, choose New Video Track from the Clip menu, or press Control+Y (Windows) or ⌘+Y (Macintosh).

3. Mark IN and OUT points in the Timeline to set the duration of the title.

4. Mark an IN or OUT in the Source monitor.

5. In the Timeline, patch the title from source V1 to record V2.

   When you patch one track to another, the system automatically monitors the selected record track, so the system is now monitoring V2. Since the sequence plays all tracks below and including the monitored track, make sure to monitor V2 to view V1 and V2.

 Click the empty area to the right of record track selector V1 to display the V1 Monitor icon and view only track V1.

6. Overwrite the title onto track V2.

7. If you have not yet rendered the title, park your blue position indicator on the title effect icon in the Timeline and choose the Render Effect button from the Tool Palette Fast menu.

Fading a Title

To fade the title:

1. Place the Position indicator in the title segment.

   To fade multiple titles in a sequence, click either Segment mode button, press the Shift key, and click the desired title segments in the Timeline.

2. Make sure the appropriate track selector is on.

3. Make sure the Timeline window is active.

4. Click the Fade Effect button from the Tool Palette Fast menu.

5. In the dialog box, enter the number of frames for the Fade Up and Fade Down.

6. Click OK.

Revising the Title

If you need to revise a title that is edited into your sequence:

1. Place the Position indicator on the title icon in the sequence.

2. Make sure the video track for the title is highlighted in the track panel.

3. Enter Effect mode by clicking the Effect Mode button in the Tool Palette.

4. Click the icon to the left of the word, "Title," to enter the Title Tool.

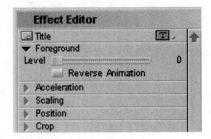

5. Revise the title.

6. Choose Close from the File menu to close the Title Tool and return to Effect mode.

7. Choose Save when prompted.

8. Close the Effect Editor.

   The modified version of the title exists in the bin holding the sequence while the original title remains in the bin where you saved it. The modified version also appears in the sequence.

9. (Option) In the title bin, delete the old title.

10. Play your title.

Review Questions

1. If a font does not appear in the Font Selection menu, what would be the reason? See "Selecting a Font" on page 11-8.

2. What is the difference between kerning and leading? See "Kerning and Leading" on page 11-11.

3. How do you create a glow? See "Adding a Glow" on page 11-17.

4. How do you edit a title so it is keyed over video? See "Editing the Title into the Sequence" on page 11-28.

5. For the Title tool, answer the following questions:

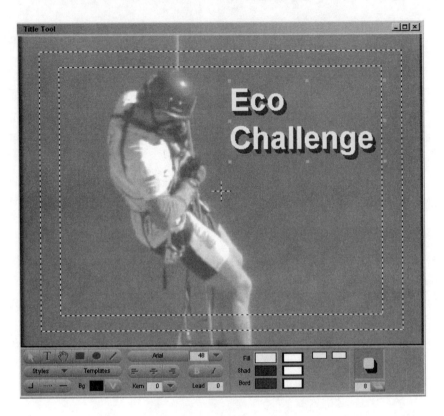

a. Which area is safe for titles?

b. How can you toggle between Selection and Text modes without clicking those buttons?

c. If you want the text 'Eco Challenge' to match the color of the helmet, what would you do?

d. If you want the top half of the text 'Eco Challenge' in green, and the bottom half in blue, what boxes do you use to create that color design?

e. What button do you select to toggle between drop and depth shadows?

Exercise 10

Creating Titles

In this exercise, you will finish the ECO Challenge advertising spot. We provide you with two versions of the exercise; perform the one that best suits your abilities and work style. For a more guided exercise, see "Creating Titles (Guided)" on this page. For a less guided exercise, see "Creating Titles (Outlined)" on page 41.

Creating Titles (Guided)

In this exercise, you will add a title, "Canyonlands Outdoor Adventure School," to your sequence.

Getting Started

To get started:

1. Create a new bin for storing your title. Keep it open.

2. Duplicate the sequence you worked on in the previous exercise, and name the duplicate.

3. Load the duplicated sequence into the Timeline.

Creating a New Title

To create the "Canyonlands Outdoor Adventure School" title for your sequence:

1. Mark an IN and OUT in your Timeline where you want your title to begin and end.

2. Place the Position indicator within the scene where you want your title to appear. This frame will be visible in the Title Tool as background.

3. Choose New Title from the Clip menu.

   A dialog box appears.

4. Click Title tool.

Using the Title Tool

The Title tool opens and displays the frame from the Timeline in the background.

1. Click in the image where you want the "Canyonlands Outdoor Adventure School" title to start.

2. Type "Canyonlands Outdoor Adventure School."

Modifying the Title

1. Click the Selection tool.

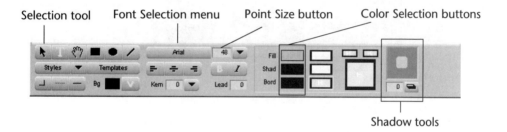

2. Select your text box by clicking on the text.

3. Choose a new font from the Font Selection menu.

4. Click the Point Size button to choose a new point size.

5. Drag the text box and reposition it.

To change the text's color:

1. Click and hold the Fill Color Selection box. Drag the box to the side so the Title Tool Color Picker stays open.

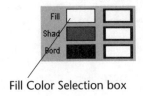

Fill Color Selection box

The Title Tool Color Picker:

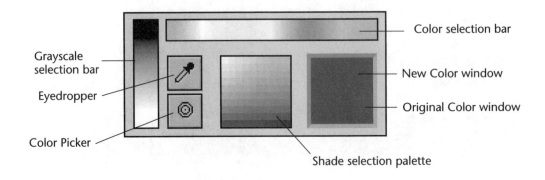

Grayscale selection bar

Eyedropper

Color Picker

Color selection bar

New Color window

Original Color window

Shade selection palette

2. To choose a color:

   a. Click or drag the cursor along the Color selection bar to the color you want.

   b. Click or drag the cursor in the Shade selection palette to choose a shade. The New Color window displays the shade.

   c. Change the color and shade until you achieve the results you want.

3. Close the Title Tool Color Picker.

To add a drop or depth shadow:

1. Click the Shadow Depth and Direction button and drag the cursor around and out to position the shadow in whatever direction and to whatever depth you desire.

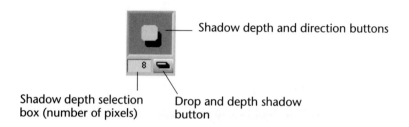

Shadow depth and direction buttons

Shadow depth selection box (number of pixels)

Drop and depth shadow button

2. Toggle the Drop and Depth Shadow button to select a drop or depth shadow.

Saving the Title

1. Choose Save Title from the File menu.

   The Save dialog box appears.

2. In the dialog box:

   a. Name the title "Canyonlands School."

   b. Select the bin for storing your title.

   c. Choose a target drive for the associated media files.

3. Click Save.

   The title will render.

4. Quit the Title Tool by choosing Close from the File menu.

   The two-minute title is automatically loaded into the Source monitor and into the target bin.

To edit the title into the sequence:

1. Mark an IN a few seconds into the title clip, so you have material for trimming and transition effects.

2. If your sequence doesn't have a V2 track, add a second video track from the Clip menu.

3. Patch the title from V1 in the Source monitor to V2 of your sequence. Turn off any audio tracks.

4. Click Overwrite.

5. Play your title to see the results.

Repositioning the Title

Sometimes, after you create the title and positioned it in the Title tool, you need to re-position it in the frame.

1. Place the Position indicator on the title icon in the sequence.

2. Make sure V2 is highlighted in the track panel.

3. Enter Effect mode by clicking the Effect Mode button, which is in the Tool Palette Fast menu.

4. Click the icon to the left of the word, "Title," to re-enter the Title tool.

Click icon. ─────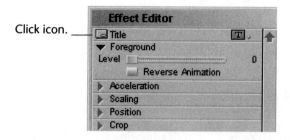

5. Activate the Selection tool, click on the text box, and reposition the title within the safe title area.

Safe title area

6. Choose Close from the File menu to close the Title Tool and return to Effect mode.

7. Choose Save when prompted.

8. Close the Effect Editor.

9. Play the result.

Fading a Title

1. Place the Position indicator over the title icon in your sequence.

2. Make sure V2 is highlighted in the track panel.

3. Click the Fade Effect button from the Tool Palette Fast Menu.

4. In the dialog box, enter the duration for the Fade Up and Fade Down and click OK.

5. Play the result.

What's Next

If time remains, continue modifying the title you just create or create others for this sequence. You might do any of the following:

• Open the title you just created and modify it by adjusting additional parameters.

• Create any other titles and add them to the sequence.

Creating Titles (Outlined)

Creating Titles

In this part of the exercise, you create an opening title for your ECO Challenge sequence, and edit it into the beginning of the sequence.

The title should provide at minimum the name of the event, "ECO Challenge." It should also draw people into the show and stylistically fit the program's content.

1. Open your sequence into the Record monitor.

2. Create a new bin for your titles.

3. Mark the portion of the sequence where you would like to place the opening title, and place the Position indicator within the marks.

4. Open a new title on your monitor.

5. Type one or more lines of text. If you want to create multiple lines of text, do one of the following:

   - To create a second line of text that will have the same properties as the first line, press Return/Enter and type the second line of text.

   - If you want to position and color each line in the title differently color, you will need to create another separate text element. Click the Text cursor in another part of the frame. Type the text.

6. Modify any the following attributes of your title, for one or more lines of text:

   - Font type and point size

   - Kerning and/or leading

   - Color

   - Drop or depth shadow

7. Save the title in the Title bin.

8. Overwrite the title to the beginning of your sequence on track V2.

9. Play the result.

Revising the Title

In this part of the exercise, you reposition at least one line of the title within the frame.

1. Open up the title you created within the Title tool. (Hint: You need to open the Effect Editor.)

2. Reposition at least one line of the title, making sure to stay within the Safe Title area.

3. Make any other changes you like.

4. Save the title and close the Title tool.

5. Fade the title up and down.

If time remains, see "What's Next" on page 11-40.

Module 12

Outputting the Sequence

Avid Xpress DV offers different methods for outputting your completed sequence. You can create an Edit Decision List (EDL) for a linear online edit; create a QuickTime file for a web site, CD-ROM, or DVD; or output to videotape, which is also called performing a digital cut. The method or combination of methods you choose depends on your situation. If you are working with film originated material and need to generate a cutlist, you can use Avid Xpress DV Matchback to generate negative cut lists for 16mm and 35mm film projects from your sequence.

This course covers creating a digital cut and outputting to DVD. See Appendix A for more information about exporting a sequence as a QuickTime file, along with other importing and exporting capabilities.

Objectives

After you complete this module, you will be able to:

- Prepare to perform a Digital Cut

- Perform a Digital Cut

- Output a sequence to DVD

Preparing for a Digital Cut

When you perform a digital cut, Avid Xpress DV plays the digital video and audio for the sequence from the storage disks and records the information onto a master tape.

When performing a digital cut to an IEEE 1394 format camera or deck, the digital cut is frame accurate. If you have a transcoder that can convert the IEEE 1394 digital signal into analog video and audio signals, you can perform a non-frame accurate digital cut to an analog Betacam or VHS deck.

Rendering Effects

You must render all effects before creating a digital cut.

See the *Effects Guide* for more information on rendering effects.

Changing to Drop-Frame or Non-Drop-Frame (NTSC Only)

If your sequence needs to be changed to drop-frame or non-drop-frame before making your digital cut, follow this procedure:

1. With your sequence in the Timeline, click in the Record monitor.

2. Choose Get Sequence Info from the File menu or press Control+I (Windows) or ⌘+I (Macintosh).

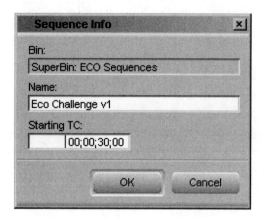

3. Click in the Starting TC box and press ; (semi-colon) on the keyboard to change to drop-frame, or press : (colon) to change to non-drop-frame.

Performing a Digital Cut

You can record your digital cut by performing an insert edit, assemble edit, or manual edit.

Performing an Insert Edit

Insert edit is the preferred method of digital cut. It requires a pre-blacked tape, which is tape with control track and timecode for at least the duration of your digital cut. Control track can be layed down on your video tape by recording a black video signal to it. As you "black" your video tape, your record deck or camera can also record proper timecode to it.

The procedure to record black and stripe timecode to a MiniDV cassette before performing the digital cut may be as simple as recording on your camera with the lens cap still in place. However, every deck and camera varies slightly in the procedure to engage the timecode. For more information on recording timecode on your video cassette consult your deck's or camera's operating manual.

To perform an insert edit:

1. Load a sequence into the Record monitor.

2. If you want to record only a portion of the sequence, mark an IN and OUT around the desired part of the sequence.

3. Load a blacked tape striped with timecode into the record deck or camera.

4. To set the parameters for an insert edit, choose Digital Cut from the Clip menu.

The Digital Cut dialog box appears.

Tracks in
sequence to be
recorded

Channels
recording to on
tape

Record Start-Time
Options pop-up
menu

Deck/Camera
controls

Deck/Camera
Selection

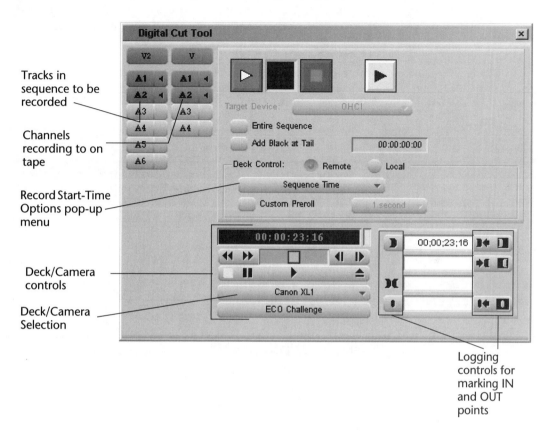

Logging
controls for
marking IN
and OUT
points

5. Make sure Deck Control Remote is selected.

6. Turn on the Remote switch on the record deck. If recording to a camera, make sure the camera is in the proper recording mode. Consult your camera's operating manual for more information.

7. Make sure your deck or camera is recognized in the Deck Selection box.

   If the Digital Cut tool displays "No Deck" in the Timecode window, choose Autoconfigure from the Deck Selection pulldown menu.

8. Select Entire Sequence if you want to record the entire sequence from start to finish.

The system ignores any marks found on the sequence. (If this option is deselected, the system records from IN to OUT, or if there are no marks, from the Position indicator to the end.)

9. (Option) Select Add Black at Tail and type the duration for the black you want to add at the end of the digital cut.

10. Choose an option from the Record Start-Time pop-up menu:

    • Sequence Time: Recording starts at the sequence's start timecode. (Generally choose this option.)

    • Record Deck Time: Recording starts at the timecode on the master tape on which the Record deck is parked.

    • Mark IN Time: Recording starts at a master tape timecode you select.

      When you choose Mark In Time, you can use the Deck controls within the Digital Cut tool to cue the tape and log IN and OUT points for frame-accurate recording.

▲ **If you are doing a digital cut of a portion of the sequence (defined by IN and OUT) and deselect Entire Sequence, the system inserts a black slug in the middle of the tape.**

11. (Option) Select Custom Preroll and choose the number of seconds from the pop-up menu to indicate how many seconds the tape rolls before the digital cut starts.

12. Select the tracks in the sequence you want to record from the left-most row of track buttons in the Digital Cut window.

13. Select the Record track buttons to the right of the Source Track buttons which specify the tracks you will record to on tape. (Choose the highest video track in the sequence, and the appropriate audio tracks.)

14. Click the Play button.

    If you have not yet loaded a tape into the record deck, the system asks you to load a tape and name it.

    The system plays the digital cut on the Edit monitor.

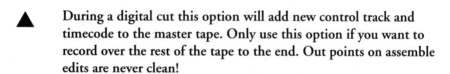

To stop the Digital Cut recording at any point, select the blue Halt Digital Cut button or press the space bar.

Performing an Assemble Edit

This option gives you the same precise control over your start time as insert edit, by only having to black a short portion of the master tape.

Assemble edit begins your digital cut at a specific timecode and commands the record deck to generate control track and timecode on the fly as the digital cut progresses. When the digital cut is complete, timecode and control track end. The result is that the end of your digital cut will not be a clean edit. Instead it will be a distorted visual edit that transitions to "snow" (or whatever else is present on the tape). (You may have encountered this situation if you ever accidentally recorded over a previously used tape on a VCR.)

When you realize your mistake and stop recording, the VCR stops recording control track. When you play back the tape to survey the damage, you notice that there is a period of distortion and "snow" before your previously recorded material reveals itself.

▲ **During a digital cut this option will add new control track and timecode to the master tape. Only use this option if you want to record over the rest of the tape to the end. Out points on assemble edits are never clean!**

▲ **Many deck-specific issues arise with the use of assemble edit. If you are not familiar with deck issues, avoid using assemble edit.**

To perform an assemble edit:

1. Load a sequence into the Record monitor.

2. If you want to record only a portion of the sequence, mark an IN and OUT around the desired part of the sequence, preferably on a cut.

3. Load a blacked tape striped with timecode into the record deck. You only need to black a short portion the tape (pre-roll plus 10 seconds) for this option to work.

4. Select Assemble Edit in the Deck Preferences settings. **You will not be able to perform an Assemble Edit without enabling the setting.**

5. To set the parameters for an assemble edit, choose Digital Cut from the Clip menu.

   The Digital Cut dialog box appears.

6. Make sure Deck Control Remote is selected.

7. Make sure the correct deck is displayed in the Deck Selection box.

8. Choose Assemble Edit from the Pop-up menu.

   This option is only available if you enable it in the Deck Preferences settings.

9. Follow the rest of the procedure from Step 8 in the previous section, "Performing an Insert Edit."

 After assemble-edit recording, a freeze frame is usually added after the OUT point for 1 second or more. This provides several frames of overlap for the next IN point before the control track and timecode break up.

Performing a Manual Edit

If you are recording to a video deck that does not support the IEEE 1394 digital video format, you will not have deck control. Instead, you must perform a manual, or "crash record" edit. To do this:

1. Load a sequence into the Record monitor.

2. If you only want to record a portion of the sequence, mark an IN and OUT around the desired part of the sequence.

3. Load a tape into the record deck.

4. Choose Digital Cut from the Clip menu.

The Digital Cut dialog box appears.

5. Select Deck Control Local.

6. Make sure the correct deck is displayed in the Deck Selection box.

7. Select Entire Sequence if you want to record the entire sequence from start to finish.

   The system ignores any marks found on the sequence. (If this option is deselected, the system records from IN to OUT, or if there are no marks, from the Position indicator to the end.)

8. (Option) Select Add Black at Tail and type the duration for the black you want to add at the end of the digital cut.

9. Select the tracks in the sequence you want to record from the left-most row of track buttons in the Digital Cut window.

10. Select the Record track buttons to the right of the Source Track buttons which specify the tracks you will record to on tape. (Choose the highest video track in the sequence, and the appropriate audio tracks.)

11. Manually press the Record button on the deck.

12. Click the Play button in the Digital Cut window.

    The system plays the digital cut on the Edit monitor.

To stop the Digital Cut recording at any point, select the blue Halt Digital Cut button or press the Space bar on the keyboard or the Stop button on the record deck.

Direct Output to DVD

You can export your finished sequence directly to a DVD disc. When the DVD is inserted into a DVD player, the DVD will automatically play back the movie. No menus or any other interactive attributes are created on the DVD.

To print your sequence directly to a DVD disc:

■ Make sure you have a DVD-burning drive attached to your system.

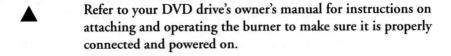 **Refer to your DVD drive's owner's manual for instructions on attaching and operating the burner to make sure it is properly connected and powered on.**

Direct Output to DVD (Windows)

1. Open the active Export Settings, and make sure that MPEG-2 is selected in the Export As field. If not, choose it from the pop-up menu. (It should be selected by default.)

2. Select the sequence that you want to export to DVD. Only one sequence may be burned to a DVD disc.

3. Choose Create DVD from the File menu.

The Create DVD dialog is displayed.

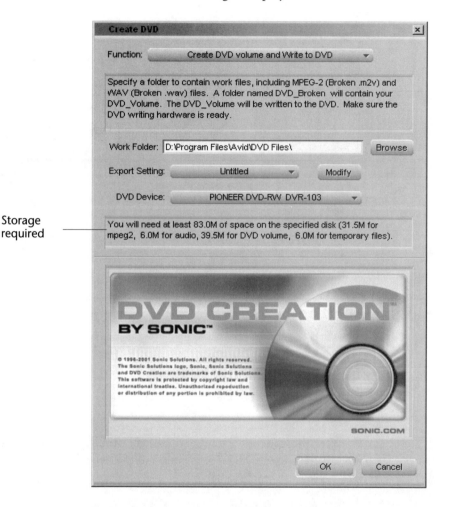

Storage
required

4. Select a location where you will create your DVD volume (using the Browse button).

The DVD volume is used to organize the files required to write the material to a DVD disc. The DVD volume is written to the location you choose on your hard drive and is then burned onto the DVD.

5. Click the Modify button.

The Export Settings for MPEG-2 appear.

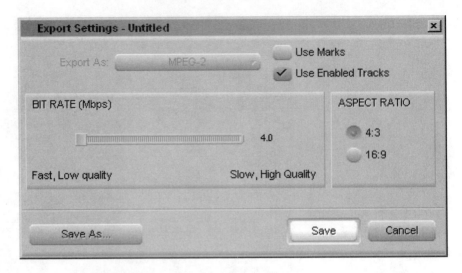

Modifying Export Settings

1. Check Use Marks to export to DVD only the information between marked IN and OUT points within the sequence.

2. Check Use Enable Tracks to export to DVD only information from the selected tracks for the sequence.

3. Adjust the Bit Rate slider to establish the quality level of the created MPEG file. Higher bit rates result in better quality, but also may require more storage space.

4. Choose 4:3 Aspect Ratio unless you are using original 16:9 anamorphic material.

5. Click Save.

6. In the Create DVD dialog box, look in the pane above the DVD Creation graphic for an estimate of the storage space you'll need on your drive.

 You must have enough storage space available on your internal hard drive to accommodate the DVD Volume before it is written to a DVD disc.

7. Click OK.

The system exports the information to the location you specified for your DVD volume and then begins the process of writing the information to your DVD disc, using the attached DVD-burning drive.

▲ **This process can take some time. Software-based MPEG encoding is an extremely complex process that can take up to 30 times the real-time duration of the sequence.**

Direct Output to DVD (Macintosh)

You can export clips and sequences to iDVD and DVD Studio Pro authoring applications. Video is exported as a QuickTime Reference file. Audio is mixed down to a stereo interleaved file and converted to a 48 kHz and AIFF file.

1. Select the sequence(s) or clip(s) that you want to export to DVD.

You may burn one or more clip, subclip, sequence, or subsequence to a DVD disc.

2. Choose Send to DVD from the File menu.

The Send to DVD dialog is displayed.

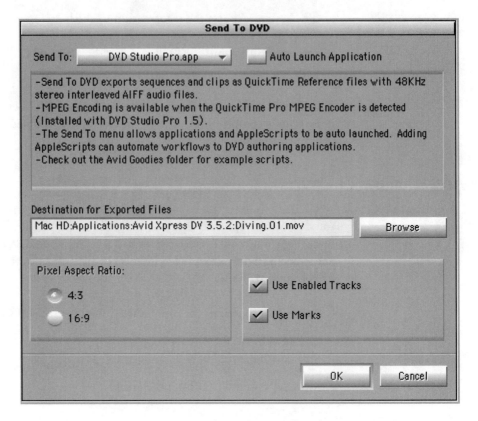

3. In the "Send to" field, choose one of the following, depending on the application you'll use:

    - iDVD.app

    - DVD Studio Pro.app

 The first time you activate "Send to," the system checks for iDVD and DVD Studio Pro. If found, they are automatically added to the Send to menu. If not found, install the application and manually add it to the menu.

4. Enable the Auto Launch Application checkbox.

5. Select a location where you will create your DVD volume (using the Browse button).

The DVD volume is used to organize the files required to write the material to a DVD disc. The DVD volume is written to the location you choose on your hard drive and is then burned onto the DVD.

6. (DVD Studio Pro only) DVD Studio Pro (1.5 and higher) comes with the QuickTime Pro MPEG Encoder. If you have it on your system:

   a. Press the QT MPEG settings.

   b. In the QuickTime MPEG Encoder window, choose the MPEG parameters for the export.

   While the QuickTime MPEG Encoder is processing, you can continue editing in Xpress DV.

7. (DVD Studio Pro only) Enable the Use QuickTime for MPEG Encoding checkbox.

8. Check Use Marks to export to DVD only the information between marked IN and OUT points within the sequence.

9. Check Use Enable Tracks to export to DVD only information from the selected tracks for the sequence.

10. Choose 4:3 Aspect Ratio unless you are using original 16:9 anamorphic material.

11. Click OK.

   The system exports the QuickTime Reference file and Stereo Interleaved AIFF files to the location you specified for your DVD volume.

12. Proceed to the "If using iDVD" or "If using DVD Studio" section.

If using iDVD:

1. Drag and drop the QuickTime Reference file into the iDVD window.

2. Change any parameters in iDVD.

3. Burn the DVD, using the attached DVD-burning drive.

If using DVD Studio Pro:

1. Drag and drop the QuickTime Reference file and Stereo Interleaved AIFF files into the DVD Studio Pro Assets window.

2. Change any parameters in iDVD.

3. Burn the DVD, using the attached DVD-burning drive..

Review Questions

1. Where does recording start for each of the three settings in the Record to Tape option in the Digital Cut window? See "Performing a Digital Cut" on page 12-4.

   a. Sequence Time

   b. Record Deck Time

   c. Mark In Time

2. What is the difference between preparing tape for an insert edit compared to an assemble edit? See "Performing a Digital Cut" on page 12-4.

3. Under what circumstance might it be preferable to perform an assemble edit as opposed to an insert edit? What risk, if any, is involved? See "Performing an Assemble Edit" on page 12-7.

4. If you need frame-accurate recording, should you crash record? See "Performing a Manual Edit" on page 12-8.

5. What format should you use to export a sequence to DVD? See "Direct Output to DVD" on page 12-10.

Appendix A

Importing and Exporting

The Avid system allows you to import and export complete sequences or selected graphic, animation, and audio files to and from compatible systems.

For example, edited sequences can be exported for use in QuickTime™ applications; multiple audio tracks can be exported for audio sweetening in any compatible digital audio workstation; and graphics files can be created and fine-tuned using third-party paint or image-processing software and imported for use in a sequence. You might also need to export the video for distribution on CD-ROM, DVD-ROM, or the web.

This appendix covers several of the available import and export options.

If you would like to know more about importing and exporting, consider taking the following Avid course:

- **Creating Graphics for Avid Xpress DV with Adobe Photoshop.***

* Available both as an instructor-led course or as a stand-alone book with exercise media on CD.

Preparing to Import Still Images

For best results, still graphics must meet a specific set of criteria *before* you import them into the Avid system. These criteria are described in the following section.

Criteria for Imported Graphics and Animations

Frame Size

The dimensions of the image expressed as <width> x <height>, usually in pixels. All graphics and animations should be properly sized for import. If not, it is likely that the image will be distorted and the quality reduced. The following table lists the proper NTSC and PAL frame sizes for graphics and animations that will be imported into an Avid system.

Table 1: Proper Frame Sizes

Format	Square Pixel 4x3	Square Pixel 16x9	Native Size* Non-Square Pixel
NTSC	640 x 480	853 x 480	720 x 480
NTSC 601** (non-DV)	648 x 486	864 x 486	720 x 486
PAL	768 x 576	1024 x 576	720 x 576

Native size refers to the actual frame size stored internally by the Avid system. These sizes conform to the industry specifications for digital video.

** *NTSC 601 refers to the frame size of full-frame ITU-R BT.601 digital video. NTSC DV does not use the full frame. Instead, it omits off the top four lines and bottom two lines of the frame. DV. All Avid systems use the full 601 frame size. PAL ITU-R BT.601 frames and PAL DV frames use the same frame size.*

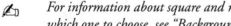 *For information about square and non-square pixels, and guidelines about which one to choose, see "Background: Square Versus Non-square Pixels" on page 36.*

■ If necessary, use the Photoshop Crop tool to resize the image to the appropriate target width and height.

Field Ordering

Field ordering defines how the file is interlaced. An odd, or upper, field ordering implies that the first line of each frame is to be used for field one. An even, or lower, field ordering implies that the first line of each frame is to be used for field two. In order for the imported element to play back correctly, the system must know how to assign the interlaced lines in the file to each video field.

If the element (graphic or animation) to be imported has been field rendered or if it contains interlaced video, it is critical that the file has the proper field ordering, especially if the animation is a QuickTime file using the Avid Codec.

Avid Xpress DV uses the following field ordering:

• NTSC and PAL: Even (Lower field first)

File Format

The Avid system accepts a variety of file formats. The most commonly used formats are TIFF, PICT, and Photoshop.

Color Space

Color space is the method used to define and store color within the file. In Photoshop this is often referred to as *color mode*. Common modes include Bitmap, Grayscale, Index, RGB, and CMYK.

Importing Still Graphics and Animation

When you import a file or sequential files, the Avid system saves the imported media as a media file on the target drive that you specify, and creates a clip for the media in the active bin. You can then manipulate and edit the object like any clip or sequence.

You can also export a video clip or frame into a compatible program, alter it or create a special effect with it, and then reimport it into the Avid system. For example, you might export a frame of your sequence, manipulate it in a graphics program, and then reimport it to use as part of an effect.

To import files into the Avid system:

1. Select the bin where you want to store the imported files.

2. Choose Import from the File menu.

   If Import is dimmed, you probably have not activated a bin.

   The import dialog box appears.

   Windows

   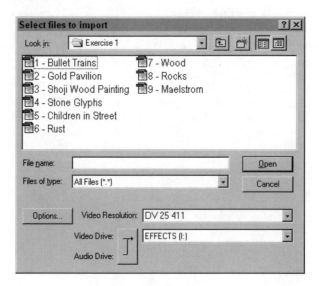

Macintosh

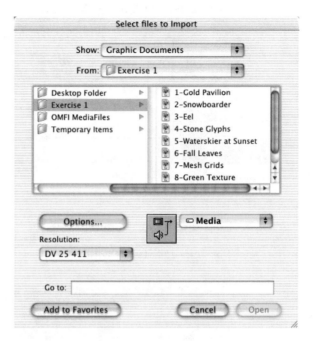

3. Navigate to the folder where the import elements are stored.

4. Select the file(s) to import. Make sure the file type is set to Graphic Files (Windows) or Graphic Documents (Macintosh).

   (Windows) Use the Control or Shift keys to select multiple files at once. The Control key allows you to select discontinuous files while the Shift key allows you to select contiguous files.

   (Macintosh)To select multiple files, use the Shift key to select multiple files at once.

   ▲ **If one of the elements you are importing is stored in sequential file format, only select the file for the first frame, not every frame. (Sequential files are a series of files where each file represents a single frame.) Sequential files will be covered in "Sequential Files" on page 31.**

5. Choose the Media Drive.

6. If you want to separate your video and audio media files to separate media drives, click on the Media Drives button.

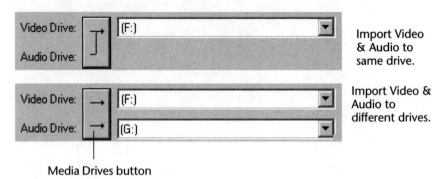

Import Video & Audio to same drive.

Import Video & Audio to different drives.

Media Drives button

7. Click the Options button.

The Import Settings window appears.

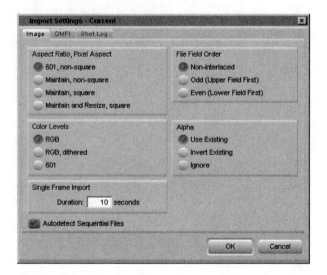

8. Use the following information to help you set the various import options.

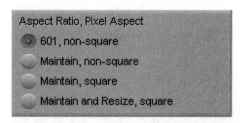

- **601, non-square** — This is the system default. This option assumes the file is properly sized for import into the Avid system and leaves the image alone. (Refer to the table on page 2 for the proper import sizes.) If the image is not properly sized, this option forces the image to fit the entire video frame, which will distort images with non-television aspect ratios.

- **Maintain, non-square** — (NTSC only) This option is designed to be used with full frame non-square NTSC images imported into an NTSC DV project. The full NTSC frame has a size of 720 x 486 (as opposed to the 720 x 480 frame size of NTSC DV). The top four lines and bottom two lines of the 720 x 486 frame are removed from the image. This conforms to the SMPTE specification for NTSC DV frames.

- **Maintain, square** — This option is designed to be used with images that are smaller than the video frame size and cannot be resized. It does not attempt to resize the image in any way, but compensates for the square pixels, centers it within the video frame and adds video black around the image. This option is designed to make it easy to bring small graphics, such as web-originated art, into the Avid system.

- **Maintain and Resize, square** — This option assumes an incorrect image size. It letterboxes the image with video black and resizes it to fit either the 720 pixel width (for wide images) or the 480 (NTSC) or 576 (PAL) height (for tall images). It also assumes the import file has square pixels and compensates accordingly.

  Use this option only in special circumstances, such as in a film animation project, where you want to maintain the original aspect ratio, and if the graphic proportions are neither standard video (1.33:1) nor 601. This option will maintain the aspect ratio of the graphic and add horizontal or vertical black bands, as appropriate.

If the graphic has an embedded alpha channel and one of the three Maintain options is chosen, the system will key out the area around the graphic instead of adding video black.

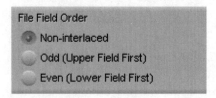

- Allows you to set the field ordering of the import file. If the file is not interlaced (like a frame created in Photoshop), set this option to "Non-Interlaced." Otherwise, select the field ordering that was used to create the file.

▲ **If you are importing an animation using the Avid DV codec, this setting is ignored and the animation's field ordering cannot be changed. Therefore, it is critical that you inform all animators and compositors you work with of the correct field dominance for the Avid system.**

See "Field Ordering" on page 3 for more information about field ordering.

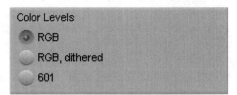

- **RGB** — Designed to be used with traditionally created computer images. The blackest black in the graphic will be assigned the value of video black and the whitest white will be assigned the value of video white.

  This option should be chosen for graphics and animations created in third party programs.

- **RGB, dithered** — Assigns values identically to RGB. Select this option if you are importing a graphic with a fine gradient. Due to the limitations of DV video encoding, banding is possible in fine gradients. This option adds a slight amount of noise to the gradient and masks the banding inherent in digital video.

- **601** — Use this option if the graphic was created specifically to use the extended signal range available in the ITU-R BT.601 video standard. Do not use this option if the graphic was not created for 601 import as illegal color values may result.

If you intend your final output to be web distribution only, choose 601 to import graphics created in RBG. This will leave your black and white values unchanged.

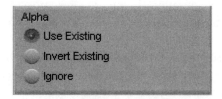

- **Use Existing** — Applies only to images that have an alpha channel; the setting has no effect on images that don't have an alpha channel. If this option is selected, the system imports the image and its alpha channel as a Matte Key effect.

  Use this option if the alpha channel was inverted by the graphic artist or animator.

- **Invert Existing** — Inverts the black and white areas in an alpha channel. By default, the Avid system expects alpha channels to be defined so that black represents the opaque areas and white represents the transparent areas.

  If your alpha channel was created with white representing the opaque areas and black the transparent, you must enable this option. Most graphic and animation programs define the alpha channel in this way.

  Use this option when importing still graphics, sequential file animations or movies, or QuickTime movies.

- **Ignore** — If this option is selected, the system disregards the alpha channel and imports only the RGB portion of the image.

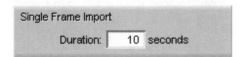

- Allows you to specify the duration in seconds for still graphics.

  The duration chosen does not impact the storage space used by the graphic. It only affects the duration of the graphic in the bin.

9. If you are importing an animation stored in sequential file format, make sure that Autodetect Sequential Files is selected. Otherwise, only the first frame of the sequence will be imported. (Sequential files will be covered in "Sequential Files" on page 31.)

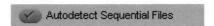

10. When you are satisfied with the Import Settings, click OK to return to the Import dialog.

11. Click OK to begin the import process.

Drag-and-Drop Method

Another way to import a file is to drag it directly from its location in a Windows or Macintosh folder to the desired bin. When you use this technique, the system imports the file using the active Import settings.

1. If you have multiple Import settings listed in the Project window, select the Import settings you want to use. (The course covers multiple Import settings in the next section, "Creating and Using Multiple Import Settings.")

2. Open the bin where you want to store the imported files.

3. Using Windows Explorer (Windows) or the Finder (Macintosh), navigate to the folder that contains the graphics.

4. Drag the file(s) from the folder to the bin.

 Although this method can save you time, you must be careful that the Import settings are appropriate for the file you are importing.

Creating and Using Multiple Import Settings

You can create multiple Import settings and easily switch between them. Import settings are accessed from the Settings list of the Project window.

Multiple import settings allow you to preconfigure the Import options for a variety of import situations. For example, you can create one setting for importing properly sized still graphics and another for web-originated graphics that must be left at their original non-standard size.

To create a new Import setting:

1. Click the Settings button in the Project window to display a list of your current settings.

2. Click an Import setting.

3. Choose Duplicate from the Edit menu.

4. Name the setting by clicking the custom name column (between the setting name and the setting type identifier), typing a name, and pressing Enter or Return.

5. Double-click the Import setting to open it.

6. Adjust the settings as desired.

7. Click OK.

8. To switch between Import settings, simply click to the right of the name of the setting you wish to use. The check mark will jump to that setting, indicating it is active. If you want to use the drag-and-drop method, you must select your setting.

▲ **When you modify the import options from the Import dialog box, the active Import setting is also updated.**

Exporting Still Frames

You can export still frames from the Avid system using any of the file formats available for import.

1. Load the clip or sequence containing the frame you wish to export into the Source or Record monitor.

2. Park on the desired frame and make sure the appropriate track is monitored.

3. Choose File > Export.

The Export dialog box opens.

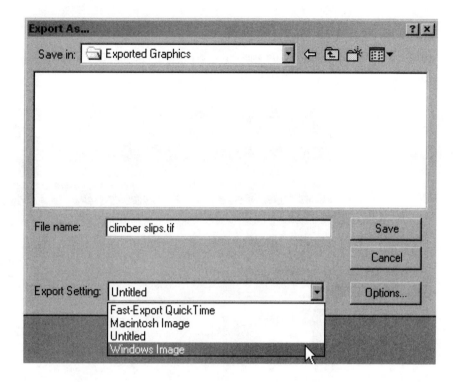

At the bottom of the Export dialog, a pop-up menu allows you to choose from a list of Export settings. When a new user is created on the Avid system the system creates four default export settings.

- Fast-Export QuickTime

- Macintosh Image

- Untitled

- Windows Image

4. Choose Windows Image or Macintosh Image.

5. Click the Options button to open the Export Settings dialog box.

The Export Settings dialog box opens.

Choosing Export Options

1. Make sure Graphic is listed in the Export As field.

   The Graphic settings are displayed in the Export Settings window.

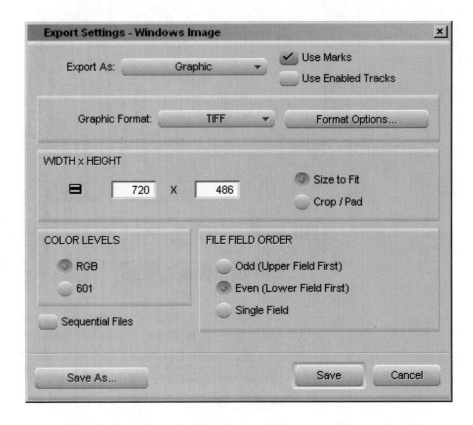

2. Use the following information to help you set the various export options.

   - **Use Marks** — Although it isn't obvious, this option does apply when exporting single frames.

     If set, the Avid system exports the frame at the IN point or, in the absence of an IN point, at the blue position indicator. If not set, the system exports the first frame of the clip.

   - **Use Enabled Tracks** — This option controls which track(s) are exported in a multilayer sequence.

- If Use Enabled Tracks is deselected, the sequence will export the sequence from the highest *monitored* track.

- If Use Enabled Tracks is selected, the sequence will export the sequence from the highest *active* track.

This option is designed to allow an editor to export a large number of audio tracks in a single group. It should be disabled when exporting graphics and video only.

- **Graphic Format** — Choose the format you wish to export to from the pop-up menu. Most graphic exports will use either TIFF or PICT.

- **Format Options** — This button displays the options available for the chosen graphic format.

  If TIFF was the chosen format and you click Format Options, the following dialog appears.

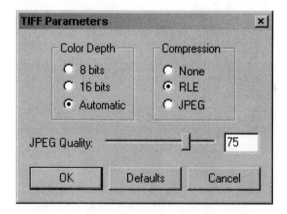

The displayed options, Automatic Color Depth and RLE Compression, are the preferred options. (Click OK.)

- **Width x Height** — Enter the size required or choose one from the Fast menu to the left. Refer to the table in the section "Frame Size" on page 2 for the recommended size.

  - Use a Square Pixel size when exporting a graphic that will be used for print or the web.

  - Use the Native Size when exporting a graphic for use in After Effects or other compositing program.

  - Use the Native Size when exporting a graphic that will be retouched and reimported into the Avid system, or if the graphic is intended for use in a DVD presentation.

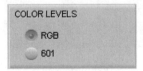 *You may also want to export the square pixel version of a graphic file to use in a square-pixel- based application like Photoshop as a previsualization reference to create other graphic buttons for use in a DVD project.*

- **Scale to Fit** or **Crop / Pad** — Determines how the image is fit into the export size. These options behave differently depending on the export size you chose.

  - Use Scale to Fit for all instances except when exporting a still to the non-DV NTSC frame sizes.

  - Use Crop / Pad when exporting a still for use in an NTSC DVD or DV project.

COLOR LEVELS

  ● RGB
  ○ 601

- **Color Levels**

  - RGB should be chosen for most graphic exports, especially when a frame is exported for use in print or on the web.

- The 601 option is most commonly used when exporting frames that will be retouched slightly and reimported into the Avid system.

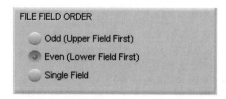

- **File Field Order**

  - The Single Field option exports only one of the two video fields and is the best option when exporting still graphics.

  - The other two options will export both video fields and is used primarily when exporting video clips.

3. Deselect the Sequential Files option.

4. Click on the Save As... button, name this setting, and click OK.

   Saving a setting allows you to easily switch between different export configurations. Use a name that makes the options easy to identify. For example, *RGB TIFF Graphic.*

5. Click Save to close the Export Settings.

Saving the File

In the Export As dialog box:

1. Navigate to the location where you want to save the graphic.

2. Enter a name for the graphic and save it.

   Don't use non-alphanumeric characters, such as \ / | * ? : < > in the file name. These characters are not allowed in filenames in Windows or Unix systems.

   The Avid system automatically assigns a three-character extension for the chosen file format. This extension is required if the file is intended to be used on a Windows or SGI system. If you are going to use the file exclusively on the Macintosh, you can remove the extension.

Create a naming convention for your files so you can easily locate individual files.

3. Click Save to save and export the graphic.

   You can open and edit the file in any program that supports this file format.

Exporting Video

In this section, you'll learn how to export and import video with the Avid system. This allows you to take advantage of third party special effects packages such as Adobe After Effects, 3D animation packages, or others. You might also need to export the video for distribution on CD-ROM, DVD-ROM, or the web.

A QuickTime movie is a single file containing all of the exported frames and their frame rate. Movies can be video only, audio only, or video and audio.

Exporting a clip or sequence as a QuickTime movie allows you to edit an image from the Avid system using an application that supports QuickTime, and then reimport the movie back into the Avid system or use the resulting QuickTime movie in a multimedia project.

Tips for Creating QuickTime Movies

Make sure you render any effects prior to export. If you do not, they render into the exported movie during the export, which increases the amount of time for export. The effects in the sequence remain unrendered after exporting.

You can streamline the export process by selecting a setting before beginning the export. After you select a setting, the parameters remain the default settings for all exported files, unless you change them during the export. This is especially useful when you batch export a number of files directly from a bin.

Exporting Video as QuickTime

1. To select the media you want to export, do one of the following:

   • To export an entire sequence or clip, open the bin containing the sequence or clip you want to export and highlight it.

   • To export a section of a sequence or clip, load the sequence into the Record monitor (or load the clip into the Source monitor) and mark an IN and OUT.

2. Select the desired sequence or clip in its bin.

   If there is more than one sequence or clip to export, place them in a single bin and select all of them.

3. Choose File > Export.

   The Export dialog box opens.

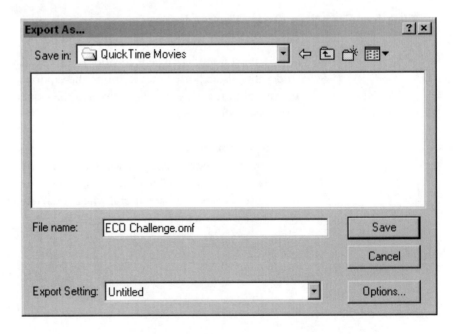

4. Navigate to the folder in which you want to save the video.

5. To use a previously saved setting, choose the setting name from the Export Setting scroll list. Proceed to the section, "Saving the File" on page 17.

6. To define your own export settings, choose Untitled and click Options.

The Export Settings window appears.

Choosing the Correct Export Type

Before exporting, you need to decide on a file format. The choice often depends upon what software or platform will be used to read the exported files, and the final destination of the movie.

Two different types of QuickTime movies can be exported from the Avid system:

- QuickTime Standard — all of the media is embedded in the movie file.

  All of the media used in the sequence is copied into the QuickTime movie. As a result, the export may take a while and the exported movie may be quite large.

  Exported QuickTime movies cannot exceed two gigabytes in size. Depending upon the codec you choose, you can reach this limit in as few as sixty seconds of video or as much as half an hour or more of video.

- QuickTime Reference — none of the media is embedded in the movie file.

  A QuickTime Reference movie is, essentially, a "wrapper" that looks like a QuickTime file, but that actually points directly to the Avid media stored on your media drives. None of the media used in the sequence is copied into the resulting QuickTime movie. Instead, a small QuickTime file is created that points to the required media files on the media drives. A QuickTime Reference movie exports very quickly.

You can open a QuickTime Reference movie on a computer desktop, but you might not be able to play it back as smoothly as the media plays back within the Avid application.

The great thing about a QuickTime Reference movie is that it takes up very little storage space and is extremely fast to export. Any other application on your Avid system that supports QuickTime should be able to open the QuickTime reference and be able to reference the Avid media files.

Only use a QuickTime reference if the applications you want to open the movie in reside on the same system or have access to the media drives where the native Avid media lives.

Exporting as a QuickTime Reference Movie

1. Choose QuickTime Reference from the Export As pop-up menu.

   The QuickTime Reference options appear.

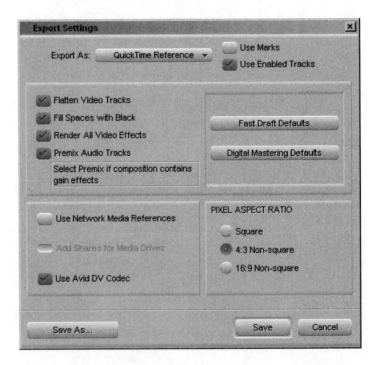

2. Use the following table to help you set the various export options.

The following table explains the various export options.

Table 2: Export Options

Export Options	If Selected:	Additional Notes
Use Marks	Only the portion within the IN and OUT points will export	In the absence of an IN point, this option will export the entire sequence.
Use Enabled Tracks This option controls which track(s) are exported in a multilayer sequence.	The video will export from the highest active track and the audio on all active tracks will be mixed together.	If deselected, the video will export from the highest *monitored* track and the audio on all monitored audio tracks will be mixed together. This option is designed to allow an editor to select a large number of audio tracks and export them in a group for audio post.
Flatten Video Tracks	All of the video tracks are flattened into a single video track.	This option should always be selected when exporting movies for external processing.
Fill Spaces with Black	Any filler holes in the video will be replaced with video black.	This option should always be selected when exporting movies for external processing.
Render All Video Effects	Any unrendered effects in the sequence are rendered prior to export. If it is deselected, any unrendered effects are ignored.	This option should always be selected when exporting movies for external processing.
Premix Audio Tracks	Be sure the audio is mixed to stereo prior to export.	This option should be turned off if the audio was previously mixed down to mono.
Use Network Media References	This option should be enabled if the movie will be compressed on another station that is connected to the editing station via a Unity network.	
Add Shares for Media Drives	This option should be enabled only if both the editing and the compression stations are on a Unity network and some of the media used by the exported movie is stored on a local drive.	Leave this option deselected unless both the editing and the compression stations are on a Unity network and some of the media used by the exported movie is stored on a local drive.

Pixel Aspect Ratio	Allows you to embed the aspect ratio of the source video into the QuickTime movie.	Very few third party programs support this option at this time.
Use Avid DV Codec	Select only if the exported movie will be processed on an Xpress DV system. If the file is to be used on other systems, deselect this option.	

3. Save the file. If you need further instructions, see "Saving the File" on page 17.

Exporting as a QuickTime Standard Movie

1. Choose QuickTime from the Export As pop-up menu.

   The QuickTime options appear.

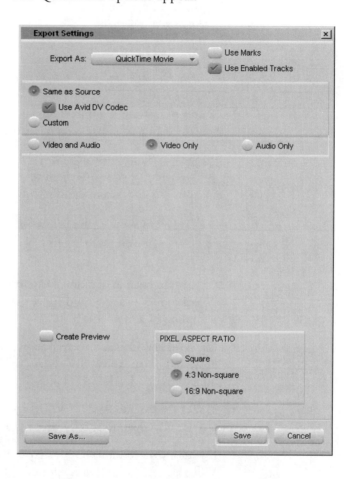

2. Use the following section to help you set the various export options.

   - **Use Marks** — If this option is selected the Avid system will only export the portion within the IN and OUT points.

     In the absence of an IN point, this option will export the entire sequence.

   - **Use Enabled Tracks** — This option controls which track(s) are exported in a multilayer sequence.

- If Use Enabled Tracks is deselected, the video will export from the highest *monitored* track and the audio on all monitored audio tracks will be mixed together.

- If Use Enabled Tracks is selected, the video will export from the highest *active* track and the audio on all active tracks will be mixed together.

This option is designed to allow an editor to select a large number of audio tracks and export them in a group.

- **Source / Custom (Compression)** — These two options specify how the exported movie is compressed.

  - Same as Source instructs Xpress DV to export the movie using the Avid DV codec. Make sure the Use Avid DV Codec button is checked under the Same as Source button.

    Use this option if you plan to export the QuickTime to another application and then reimport it back into the Avid system.

  - Custom enables additional export options and allows the editor to set the size and codec used. We will discuss this option in a moment.

- **Use Avid DV Codec** — Select only if the exported movie will be processed on an Xpress DV system. If the file is to be used on other systems, deselect this option.

- **Tracks (Video and Audio / Video Only / Audio Only)** — These options allow you to specify which tracks are to be exported.

  If your movie contains both video and audio, be sure that the Video and Audio option is selected.

- **Create Preview** — This option appends a QuickTime movie preview frame to the file.

  This data is ignored by most programs and this option can remain disabled.

- **Pixel Aspect Ratio** — This option allows you to embed the aspect ratio of the source video into the QuickTime movie.

Very few third party programs support this option at this time.

3. If you don't need to set custom compression (covered in the next section), save the file. If you need further instructions, see "Saving the File" on page 17.

Setting Custom Compression Options

■ Click Custom to enable additional options in the Export Settings dialog.

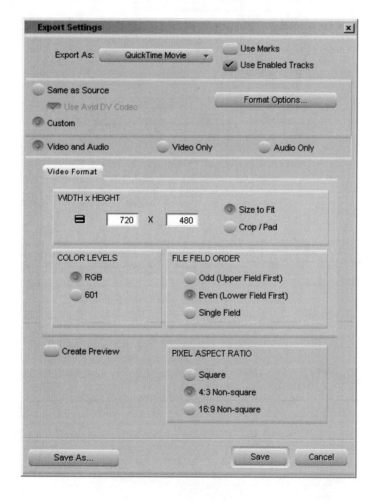

The following section discusses the Custom options enabled.

Format Options

This button opens the standard QuickTime compression dialog allowing you to select the desired video and audio codecs.

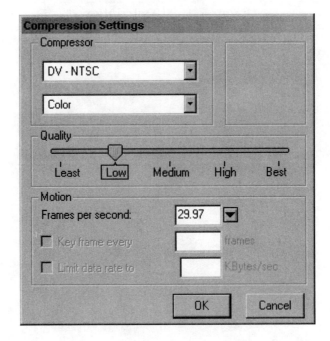

- **Video Settings** — Opens the video compression settings, allowing you to select the desired QuickTime codec and frame rate.

The codec you choose will determine the quality and usability of the final movie. Many of the codecs are designed for specific uses, such as streaming video, graphics, and so on. The following table lists the preferred video codecs for Avid systems, and all are available with QuickTime 5. (Additional codecs may also be installed.)

Codec	Usage	Description
DV - NTSC / DV - PAL	Preferred codec for DV	Reads and writes the native video codec used in consumer and prosumer cameras. Requires a frame size of 720 x 480 (NTSC) or 720 x 576 (PAL). Does not support an alpha channel.
Avid Meridien Compressed / Avid Meridien Uncompressed	Compatibility with Avid Meridien-based systems	The preferred codec for exporting and importing into Media Composer release 8.0 and later. Saves the video at the resolution you choose. Supports an alpha channel. For more information, see the following section on the Avid codecs.
Avid ABVB Nuvista	Compatibility with Avid ABVB-based systems	Provides the ability to read or write movies using the AVR compression used by Media Composer release 7.x and earlier. Supports an alpha channel (ABVB AVR resolutions only).

- **Filter** — Allows you to apply a QuickTime effect filter.

These filters are a standard part of QuickTime and will significantly increase the export time, if applied.

- **Size** — Lets you specify the export frame size.

This option is part of the standard QuickTime interface, but is not the appropriate place to specify the export frame size.

- **Sound Settings** — Lets you specify the audio compression, sample rate, and bit depth.

Should be set to 44.1 kHz, 16 bit, or 48 kHz, 16 bit, or 32 kHz, 16 bit to maintain full audio quality. Compression should only be used when creating final output for web or CD-ROM.

Video Format

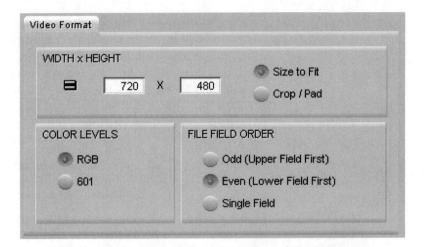

- **Width x Height** — Allows you to specify the frame size for export. Any frame size can be chosen, but the fast menu provides a list of commonly used export sizes.

- **Size to Fit** and **Crop / Pad** — If a frame size that does not match the video aspect ratio is chosen, these options determine how the video frame is fit into the chosen frame size.

  - Size to Fit forces the image to fit the chosen frame size and will distort the image if a non-video aspect ratio is chosen.

  - Crop / Pad does not distort the image. Instead, it either removes extraneous scan lines (for example, when the 720 x 486 NTSC frame size is chosen) or adds lines of black to fill out the chosen frame size.

  - **Color Levels** — Specifies the Color Levels the exported movie will contain. Choose 601 for all video exports.

- **File Field Order** — Determines the field order of the exported movie.

  - Odd (Upper Field First) and Even (Lower Field First) will adjust the field ordering, if necessary, to conform to the chosen option.

  - Single Field exports the information in field 1 only.

See the table in "Field Ordering" on page 3 for more information.

4. Save the file.

The Avid DV Codec

Xpress DV includes a DV codec which is designed to allow for the highest possible image quality in an exported movie. However, the Avid DV codec is not installable on other systems. Therefore, you should only use it if you plan to use the exported file in another program on an Xpress DV system. If you attempt to open the exported file on another system, the file will be unreadable.

If you plan to use the exported file on other systems, be sure to deselect the Use Avid DV Codec option in the Export dialog. Xpress DV will use the Apple DV instead. This will not affect the time required to export a movie.

Sequential Files

Sequential files are a series of files where each file represents a single frame. The file name includes a number that indicates the order of the frames. (For example, movie.001.tif, movie.002.tif, movie.003.tif, and so on.).

Tips for Using Sequential Files

When you export a sequence as sequential files, keep in mind the following points:

- For the Color Levels option, the following guidelines should help you determine whether to use RGB or 601 levels (RGB is the default).

  Use RGB Graphics levels when:

  - Exporting a frame or frames that you plan to modify radically and reimport.

    One example is when you need to apply a stylize effect in Adobe

Photoshop. Using RGB levels clips the signal at video black and video white, which is necessary in this case. If you use 601 levels, the effect you apply might cause the signal to extend beyond video black and white.

- Exporting a frame to be used in a prepress environment.

Use 601 levels when:

- Exporting a frame or frames that you plan to modify subtly and reimport.

  This method is appropriate when you need to fix a dropout or touch out negative grit. Using 601 levels maintains all of the captured signal. If you use RGB levels, the system clips all values below video black and above video white, which may introduce undesirable artifacts and cause the modified frame not to match back perfectly.

- Using or creating video that requires superblack, such as a luma key element.

- Check the Sequential Files checkbox.

- Due to the large number of files possible with sequential file exports (1800 files per minute of NTSC video, 1500 files per minute of PAL video), we recommend that you always export into an empty folder.

- Exporting sequential files may take between one and ten seconds per frame, depending upon your hardware.

Drag-and-Drop Method

As with still graphics, you can use the drag-and-drop technique to export a sequence as a QuickTime movie. Just drag the desired sequence from its bin to a new location on the desktop. When you use this technique, the system uses the active Export Settings. Although this method can save you time, you must be careful that the Export Settings are appropriate for the current sequence, as described in the previous sections.

Importing Audio from an Audio CD

Sometimes it's necessary to bring in audio files from an audio CD. Perhaps you have a library of music CDs or you need to bring in some sound effects.

To import the audio into the Avid system:

1. Insert the audio CD into the CD-ROM drive.

2. In Avid Xpress DV, select a bin.

3. Choose Import from the File menu.

   If Import is dimmed, you probably have not activated a bin.

The Import window opens.

Windows

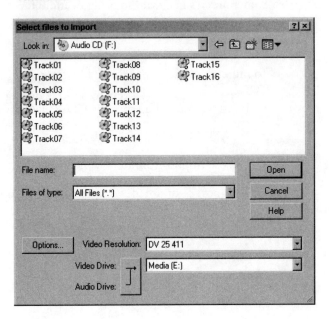

Macintosh

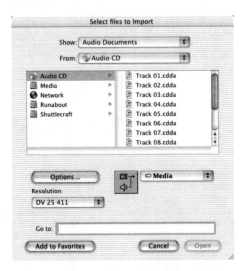

4. Use the Directory pop-up menu to navigate to the CD-ROM drive.

5. Select the track(s) in the folder.

6. Click Open.

   The audio tracks are imported into the selected bin. A clip is created for each track, and the audio may now be edited into a sequence.

   If your project is using 48 kHz audio, the audio file will be converted from 44.1 kHz to 48 kHz during import.

Background: Square Versus Non-square Pixels

Any computer-based or video-based image is composed of pixels. These pixels may be square or non-square in shape. For importing and exporting, particularly for importing and exporting video, you need to understand the ramifications of these two types of pixels.

The basic point to remember is that video traditionally uses non-square pixels and computers use square pixels. If you create an image in Photoshop, which uses square pixels, you have to create it a particular way so you can import it into the Avid system, which uses non-square pixels. Read on for further explanation.

Square Versus Non-square Pixels

Avid Xpress DV uses the DV frame size, which is 720 x 480 pixels for NTSC and 720 x 576 for PAL. If you calculate the aspect ratio of these resolutions, you notice that it differs from the video aspect ratio of 1.33:1. Why does a 720 x 480 frame appear to have a wider aspect ratio? If we assume that the frame has square pixels, it is indeed wider. However the DV 720 x 480 frame uses non-square pixels.

Traditionally, analog NTSC signals have always used non-square pixels, where the pixels were more tall than wide. It was not until computer-based video arrived in the 1980s that NTSC signals were recorded with square pixels. This was because computers used square pixels, and working with non-square pixels and playing a visibly correct image was beyond the technology of the day. Today, many graphics and animation programs, including Adobe Photoshop, continue to use the square pixel format.

Digital videotape, on the other hand, has always used non-square pixels to conform with the analog signal. Avid systems use this same non-square pixel so that it conforms with the DV frame size.

The following illustration shows the difference between square pixels and non-square NTSC and PAL pixels. Each of the three images is the same size. Notice that the square pixel circle has exactly the same number of pixels horizontally and vertically, while the NTSC circle has more pixels horizontally. This is because DV NTSC pixels are more tall than wide. The PAL circle has fewer pixels horizontally than vertically because DV PAL pixels are more wide than tall.

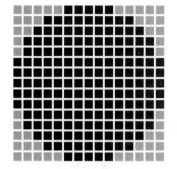 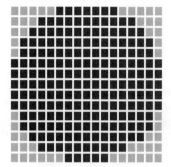 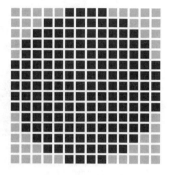

Computer Pixels
(Square)

NTSC DV Pixels
(Nonsquare)

PAL DV Pixels
(Nonsquare)

You can import and export with either square pixels or non-square pixels. The system determines which kind of pixels the imported image uses by the frame size of the image. If the file is 720 x 480 (NTSC) or 720 x 576 (PAL), the system assumes non-square pixels. If the frame size is anything else, the system assumes square pixels and resizes the image to fit the DV frame size.

When you open an image that is saved with DV non-square pixels in a program such as Photoshop, which always displays using square pixels, the image appears stretched (NTSC) or squeezed (PAL). This is normal, and is due to square pixels displaying a non-square pixel image.

Image Viewed in
Media Composer

Image Viewed in
Photoshop (NTSC)

Image Viewed in
Photoshop (PAL)

Resizing a Graphic Image Before Importing

Depending on whether you work in NTSC or PAL video, you need to resize an image in the graphics program to 720 x 540, 648 x 480, or 768 x 576 before importing. These sizes have an aspect ratio of 1.33:1. These sizes also assume a square pixel will be used to display the image.

Non-square and Square Pixel Guidelines

The following guidelines should help you determine whether to use non-square or square pixels when importing and exporting.

Use non-square pixels when:

- Importing or exporting using the Avid DV codec.

  The Avid DV codec requires non-square pixels.

- Preparing an animation that will use field rendering.

  In video, fields represent different periods of time. In NTSC, fields 1 and 2 are 1/60th of a second apart; in PAL, fields 1 and 2 are 1/50th of a second apart. Field rendering is a process in which an image is rendered for each field and the two are combined into a single video frame. To preserve field data properly, you must render it with the correct number of scan lines (480 for NTSC, 576 for PAL).

  Square pixels can be used for field rendering if the frame size you are rendering to is 648 x 480 (NTSC) or 768 x 576 (PAL).

- Exporting video out of the Avid system.

  Because the DV frame is the native frame size for the Avid system, if you export using the proper non-square pixel size, there is no risk of artifacting due to a resize from non-square to square pixels.

Use square pixels when:

- Preparing a still graphic for import.

  Sizing to a square pixel 1.33:1 aspect ratio is the simplest method and is appropriate for still graphics.

- Preparing an animation that does not use field rendering.

  As long as you are not field rendering, square pixel frame sizes are appropriate for import. You can also use non-square pixel frames, if desired.

- Exporting a still graphic for use in a prepress environment.

  Any image you plan to export for use in print should be at a square pixel size so it does not appear distorted when printed. However, it is important that you export only one field.

Appendix B

Media Management

An important component of editing on an Avid system is managing media and available storage space in the system. Avid systems provide many functions and tools to aid with the process. In this appendix, we cover some of them.

Retrieving Bins from the Attic

The Attic is a folder on the C: drive (Windows) or Avid drive (Macintosh) which contains folders for each of your projects in which the system saves backup copies of any open bins in a project. Whenever you save or auto-save, a backup copy is placed in the project folder within the Attic folder, with '.bak' and a number added to the bin name. Each new backup is placed in this folder until the number of copies in the folder reaches a maximum (which you can set). Once the maximum is reached, subsequent backup files replace older versions of the same file.

The Attic folder is useful when you have lost information in a bin, or if you wish to return to an earlier version of your sequence.

To retrieve a bin from the Attic folder:

1. (Option) In Avid Xpress DV, move any needed clips from the bin you will replace to another bin, and delete the bin you will replace.

2. Close all open bins.

3. If you are experiencing any technical problems, quit Avid Xpress DV.

4. Open the Attic folder (in C:\Program Files\Avid\Avid Xpress DV) for Windows, or the highest level in the Avid disk for Macintosh), and then the folder for the project.

5. Identify the bin you wish to retrieve by its name and Last Modified date (in this case the date and time the bin was saved into the Attic).

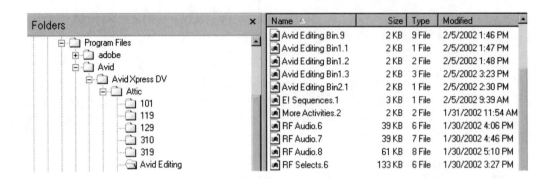

6. Make a copy of the bin, by doing one of the following:

    *   (Windows) Press Control+C (Copy), click anywhere in the folder, and then press Control+V (Paste).

    *   (Macintosh) Press ⌘+D.

7. Rename the copy.

8. Drag that bin into the appropriate Project folder in the Avid Projects folder.

9. Drag the original bin from the Project folder to the trash.

10. Return to Avid Xpress DV. If you previously quit the application:

    a. Launch Avid Xpress DV.

    b. Open the Project.

    c. Open the backup bin by choosing Open Bin from the File menu.

    d. In the dialog box that appears, navigate through the project folders until you locate the backup bin and select it.

If you did not close the bin for which you are retrieving a backup (step 2), you will get an error message stating that you cannot have more than one copy of a bin open at the same time.

Locking Items in the Bin

You can lock any item in the bin — including source clips, master clips, subclips, and sequences — to prevent deletion. Locked items can still be edited and modified.

To lock items:

1. Display the Lock heading in the bin by choosing Headings from the Bin menu, clicking the Lock heading, and clicking OK.

2. Click a clip, subclip, or sequence to select it.

3. Select additional items if necessary.

4. Choose Lock Bin Selection from the bottom of the Clip menu.

A lock icon appears for each locked clip in the Lock column of the default Statistics Bin view.

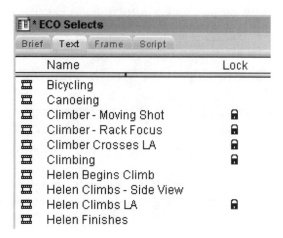

To unlock previously locked items:

1. Select the items in the bin.

2. Choose Unlock Bin Selection from the Clip menu.

Deleting Clips and Media Files

Let's revisit some of the information learned in Module 1; it's particularly relevant now. Master clips, subclips, and sequences consist of statistical data that occupies very little drive space on the internal disk, while the media files associated with them take up substantial room on the external media drives. If you need to free up a lot of drive space to work on a new project, you can delete the media used in an old project *as long as you save the master clips, subclips, and sequences.* Deleting media files will not harm the related master clips, subclips, and sequences.

As long as you have the master clips, subclips, and sequences, you can always batch record and re-edit the program again, if necessary. You can redigitize media as long as it has timecode and you keep the clip information.

After deleting audio and video media files, the associated clips and sections of sequences play silence and display the Media Offline frame. Offline audio-only clips will display a black frame and play without sound. They will not display the Media Offline message.

 If you are unsure if the audio is silent or offline, choose Show Offline Clips in the Bin Fast menu.

Two Ways to Delete Clips and Media Files

There are two ways to delete clips and media files; you can delete from the bin or from the Media Tool. In this section, we discuss the first method; in the next section we discuss Media Tool.

You can use either method to delete clips and/or the media files linked to the clips. Using the Media Tool gives you more options, as you shall see.

Deleting from a Bin

When deleting clips from a bin you have the option to delete the master clip, its associated media files, or both.

- "Delete associated media files" is used for clearing space on the drives without losing any information about the clip. This will enable you to redigitize all the offline clips in the future based on their text information and timecode.

- Deleting both the master clip and its associated media files is done when a clip will not be needed anymore for a project.

 If you delete the clips and sequences of the deleted media files and have no backups, you will not be able to rerecord the material later, unless you log everything again. You should always make a backup copy of the project and bins, just in case you need them some time in the future.

To delete media files associated with master clips, sequences, and effects from a media drive:

1. Click to activate the bin, and select the clips whose media files you want to delete.

2. Choose Delete from the Edit menu, or press the Delete key, to open the bin's Delete dialog box.

3. Select the media objects that you want to delete, as shown in the following figure.

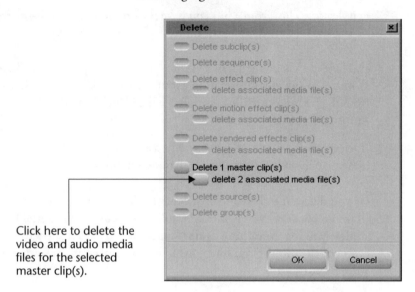

Click here to delete the video and audio media files for the selected master clip(s).

*   Selecting only "Delete 1 master clip(s)" will delete only the clip, which contains the text instructions such as its start and end timecode. The clip will disappear from the bin but the media is still stored on the external drives. You should avoid doing this.

*   Selecting only "Delete 2 associated media file(s)" will delete the actual recorded picture and sound associated with the clip. The clip will remain in your bin with all its text information; however, Frame view will display the message Media Offline. That means that the Avid system cannot currently find a media file on the external drives which correspond to the timecode information of the clip.

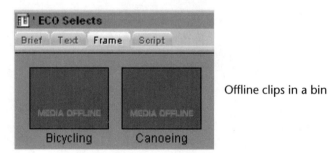

Offline clips in a bin

- Selecting both options will delete both the text information of the clip and all its associated media files.

▲ **Remember not to delete the selected master clips and/or sequences if you will need to rerecord them later.**

▲ **You cannot undo the deletion of media files. Make sure no one else needs the media files you are planning to delete, and make sure no other project is using these media files.**

4. Click OK.

   A confirmation dialog box appears.

5. Click Delete.

The Media Tool

The Media tool allows you to see the media files on all hard drives online in a display that is similar to your bin formats. You can use the Media tool to view or delete the available media files or specific tracks contained in the media file. The Media tool also allows you to track down all media files used in a particular project or sequence.

Setting the Media Tool Display

You can set the Media tool to display different types of files from the current or other existing projects. To set the Media tool display:

1. Choose Media Tool from the Tools menu.

The Media Tool Display dialog box appears.

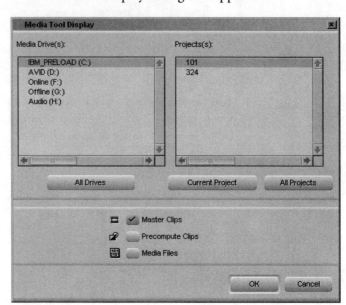

2. Select one or more media disks. To include all disks, select All Drives.

3. Select one or more projects. To include all projects, select All Projects.

4. Select one or more file types you want to view (Master Clips, Precompute Clips, and Media Files).

   • A master clip can have many associated media files: one or more video and up to eight audio media files.

   • Precompute Master Clips are rendered effects.

 You will rarely need to display Media Files.

Sorting, Sifting, and Managing Data in the Media Tool

The Media tool provides the same database functionality as a bin. You can:

• Sort single or multiple columns in ascending or descending order as you would in a bin

- Perform a custom sift as you would in a bin

- Add, hide, or delete column headings as you would in a bin

- View clips in Frame, Text, Brief, or Script view

- Click and drag master clips from the Media tool into bins

Deleting From the Media Tool

Delete from the Media tool to:

- Delete media files for specific tracks associated with a master clip.

  For example, you might unintentionally leave the video track selected when recording a voice-over. You could delete the unwanted video track and leave the audio online.

  This capability is not available by deleting from a bin.

- Delete all of the media files for a specific project or sequence.

  This would be less time consuming than opening every bin for a project and deleting the associated media files.

 You cannot undo deletion of media files. Make sure no one else needs the media files you are planning to delete, and make sure no other project is using these media files.

To delete media files from the Media tool:

1. Display the Master Clips and/or Precompute Master Clips from your project, depending on what you want to delete.

2. In the Media tool, select the item(s) whose media files you want to delete.

3. Press the Delete key to open the Media tool's Delete Media dialog box.

4. Select the media objects that you want to delete.

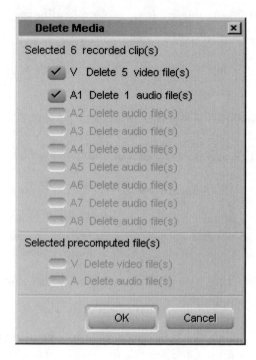

Notice that the Delete Media dialog box allows you to select media files by media type. This capability makes it possible to delete all of the video and batch record at a new resolution without affecting mixed audio tracks.

5. Click OK.

A confirmation dialog box appears.

6. Click Delete.

The media files are deleted from the drive. The master clips remain stored in their bins.

Identifying Media Relatives

With Avid Xpress DV, you can identify the media objects (master clips, subclips, precomputes, sequences) that share the same media files, regardless of whether the media files are present on the system. Media objects that share the same media files are called *media relatives*.

Identifying media relatives can be useful if you want to know:

- Which master clip a subclip was drawn from

- Which subclips and media are "related" to a specific master clip

- All of the master clips, subclips, and precomputes associated with a sequence or project

- Which media files to delete from a project without taking offline any of the media used in a sequence

Identifying Media Relatives

To identify the media relatives of a clip or sequence:

1. Open the bins that contains the master clips, subclips, and sequences of the media files that you want to find, making sure that all items are deselected. (You can open them in the SuperBin or in individual bins.)

2. Select the master clip(s), subclip(s), or sequence(s) for which you want to identify the media relatives.

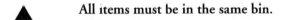 **All items must be in the same bin.**

3. Choose Select Media Relatives from the Bin menu.

   The media relatives of the selected items are highlighted in all open bins.

Deleting Unused Media from a Project

You can use Select Media Relatives to select and delete media files that were not used in a project. This is useful if you want to delete any media files that were not used in order to open drive space. In this procedure, you use a bin and the Media tool together to identify media relatives in both places.

To identify and delete unused media files associated with a particular sequence:

1. Open the bins that contain the master clips, subclips, and the sequence of the media files that you want to find, making sure that all items are deselected.

2. Open the Media tool and select Current Project and Digitized Master Clips in the Media Tool Display dialog box.

3. Resize and position the bin(s) and the Media Tool window so that you can see both of them.

4. Select the sequence for which you want to identify the media relatives.

5. Choose Select Media Relatives from the Bin menu.

   The media relatives of the selected items are highlighted in the Media tool and in all open bins.

6. Choose Reverse Selection from the Media Tool Fast menu.

   This reverses the current selection, highlighting all the media files in the Media Tool that are unrelated to your clips and sequences.

7. Press the Delete key.

 If you are using master clips in your sequence that come from tapes associated with another project, the Current Project selection in the Media Tool Display dialog box will not show those clips.

Glossary

3/4-inch U-matic. One of the first composite videocassette formats, in which the composite signal is recorded onto 3/4-inch tape. Used for many years, particularly in field recording, the U-matic format is slowly being replaced by more advanced and lightweight systems.

4:2:2 digital video. A digital video system defined by the ITU-R 601 (CCIR 601) technical documentation. 4:2:2 refers to the comparative ratio of sampling of the three components of the video signal: luminance and two color channels.

add edit. An edit added between consecutive frames in a sequence segment within the Timeline. An add edit separates segment sections so the user can modify or add effects to a subsection of the segment.

AES/EBU. Audio Engineering Society/European Broadcasting Union. A standards-setting organization that defined a digital signal format for professional audio input to the Avid video-based editing systems using the SA 4 card. This signal format is typically used when you input sound directly to Avid video-based editing systems with a digital audiotape (DAT) machine, thereby bypassing the videotape recording process.

AIFF-C. Audio Interchange File Format-Condensed. A sampled-sound file format that allows for the storage of audio data. This format is primarily used as data interchange format but can be used as a storage format as well. OMF Interchange includes AIFF-C as a common interchange format for noncompressed audio data.

alpha channel. An 8-bit, grayscale representation of an image used to create a mask for keying images.

A-mode. A linear method of assembling edited footage. In A-mode, the editing system performs edits in the order in which they will appear on the master, stopping whenever the edit decision list (EDL) calls for a tape that is not presently in the deck.

analog recording. The common form of magnetic recording where the recorded waveform signal maintains the shape of the original waveform signal. All videotape source footage is analog. When recorded (via telecine transfer), footage is converted from the analog format to a digital format.

anti-aliasing. A computerized process of digitally smoothing the jagged lines around graphic objects or titles.

aspect ratio. The numerical ratio of a viewing area's width to its height. In video and television, the standard aspect ratio is 4:3, which can be reduced to 1.33:1 or simply 1.33. HDTV video format has an aspect ratio of 16:9. In film, some aspect ratios include: 1.33:1, 1.85:1, and 2.35:1.

assemble edit. An edit where all existing signals on a tape (if any) are replaced with new signals. Assemble editing sequentially adds new information to a tape and a control track might be created during the edit. The edit is made linearly and is added to the end of previously recorded material.

Attic folder. The folder containing backups of your files or bins. Every time you save or the system automatically saves your work, copies of your files or bins are placed in the Attic folder, until the folder reaches the specified maximum. The Attic folder copies have the file name extension .bak and a number added to the file name. The number of backup files for one project can be changed (increased or decreased) in the Bin Settings dialog box.

audio timecode. Longitudinal timecode (LTC) recorded on an audio track.

AutoSave. A feature that saves your work at intervals you specify. Backups are placed in the Attic folder.

Avid disk. The disk that contains the operating system files. The computer needs operating system information in order to run.

Avid Projects folder. The folder containing your projects.

backtiming. A method of calculating the IN point by subtracting the duration from a known OUT point so that, for example, music and video or film end on the same note.

backup. A duplicate copy of a file or disk in another location if the original file or disk becomes corrupted.

batch record. The automated process in which groups of clips, sequences, or both are digitized (recorded digitally).

Betacam, Betacam SP. Trademarks of Sony Electronics, Inc. Two component videotape and video recording standards. Sony Betacam was the first high-end cassette-based system, recording video onto 1/

2-inch magnetic tape. The SP version arrived 3 years after the first Betacam, improving on signal-to-noise ratios, frequency responses, the number of audio channels, and the amount of tape available on cassettes. SP is now the only type sold.

bin. A database in which master clips, subclips, effects, and sequences are organized for a project. Bins provide database functions to simplify organizing and manipulating material for recording and editing.

black and code. Video black, timecode, and control track that are prerecorded onto videotape stock. Tapes with black and code are referred to as striped or blacked tapes.

black burst. A video signal that has no luminance or chrominance components (except burst) but contains all the other elements of a video signal. Black burst is the reference signal commonly used for timing audio and video samples.

black burst generator. An electronic device that emits a signal that registers as pure black when recorded on videotape.

black edits. 1. A video source with no image.
2. A special source you can fade into, out of, or use for other effects.

B-roll. An exact copy of the A-roll original material, or new original material on a separate reel, for use in A/B-roll editing.

bumping up. The transfer of a program recorded on a lower quality videotape to a higher quality videotape (such as from 3/4-inch to 1-inch videotape, or S-VHS to MII).

burn-in. A visible timecode permanently superimposed (burned in) on footage, usually in the form of white numbers in a black rectangle. Burned-in timecode is normally used for tracking timecode during previews or offline editing. A videotape with burn-in is also called a burn-in dub or window dub.

channel. 1. A physical audio input or output.
2. One of several color components that combine to define a color image. An RGB image is made up of red, green, and blue color channels. In color correction, you can redefine color channels by blending color components in different proportions.

character generator. An electronic device, or computer device and software combination, that creates letters and numbers that can be superimposed on video footage as titles.

chroma. Video color.

chrominance. The saturation and hue characteristics of a composite video signal; the portion of the video signal that contains color information. Adjust chrominance and other video levels before recording.

clip. 1. A segment of source material recorded into your system at selected IN and OUT points and referenced in a project bin. The clip contains pointers to the media files in which the actual digital video and audio data is stored.

2. In a record in a log, which stands for one shot, the clip includes information about the start and end timecode for the shot, the source tape name, and the tracks selected for editing.

3. In OMFI, a general class of objects in the OMF Interchange class hierarchy representing shared properties of source clips, filler clips, attribute clips, track references, timecode clips, and edge code clips. A clip is a subclass of a component.

codec. *Compressor/dec*ompressor. Any technology for compressing and decompressing data. Codecs can be implemented in both software and hardware. Some examples of codecs are: Cinepak, MPEG, and QuickTime.

color bars. A standard color test signal, displayed as a video pattern of eight equal width columns (that is, "bars") of colors. SMPTE color bars are a common standard. You adjust video levels against the color bars on your source videotape before recording.

component video. The structuring of the video signal whereby color and luminance signals are kept separate from one another by using the color-subtraction method Y (luminance), B–Y (blue minus luminance) and R–Y (red minus luminance), with green derived from a combination. Two other component formats are RGB and YUV.

composite video. A video signal in which the luminance and chrominance components have been combined (encoded) as in standard PAL, NTSC, or SECAM formats.

composition. The standard term used by OMF Interchange to refer to an edited sequence made up of a number of clips. The OMF equivalent of a sequence in an Avid system.

compression. 1. In audio, the process of reducing the dynamic range of the audio signal.

2. In video, a lack of detail in either the black or the white areas of the video picture due to improper separation of the signal level.

3. A reduction of audio signal details, video signal detail, or both to reduce storage requirements during transformation from analog to Avid digital format. In JPEG compression, for example, algorithms for variable frame length analyze the information in each frame and perform reductions that maximize the information retained. Compression does not remove any frames from the original material.

conform. To prepare a complete version of your project for viewing. The version produced might be an intermediate working version or the final cut.

Console. A display that lists the current system information and chronicles recently performed functions. It also contains information about particular items you are editing, such as the shots in your sequence or clips selected from bins.

contrast. The range of light-to-dark values present in a film or video image.

control track. The portion of the video recording used to control longitudinal motion of the tape during playback. Control track can be thought of as electronic sprocket holes on the videotape.

CPU. Central processing unit. The main computational section of a computer that interprets and executes instructions.

crossfade. An audio transition in which the outgoing sound gradually becomes less audible as the incoming sound becomes more distinct. Also called an audio dissolve.

cue. To shuttle a videotape to a predetermined location.

cut. 1. An instantaneous transition from one video source to another.
2. A section of source or record tape.

D1, D5. Two digital videotape recording formats that conform to the ITU-R 601 (CCIR-601) standard for uncompressed 4:2:2 digital component video. D5 is very similar to D1 in that it is a component digital recorder. However, D1 records with 8-bit accuracy; D5 records with 10-bit accuracy.

D2, D3. Two digital videotape recording formats for composite video. The main difference between D2 and D3 is that D2 uses 3/4-inch digital videotape, and D3 uses 1/2-inch digital videotape.

DAE. Digidesign Audio Engine. A trademark of Avid Technology, Inc. The application that manages the AudioSuite plug-ins.

DAT. Digital audiotape. A digital audio recording format that uses 3.8mm-wide magnetic tape in a plastic cassette.

decibel (dB). A unit of measurement for audio volume level.

deck controller. A tool that allows the user to control a deck by using standard functions such as shuttle, play, fast forward, rewind, stop, and eject.

depth shadow. A shadow that extends solidly from the edges of a title or shape to make it appear three-dimensional.

digital cut. The output of a sequence, which is usually recorded to tape.

digital recording. A method of recording in which the recorded signal is encoded on the tape in pulses and then decoded during playback.

digital television. DTV. The technology enabling the terrestrial transmission of television programs as data.

digitally record. To convert analog video and audio signals to digital signals.

dip. An adjustment to an audio track in which the volume gain level decreases or "dips" to a lower level, rather than fading completely.

direct digital interface. The interconnection of compatible pieces of digital audio or video equipment without conversion of the signal to an analog form.

dissolve. A video or audio transition in which an image from one source gradually becomes less distinct as an image from a second source replaces it. An audio dissolve is also called a segue.

drop-frame timecode. A type of SMPTE timecode designed to match clock time exactly. Two frames of code are dropped every minute on the minute except the tenth minute, to correct for the fact that color frames occur at a rate of 29.97 fps, rather than an exact 30 fps. Drop-frame timecode is recorded with semicolons between the digits; for example, 1;00;10;02.

drop shadow. A shadow that is offset from a title or shape to give the feeling of spatial dimension.

dupe. Duplicate. A section of film or video source footage that has been repeated (duplicated) one or more times in an edited program.

DV. Digital video that is transferred through equipment conforming to IEEE Standard 1394. This equipment is sometimes called FireWire or I-Link.

DVE. Digital video effect.

dynamic range. An audio term that refers to the range between the softest and loudest levels a source can produce without distortion.

EBU. European Broadcasting Union. A standards-setting organization in which only users (not vendors) have a voice.

edit. To assemble film or video, audio, effects, titles, and graphics to create a sequence.

edit controller. An electronic device, often computer-based, that allows an editor to precisely control, play, and record to various videotape machines.

edit rate. In compositions, a measure of the number of editable units per second in a piece of media data (for example, 30 fps for NTSC, 25 fps for PAL, and 24 fps for film).

EDL. Edit decision list. A list of edits made during offline editing and used to direct the online editing of the master.

effects. The manipulation of an audio or video signal. Types of film or video effects include special effects (F/X) such as morphing; simple effects such as dissolves, fades, superimpositions, and wipes; complex effects such as keys and DVEs; motion effects such as freeze frame and slow motion; and title and character generation. Effects usually have to be rendered because most systems cannot accommodate multiple video streams in real time.

energy plot. The display of audio waveforms as a graph of the relative loudness of an audio signal.

extract. To remove a selected area from an edited sequence and close the resulting gap in the sequence.

fade. A dissolve from full video to black video or from full audio to no audio, or vice versa.

field. One-half of the scan lines in an interlaced video frame. In most systems, the odd-numbered lines form one field, and the even-numbered lines form the second. NTSC video contains approximately 60 fields (30 frames) per second, and PAL video contains 50 fields (25 frames) per second.

file system. A way of organizing directories and files on a disk drive, such as FAT or NTFS for Windows computers.

filler clip. A segment of a sequence that contains no audio or video information. Filler can be added to the Source monitor (or pop-up monitor) and edited into a sequence.

format. To prepare a disk drive or floppy disk for use. For Windows computers, you format a disk drive by copying a file system (either FAT or NTFS) to the drive.

formatting. The transfer and editing of material to form a complete program, including any of the following: countdown, test patterns, bars and tone, titles, credits, logos, space for commercial, and so forth.

fps. Frames per second. A measure of the film or video display rates (NTSC = 30 fps; PAL = 25 fps; SECAM = 25 fps; Film = 24 fps).

frame. One complete video picture. A frame contains two video fields, scanned at the NTSC rate of approximately 30 fps or the PAL rate of 25 fps.

frame offset. A way of indicating a particular frame within the group of frames identified by the edge number on a piece of film. For example, a frame offset of +12 indicates the twelfth frame from the frame marked by the edit.

gain. 1. A measurement of the amount of white in a video picture.
2. Audio levels or loudness.

gamma. A measurement of the midpoint in the luminance range of an image. Used in color adjustments to control the proportions of brighter and darker areas in an image. Also called the gray point.

gang. Any combination of multiple tracks that are grouped. An edit that is performed on one track is also performed on tracks that are ganged together.

generation. The number of times material has been rerecorded. The original videotaped material is the first generation. A copy of the original is a second-generation tape, and so on. Each generation shows a gradual loss of image quality. With digital copies, there is little or no loss in quality.

genlock. In Broadcast, a system whereby the internal sync generator in a device (such as a camera) locks onto and synchronizes itself with an incoming signal.

gigabyte (GB). Approximately one billion bytes (1,073,741,824 bytes) of information.

handles. Material outside the IN and OUT points of a clip in a sequence. The Avid system creates handles when you decompose or consolidate material. The Decompose and Consolidate features can create new master clips that are shorter versions of the original master clip. The handles are used for dissolves and trims with the new, shorter master clips.

hard disk. A magnetic data recording disk that is permanently mounted within a disk drive.

hard recording. The immediate recording of all audio, video, timecode, and control tracks on a magnetic recorder. Because hard recording creates breaks in any existing timecode or control track on the tape, this procedure is often performed on blank tape when an edit is not required or in emergency circumstances. Also called crash recording.

HDTV . High-definition television. A digital video image having at least two times the resolution of standard NTSC or PAL video. The HDTV aspect ratio is 16:9. (Analog TV has a ratio of 4:3.)

head frame. The first frame in a clip of film or a segment of video.

headroom. 1. In video, the room that should be left between the top of a person's head and the top of the frame when composing a clip.
2. In audio, the amount of available gain boost remaining before distortion is encountered.

hertz (Hz). The SI unit of frequency equal to one cycle per second.

Hi Con. A high-contrast image used for creating matte keys.

hue. An attribute of color perception. Red, green, blue form the color model used, in varying proportions, to produce all the colors displayed in video and on computer screens. Also called a color phase.

initializing. The setting of the computer edit program to proper operating conditions at the start of the editing session.

IN point. The starting point of an edit. Also called a mark IN.

interface. 1. The computer software or hardware used to connect two functions or devices.
2. The program access level at which a user makes selections and navigates a given system.

IRE. A unit of measurement of the video waveform scale for the measurement of video levels, originally established by the Institute of Radio Engineers. The scale is divided into 140 IRE units, 100 above the blanking reference line and 40 below it.

ITU-R BT.601. The standard for standard-definition component digital video, published by the International Telecommunication Union as ITU-R BT.601-5 (formerly CCIR 601). This standard defines digital component video as it is derived from NTSC and PAL. It forms the basis for HDTV formats as well.

jam syncing. The process of synchronizing a secondary timecode generator with a selected master timecode.

JFIF. JPEG File Interchange Format. A file format that contains JPEG-encoded image data, which can be shared among various applications. JFIF resolutions store data at a constant rate; for example, JFIF 300 uses 300 KB for each frame it stores. JFIF resolutions comply with the ISO-JPEG interchange format and the ITU-R 601 standard.

JPEG. Joint Photographic Experts Group. Also, a form of compression developed by Avid Technology, Inc.

kerning. The spacing between text characters in print media, such as titles.

keyframes. The frames used in an effect. Opacity levels, outgoing and incoming frame proportions, and acceleration settings can be applied to specified keyframes within an effect.

kilobyte (KB). Approximately one thousand bytes (1024 bytes) of information.

kilohertz (kHz). One thousand cycles per second.

layback. The process of transferring a finished audio track back to the master videotape.

layered tracks. The elements of an effect created by combining two or more tracks in a specified way, such as nesting one track as a layer within another.

leader. A length of film, tape, or a digital clip placed at the beginning of a roll, reel, or sequence to facilitate the cueing and syncing of material.

level. A quantitative measure of a video or an audio signal. A low level indicates the darker portions in video and the soft or quieter portions in audio; conversely, a high level indicates a brighter video image or a louder audio signal. The level of audio signal correlates directly with the volume of reproduced sound.

lift. To remove selected frames from a sequence and leave black or silence in the place of the frames.

linear editing. A type of tape editing in which you assemble the program from beginning to end. If you require changes, you must rerecord everything downstream of the change. The physical nature of the medium (for example, analog videotape) dictates how you place material on the medium.

line feed. A recording or live feed of a program that switches between multiple cameras and image sources. Also known in sitcom production as the director's cut.

locator. A mark added to a selected frame to qualify a particular location within a sequence. User-defined comments can be added to locators.

log. To enter information about your media into bins at the beginning of the editing process. Logging can be done automatically or manually.

looping. The recording of multiple takes of dialog or sound effects.

lossless compression. A compression scheme in which no data is lost. In video compression, lossless data files are usually very large.

lossy compression. A compression scheme in which data is thrown away, resulting in loss of image quality. The degree of loss depends on the specific compression algorithm used.

LTC. Longitudinal timecode. A type of SMPTE timecode that is recorded on the audio track of a videotape.

luminance. The measure of the intensity of the combined color (white) portion of a video signal.

mark IN/OUT. 1. The process of entering the start and end timecodes for a clip to be edited into a sequence.
2. The process of marking or logging timecode numbers to define clips during a logging or recording session.

master. The tape resulting from editing. The finished program.

master clip. In the bin, the media object that refers to the media files recorded from tape or other sources.

master shot. The shot that serves as the basic scene, and into which all cutaways and closeups will be inserted during editing. A master shot is often a wide shot showing all characters and action in the scene.

matchback. The process allowing you to generate a film cut list from a 30-fps video project that uses film as the source material.

match-frame edit. An edit in which the last frame of the outgoing shot is in sync with the first frame of the incoming shot, such that the incoming shot is an extension of the outgoing shot.

media. The video, audio, graphics, and rendered effects that can be combined to form a sequence or presentation.

media data. Data from a media source. Media data can be:

1. Analog data: film frames, Nagra tape audio, or videotape video and audio.

2. Digital data: either data that was recorded such as video frame data and audio samples, or data created in digital form such as title graphics, DAT recordings, or animation frames.

media files. Files containing the compressed digital audio and video data needed to play Avid clips and sequences.

megahertz (MHz). One million cycles per second.

mix. 1. A transition from one video source to another in a switcher.

2. The product of a recording session in which several separate sound tracks are combined through a mixing console in mono or stereo.

mixdown audio. The process that allows the user to combine several tracks of audio onto a single track.

monitor. 1. In video, a picture tube and associated circuitry without tuner or audio sections. The monitor includes the display of source media, clips, and sequences. In Avid products, virtual monitors are displayed on the screen in which source media, clips, and sequences can be edited.

2. In audio, to monitor specific audio tracks and channels, or another name for the speakers through which sound is heard.

MOS. The term used for silent shooting. From the pseudo-German, "Mit Out Sprechen"— without talking.

multicamera. A production or scene that is shot and recorded from more than one camera simultaneously.

multiple B-roll. A duplicate of the original source tape, created so that overlays can be merged onto one source tape.

multitrack. A magnetic tape or film recorder capable of recording more than one track at a time.

noise. 1. In video, an aberration that appears as very fine white specks (snow) and that increases over multiple generations.

2. In audio, a sound that is usually heard as a hiss.

non-drop-frame timecode. An SMPTE timecode format that continuously tracks NTSC video at a rate of 30 fps without dropping frames to compensate for the actual 29.97-fps rate of NTSC video. As a result, non-drop-frame timecode does not coincide with real time. Non-drop-frame timecode is recorded with colons between the digits; for example, 1:00:10:02.

nonlinear. Pertaining to instantaneous random access and manipulation of any frame of material on any track and on any layer of an edit sequence.

nonlinear editing. A type of editing in which you do not need to assemble the program from beginning to end. The nature of the medium and the technical process of manipulating that medium do not dictate how the material must be physically ordered. You can use nonlinear editing for traditional film cutting and splicing, and for recorded video images. You can make changes at the beginning, middle, or end of the sequence.

NTSC. National Television Standards Committee. The group that established the color television transmission system used in the United States, using 525 lines of information scanned at a rate of approximately 30 fps.

offline. Pertaining to items that are unavailable to the computer, such as offline disks or media files.

offline edit. The preliminary or rough-cut editing that produces an <Italic>EDL (edit decision list).

OMFI. Open Media Framework Interchange, a registered trademark of Avid Technology, Inc. A standard format for the interchange of digital media data among heterogeneous platforms. The format is designed to encapsulate all the information required to interchange a variety of digital media, such as audio, video, graphics, and still images as well as the rules for combining and presenting the media. The format includes rules for identifying the original sources of the digital media, and it can encapsulate both compressed and uncompressed digital media data.

online edit. The final edit using the master tapes and an edit decision list (EDL) to produce a finished program ready for distribution; usually associated with high-quality computer editing and digital effects.

OUT point. The end point of an edit, or a mark on a clip indicating a transition point. Also called a mark OUT.

outtake. A take that is not selected for inclusion in the finished product.

overlap edit. An edit in which the audio and video signals are given separate IN points or OUT points, so the edit takes place with one signal preceding the other. This does not affect the audio and video synchronization. Also called an L-cut, delay edit, or split edit.

overwrite. An edit in which existing video, audio, or both is replaced by new material.

PAL. Phase Alternating Line. A color television standard used in many countries. PAL consists of 625 lines of information scanned at a rate of 25 fps.

partition. A method of assigning disk space that creates two or more virtual disks from a single physical disk (similar to creating a directory).

patching. The routing of audio or video from one channel or track in the sequence to another.

pop-up monitor. An ancillary monitor used to view and mark clips and sequences.

position bar. The horizontal rectangular area beneath the Source monitor, Record monitor, Playback monitor, Composer monitor, and Source pop-up monitor that contains the position indicator.

position indicator. A vertical blue line that moves in the position bar and in the Timeline to indicate the location of the frame displayed in the monitor.

postroll. A preset period of time during a preview when a clip will continue to play past the OUT point before stopping or rewinding.

precomputed media. A computed effect stored in a file and referenced by a composition or sequence. Applications can precompute effects that they cannot create during playback.

preroll. The process of rewinding videotapes to a predetermined cue point (for example, 6 seconds) so the tapes are stabilized and up to speed when they reach the selected edit point (during recording of source material from a video deck).

preview. To rehearse an edit without actually performing (recording) it.

progressive media. Media composed of single frames, each of which is vertically scanned as one pass.

project. A data device used to organize the work done on a program or series of programs. Bins, rundowns, and settings are organized in the Project window. The project bins contain all your clips, sequences, effects, and media file pointers.

RAM. Random access memory. Computer memory that is volatile and unsaved — information in RAM clears when the computer is turned off.

random access. The ability to move to a video point instantly, without having to shuttle.

real time. The actual clock time in which events occur.

record. To convert analog video and audio signals to an Avid compressed digital signal format.

reel. A spool with a center hub and flat sides on which magnetic tape is wound. Generally, a spool of tape is referred to as a reel, and a spool of film is referred to as a roll.

rendering. The merging of effect layers to create one stream of digital video for playback in real time.

replace edit. An edit in which a segment in the sequence is overwritten or replaced with source material of matching duration.

resolution. The amount and degree of detail in the video image, measured along both the horizontal and vertical axes. Usually, the number of available dots or lines contained in the horizontal and vertical dimensions of a video image. Also, the number of color or grayscale values that can be added, usually stated in bits, such as 8-bit or 24-bit. Sometimes dots per inch (dpi) is referred to as the resolution, although it is more properly called the screen density.

RGB. Red, green, and blue. In computer systems, the additive primary colors used to create all other colors on a computer monitor.

rough cut. A preliminary edit of a program, usually the result of an offline edit.

safe action area, safe title area. The regions of the video image considered safe from cropping for either the action or on-screen titles, taking into account variations in adjustments for video monitors or television receivers. Safe action is 90% of the screen measured from the center, and safe title is 80%.

sample data. The media data created by recording from a physical source. A sample is a unit of data that the recording device can measure. Applications can play digital sample data from files on disk.

sample plot. The representation of audio as a sample waveform.

sample rate. The frequency of the sample units.

saturation. A measurement of chrominance. Saturation is the intensity of color in the video signal.

scale bar. A control in the Timeline window that allows you to expand and contract the Timeline area centered around the blue position indicator.

scroll bar. A rectangular bar located along the right side or the bottom of a window. Clicking or dragging in the scroll bar allows the user to move or pan through the file.

scrubbing. The process of shuttling through audio at various speeds as the audio pitch changes.

SECAM. Séquential Couleur à Memoire. A color television broadcast standard developed in France and several Eastern European countries.

segment. A section of a track or clip within a sequence in the Timeline that can be edited.

sequence. An edited composition that often includes audio and video clips and rendered effects connected by applied transitions. The Avid system contains a Timeline that graphically represents the edited sequence.

shot log. A listing of information about a roll of film or a reel of videotape, usually in chronological order.

shuttling. The viewing of footage at speeds greater than real time.

sifting. The displaying of clips that meet specific criteria in a bin.

silence. Blank (black) space in the audio tracks in a Timeline that contains no audio material.

SMPTE timecode. A frame-numbering system developed by the Society of Motion Picture and Television Engineers that is used primarily for electronic editing and timing of video programs. It assigns a number to each frame of video, telling the elapsed number of hours, minutes, seconds, and frames; for example, 01:42:13:26.

soft wipe. A wipe effect from one image to another that has a soft, diffused edge.

sorting. The arranging of clips in a bin column in numerical or alphabetical order, depending on the column the user selects.

Sound Designer II. A trademark of Avid Technology, Inc. An audio file format used for the import and export of digital audio tracks.

source clip. One of the lowest level building blocks of a sequence composition.

source mode. A method of assembly that determines in what order the edit controller reads the edit decision list (EDL) and assembles the final tape. There are five different types of source mode: A-mode, A-mode, B-mode, C-mode, D-mode, E-mode.

speed. The point at which videotape playback reaches a stable speed, all servos are locked, and there is enough preroll time for editing or recording.

splice. An edit in which the material already on the video or audio track is lengthened by the addition of new material spliced in at any point in the sequence.

split-screen. The video special effect that displays two images separated by a horizontal or vertical wipe line.

stepping. The movement forward or backward one frame at a time. Also called jogging.

storyboard. A series of pictures (traditionally sketches) designed to show how a production will look. Comic books are essentially storyboards. Storyboards and subsequent sequences can be created by manipulating images from the recorded footage in a bin.

streaming. A technology that allows users to watch a video clip or movie over the Internet while the video is being copied to their computers.

striped stock. Film stock to which a narrow stripe of magnetic recording material has been applied for the recording of a sound track.

subclip. 1. An edited part of a clip. In a sequence, a subclip can be bound by any variation of clip beginnings, endings, and mark points.
2. A subclip created by marking IN and OUT points in a clip and by saving the frames between the points. The subclip does not contain pointers to media files. The subclip references the master clip, which alone contains pointers to the media files.

sync (synchronization). 1. The pulses contained within a composite video signal to provide a synchronization reference for signal sampling. Also, a separate signal that can be fed to various pieces of equipment.
2. The sound recorded on a separate audiotape but synchronized with videotape or film shot simultaneously.

tail frame. The last frame in a clip of film or a segment of video.

TBC. Time-base corrector. An electronic device that improves video signal stability by correcting time-base errors inherent in mechanical videotape recorders.

three-point editing. The basic principle that an edit event requires only three marks between the source and record sides to automatically calculate the fourth mark and complete the edit.

TIFF. Tag Image File Format. A tag-based system developed by Aldus Corporation for storing and interchanging raster images. The OMF Interchange standard includes TIFF as a common format for graphic interchange, and it includes TIFF with extensions as a common format for video frame data.

timecode. An electronic indexing method used for editing and timing video programs. Timecode denotes hours, minutes, seconds, and frames (00:00:00:00) elapsed on a videotape. Address track timecode is recorded simultaneously with the video picture. Longitudinal timecode (LTC) is recorded on an audio track. Vertical interval timecode (VITC) is recorded in the vertical blanking interval of the video track. SMPTE timecode is the prevalent standard.

Other timecodes exist that include film timecode and audio timecode used during film projects. During editing, the Avid system can display and track several types of timecode.

Timeline. The graphical representation of every macroscopic and microscopic edit made to a sequence, including all nested effects and layered tracks.

time-of-day timecode. The timecode that approximately matches the actual time of day (clock time).

title bar. The name given to a project or bin, located at the top of a window.

tone. A constant audio frequency signal recorded at the start of a tape at 0 VU (volume units) to provide a reference for later use. Usually recorded in conjunction with color bars.

track. 1. The section of tape on which a signal is recorded. Also called a channel.

2. The sound portion of a video program.

3. A region of a clip or sequence on which audio or video is placed.

4. A playback channel represented in a sequence as either a video track or an audio track. Tracks are composed of one or more segments connected by transitions.

tracking. The positioning of video heads during playback of a tape so that the heads reproduce the strongest possible signal. Tracking is adjusted on the deck prior to recording.

track selector. A method of selecting one of the tracks from a track group; only the selected track is to be played. For example, a track selector can indicate which of four alternate views of the same scene is to be played.

transition. A representation of what is to take place as one segment ends and the next one begins. The simplest transition is a cut, which occurs in video when the first frame of the starting segment directly follows the last frame of the segment that is ending.

transition effect. A wipe, dissolve, or digital video effect (DVE) applied to an edit transition.

trim. The process of adjusting transitions in a sequence from the Timeline.

uncompressed video. A recorded video stream that is not processed by a data compression scheme. The video signal remains uncompressed at all stages of the process: input, storage, and output. Uncompressed video conforms to the ITU-R BT.601 standard.

Undo/Redo. The process that allows a return to the state of the edit immediately preceding the last edit or a repeat of an "undo" edit.

up cut. In editing, to cut the end of the previous scene, often by mistake. In general, to cut short.

VCR. Videocassette recorder. A video recorder that uses consumer-grade videotape formats such as VHS, Betamax, and Hi8.

vectorscope. A visual display that shows the electronic pattern of the color portion of the video signal. It is used to adjust the color saturation and hue by using a stable color reference such as color bars. The Avid Vectorscope monitor uses a single-line display.

VHS. Video Home System. The 1/2-inch videocassette format developed by JVC for consumer and industrial use.

video. 1. The visual portion of a program or sequence.

2. All television other than broadcast television.

video stream. 1. In analog editing systems, also called a video playback source.

2. In digital editing systems, a stream of data making up a digital video image.

VITC. Vertical interval timecode. The timecode inserted in the vertical blanking interval.

VU meter. Volume unit meter. An instrument used to measure audio levels.

WAVE. RIFF Waveform Audio File Format. A widely used format for audio data. OMF Interchange includes it as a common interchange format for audio data.

waveform. 1. In video, a visual display that shows the electronic pattern of the video signal. It is used to adjust the setup and gain by using a stable reference such as color bars. The Avid waveform uses a single-line display.

2. In audio, a visual representation of changing frequencies.

white point. The luminance value in a video image that you set to be equal to reference white when making a color adjustment.

wild sound, wild track. A recording of sound on either videotape or audiotape made without an accompanying picture.

YUV. The letter designations for luminance, luminance minus red, and luminance minus blue. YUV are the luminance and color difference signals of the component video standard for PAL. Also called YCrCb.

Index

Avid Educational Services Course Offerings 08/01/02

The following list includes Avid Educational Services' current course offerings. To register for a class, receive a catalog, or find the Avid Authorized Education Center nearest you, in North America call 800-867-2843 (AVID), Worldwide call 978-275-2071. For up-to-date course schedules, visit our web site at www.avid.com/training.

*Courses with an asterisk (*) following the name are available both as an instructor-led course and a stand-alone book with exercise media on a companion CD-ROM or DVD-ROM.

**Courses with a double asterisk (**) following the name are available only as a stand-alone book (with exercise media on a companion CD-ROM or DVD-ROM) or as an interactive CD-ROM.

101 | Avid Media Composer Editing

This three-day course introduces the concepts of nonlinear editing and includes all basic features of the Avid Media Composer system for Macintosh and Windows. Session time is divided between demonstration and hands-on practice, with ample time for experimentation with sample material. Students will use Avid Media Composer to digitize and organize source footage, edit sync and non-sync material, trim sequences, edit audio, create titles, and output work. The final product will be a finished program. This course is also appropriate for Avid Symphony users. Prerequisites: Designed for the novice Avid Media Composer editor, no familiarity with the system is necessary. Completion of a Macintosh or Windows introductory course or equivalent is required, and a background in editing, production, or post-production is strongly suggested.

Editing Essentials for Avid Media Composer and Avid Xpress**

This self-paced book, with alternating content modules and hands-on exercises, provides an in-depth overview of editing techniques for Avid Media Composer and Avid Xpress. Learn how to digitize and organize source footage, edit sync and non-sync material, trim sequences, edit audio, create titles, and output work. Prerequisites: Designed for the novice Avid Media Composer or Avid Xpress user, no familiarity with the system is necessary. Completion of a Macintosh or Windows introductory course or equivalent is required, and a familiarity with the editing process is strongly suggested. The book includes instructions for Windows and Macintosh platforms.

102 | Film Editing on Avid Media Composer

This practical three-day course prepares editors and assistant editors for film editing on Avid Media and Film Composer. Each day combines instructor-led lecture, demonstration, and hands-on practice. Topics include: Understanding the telecine process, organizing a session, logging, digitizing, editing sequences, and managing system storage. In addition, participants will learn how to create EDLs, cut lists, change lists, and digital cuts. Prerequisites: This course requires little or no familiarity with Avid Media Composer. Completion of a Macintosh or Windows introductory course or equivalent is required, as well as experience in a film editing environment.

106 | Avid Educator's Workshop

This five-day course, specifically designed for educators, introduces the concepts of nonlinear editing including all basic editing features as well as an in depth overview of the techniques necessary to teach, manage, and administer the Avid Media Composer or Avid Xpress system. The course is also appropriate for Avid Xpress DV users. Session time is divided between demonstration, hands-on practice, with ample time for experimentation with sample material, and group discussions of issues relevant to educators. Participants will use the Media Composer system to digitize and organize source footage, edit sync and non-sync material, trim sequences, edit audio, create effects and titles, and output work. The last two days of the course will focus on advanced project and system management techniques, importing and exporting graphics and video, basic troubleshooting, and system maintenance. Prerequisites: The participant should be an educator (college professors and other instructors, and technical staff) with a background in video production and/or post production but not familiar with the complexity of digital nonlinear editing on the Avid Media Composer system. Completion of a Macintosh or Windows introductory course or equivalent is recommended.

110 | Introduction to Avid Media Composer Effects

This two-day course introduces basic effects and is a prerequisite for the 305 Advanced Avid Media Composer Effects and the 310 Creating Graphics and Mattes with Avid Media Composer and Adobe Photoshop course. Class time is divided between demonstration and hands-on-practice Topics include: creating multilayered effects, keyframing effects, creating effect templates, creating motion effects and timewarps, using the 3D Effects option, and nesting layers. This course is also appropriate for Avid Symphony users. Prerequisites: Students should have completed the 101 Avid Media Composer Editing course.

117 | Avid Xpress Editing

This three-day course introduces the basic features of the Avid Xpress for Macintosh and Windows systems. Class time is divided between demonstration and hands-on practice, with ample time for experimentation on sample material. Participants will use Avid Xpress to: input source footage, create and trim sequences, edit audio, create titles, and output a finished program. The course is designed for experienced or novice editors, graphic designers, or interactive media developers. Experience with Avid Xpress or other Avid systems is not necessary. Completion of a Macintosh or Windows introductory course (depending on your system) or equivalent is recommended and a background in editing, production, or postproduction is strongly suggested.

119 | Avid Xpress DV Editing*

This two-day course is an in-depth introduction to the techniques of nonlinear editing on the Avid Xpress DV system. The class progresses through all the basic phases of creating a sequence on Avid Xpress DV, including inputting source footage, assembling and trimming sequences, editing audio, creating titles, and outputting a finished program. Class time is divided between demonstration and hands-on practice. The course is designed for video editors and developers of interactive media. Prerequisites: Experience with Avid Xpress or other Avid systems is not necessary. Completion of a Windows introductory course or equivalent experience is recommended; a background in editing, production, or postproduction is also recommended.

Avid Xpress DV Training CD-ROM**

This self-paced, interactive demonstration on CD-ROM provides comprehensive instruction on the basic techniques of nonlinear editing on the Avid Xpress DV system. No previous knowledge of the Avid Xpress DV system is required.

129 | Introduction to Avid Xpress DV Effects *

This one-day course introduces basic effects and is a prerequisite for the 329 Creating Graphics for Avid Xpress DV with Adobe Photoshop course. Class time is divided between demonstration and hands-on-practice. Topics include: creating multilayered effects, keyframing effects, creating effect templates, and nesting layers. Prerequisites: Students should have completed the 119 Avid Xpress DV Editing course or have equivalent experience.

139 | Color Correction for Avid Xpress DV *

This one-day course, designed for the intermediate user, explains how to color correct a sequence on the Avid Xpress DV system. The editor will learn how to color correct each shot in a sequence, use Avid Xpress DV's internal video scopes, make sure the color and luminance are within safe broadcast limits, and create a treatment for the entire sequence. Class time is divided between demonstration and hands-on practice. Prerequisite: Completion of the 119 Avid Xpress DV Editing course or the equivalent of six months' experience editing on the system is required.

201 | Advanced Techniques for Avid Media Composer

This two-day course is designed for experienced Avid Media Composer (or Symphony) editors who want to become more productive by mastering the system's sophisticated editing features and shortcuts. Students also learn advanced techniques to help streamline system, media, and project management. Sessions include instructor-led demonstration and hands-on practice. Topics include: editing features (such as Sync Point Editing and Replace Edit), advanced trimming techniques, editing and viewing options, sync audio methods, keyboard shortcuts, user settings, and digitizing and redigitizing tips. Project, media, and system management topics include: improving Avid Media Composer performance and moving and deleting media. Prerequisites: Completion of the 101 Avid Media Composer Editing course or the equivalent of six months' experience editing on the system is required. A background as editor, assistant editor, director, or producer is necessary.

205 | Avid Media Composer Troubleshooting (Macintosh)

Avid Media Composer and Film Composer editors using the Macintosh platform will learn how to troubleshoot basic technical problems in this two-day course. Topics include: signal flow, Macintosh-related problems, software and hardware problems, and issues involving external peripheral devices. This is an ideal class for post-production facility managers, Avid Media Composer System owners, and assistant editors. Completion of the 101 Avid Media Composer Editing course or equivalent experience and an introductory Macintosh course or equivalent are required.

305 | Advanced Avid Media Composer Effects

This two-day course focuses on designing multilayered and multinested effects on Avid Media Composer for maximum quality and optimal render time. Hands-on exercises help students create and combine effects to achieve real-world results. Topics include: effect shortcuts and tips, advanced keyframing, nesting and keying, render time reduction, and effect media management. This course is also relevant for Avid Symphony users. Prerequisites: Students should have completed both 101 Avid Media Composer Editing and the 110 Introduction to

Avid Media Composer Effects courses. They should also have several months' experience on the Avid Media Composer system.

310 | Creating Graphics and Mattes with Avid Media Composer and Adobe Photoshop

Designed for the advanced Avid Media Composer editor, this three-day course demonstrates how to prepare still and moving graphics for import into Avid Media Composer. Students will also learn how to use Intraframe Editing to create paint effects and animated mattes. Class time is divided between demonstration and hands-on-practice. Topics include: preparing and importing graphics, creating and using alpha channels, layers, and matte keys, using Adobe Photoshop to treat logos and web graphics for use in a video program, and using Avid Media Composer's Paint and AniMatte effects. Third party packages used in the class include Adobe Photoshop 6.0. This course is also relevant for Avid Symphony users. Prerequisites: Completion of the 101 Media Composer Editing course and the 110 Introduction to Avid Media Composer Effects course are required.

329 | Creating Graphics for Avid Xpress DV with Adobe Photoshop*

Designed for the advanced Avid Xpress DV editor, this two-day course demonstrates how to prepare still and moving graphics for import into Avid Xpress DV. Class time is divided between demonstration and hands-on practice. Topics include: preparing and importing graphics, creating and using alpha channels, layers, and matte keys, and using Adobe Photoshop to treat logos and web graphics for use in a video program. Third party packages used in the class include Adobe Photoshop 6.0. Prerequisites: Completion of the 119 Avid Express DV Editing course and the 129 Introduction to Avid Xpress DV Effects course are required.

320 | Finishing on Avid Media Composer and Avid Symphony Systems

This two-day course introduces the principles and practices of onlining (or finishing) programs on Avid systems. The course focuses on video signal and onlining techniques for both Media Composer and Symphony systems. Students acquire a thorough working knowledge of video and audio signals, calibration techniques, and the conforming process as a whole.

324 | Avid Symphony Finishing Effects and Color Correction

Designed for the intermediate to advanced user, this two-day course teaches the editor how to perform color correction and apply Symphony-specific effects. The editor will learn how to perform shot-to-shot and secondary color correction, perform motion tracking and stabilization, perform real-time compositing using the Ultimatte keyer, reformat a program for different delivery aspect ratios, and apply pan and scan to a reformatted program.

400 Macintosh | Avid System Support for Macintosh

This five-day course is the foundation of the program for prequalified candidates pursuing certification as an Avid Certified Support Representative. Students learn techniques to minimize system downtime and maximize productivity, focusing on software problems on Media Composer systems. Lab work and role playing give students practical experience. Topics include: basic Macintosh, SCSI, storage, software and hardware troubleshooting; system software and hardware; signal flow; and system integration. After completing the class, participants will be able to identify Macintosh and Media Composer hardware and software problems, use basic tools for troubleshooting, and provide first-line support to Avid's customer base. Prerequisites: Students must first be accepted to the ACSR program by application. They also need to complete the 101, 102, 201, and 305 classes or equivalent.

400 Windows | Avid System Support for Windows

This five-day course focuses on the integration and support of Avid Symphony systems. Avid Symphony hardware components and configurations are presented and explained. Windows and Avid software are covered. Troubleshooting concepts, models and tools are also described. Lab work and exercises give students practical experience in integrating systems and applying troubleshooting techniques. Topics include: identifying, understanding, and working with PC and Avid Symphony hardware and software; installation and configuration of Avid Symphony systems; troubleshooting and resolving problems on Avid Symphony systems. Prerequisites: Students must first be accepted in to the ACSR program by application. Requires prior completion of courses including 101, 110, and 201. Also requires completion of a Windows course or the equivalent experience and successful completion of a Windows pre-test.

402 Unity | Avid Unity MediaNet System Support

This five-day course focuses on the installation, administration, and architecture of Avid Unity MediaNet. Students will learn how to connect, configure and troubleshoot Avid Unity MediaNet, as well as other products within a post-production workgroup environment such as Avid MediaManager, Avid TransferManager, and ProTools on Unity. Lab work and exercises give students practical experience in integrating systems and applying troubleshooting techniques. Topics include: identifying and understand installation, configuration and troubleshooting procedures for Avid Unity MediaNet, Avid MediaManager and Avid TransferManager; working with networking hardware and software; and identifying hardware and software necessary to run ProTools on Unity. Prerequisites: Students must have Macintosh and/or Windows ACSR active status.

403 | Avid Unity for News

This two-day course teaches you how to install, administer, and troubleshoot broadcast products often found in an Avid Unity MediaNet news environment. Students must have Macintosh and/or Windows ACSR active status. This course is offered only as an add-on to the 402 course.

410 Macintosh | ACSR Macintosh Recertification

This two-day course focuses on the new technologies, software, and hardware that a current Avid Certified Support Representative (ACSR | Macintosh) may not be familiar with. Students will learn about new and updated topics relating to Avid Macintosh based systems. Prerequisite: Students must be Avid Certified Support Representatives (ACSRs) to participate.

410 Windows | ACSR Windows Recertification

This two-day course focuses on the new technologies, software, and hardware that a current Avid Certified Support Representative (ACSR | Windows) may not be familiar with. Students will learn about new and updated topics relating to Avid Windows-based systems. Prerequisite: Students must be Avid Certified Support Representatives (ACSRs) to participate.

500 | The Avid Master Editor Workshop

This intensive 5-day course provides a select group of editors a concentrated learning environment, focusing on ways to improve technical proficiency and enhance the creative application of the Avid Media Composer system capabilities. Highly respected special guest speakers and industry professionals will share their unique approaches to the art and technique of editing, focusing on the innovative use of nonlinear editing in the film and television industry. Potential students must submit an application and demo reel to be reviewed by Educational Services Workshop Review Committee. Please contact Avid Educational Services for additional information.

T3-101 | Train-the-Trainer: Avid Media Composer, Xpress, and Xpress DV Editing

As part of the Avid Certified Instructor (ACI) program, this five-day course prepares instructional professionals to teach the 101 Avid Media Composer Editing, 117 Avid Xpress Editing, and 119 Avid Xpress DV Editing courses. Students acquire the teaching skills through lecture, interactive role playing, hands-on sessions, and written and oral examinations. Topics of discussion include presentation skills, course curriculum, and teaching methodology. The instructor will show beginning instructors how to give presentations, lead hands-on exercises, and answer questions about Avid products from a diverse audience. During the class, students review and present course modules on inputting material into the system, editing a sequence, and outputting a finished program. Prerequisites: Students must first be accepted to the class by application.

135 | Introduction to Digidesign ProTools

This course introduces ProTools basic recording and editing functions. It is designed for audio engineers and editors who want to learn the ProTools feature set and incorporate its use into their audio and video applications. This three-day course features instructor-led demonstrations and student exercises. Topics include: recording audio; nonlinear editing; editing narration and sound effects; hardware system overview, using SMPTE timecode and fades; and managing regions and tracks. During the class, students will conduct a basic audio-editing session including inputting source material, editing tracks, and adding effects. Prerequisites: This course is for editors, audio/video engineers broadcast professionals and musicians. It requires basic Macintosh skills and a general understanding of audio and/or acoustics. Note: Mixing and the use of plug-ins are not covered in this course.

235 | Digidesign Pro Tools Mixing

This two-day course is designed for audio engineers, editors and musicians who want to learn how to effectively use the Digidesign Pro Tools mixing feature set and to incorporate it into audio and video applications. Topics include: Applying AudioSuite and TDM plug-ins; using Inserts and Sends; submixing and bouncing tracks; recording, editing, and creating automation, conducting a basic Digidesign Pro Tools mixdown and layback. Prerequisites: This is an intermediate level course. It is recommended for editors, audio engineers and musicians. Students must have completed 135 Introduction to Digidesign Pro Tools Editing prior to taking this course or have equivalent knowledge. A basic understanding of mixing boards and prior mixing experience is helpful.

DS-101 | Avid|DS Editing and Basic Effects

This three day course introduces students to the Avid|DS SD and HD workflow processes. Students will familiarize themselves with the Avid|DS editing, audio, and media management techniques. They will also get an introduction to Effects and Animation. Topics include: Capturing media, Story-boarding, Editing a scene with dialogue, Multicamera Editing, Transitions, Media Management, DVE, Color Correction, Titling, Customizing the interface, Audio Effects, Mixing Audio, and Conforming. Prerequisites: None.

DS-120 | Conforming on Avid|DS for Avid Media Composer Editors

Designed for the experienced Avid Media Composer editor, this one-day class teaches how to conform Avid Media Composer sequences on Avid|DS. Topics include: Preparing for the Avid|DS conform, conforming in High Definition, understanding how effects conform, and manipulating effects and graphics in Avid|DS. Prerequisites: Students should have completed the DS-101 course and be experienced Avid Media Composer editors.

DS-201 | Avid|DS Graphics and Effects

This two day course introduces the students to more advanced Graphics, Effects, and animation techniques. Topics include: Multiple Effects and Animation, Effects tree, Handwriting, Scratch removal, Warp Effect, Timewarping, Mix and Match, Luma Keyer, Blue/Green Keyer, and Advanced Titling. Prerequisites

DS-301 | Avid|DS Compositing and Effects

This three-day course explores the compositing and graphic tools used in Avid|DS system. Students will become familiar with the compositing and the 3D DVE layouts and workflow. Specific features of the Graphics layout are also covered. Topics include: Blue Green Keyer, Multiple Mattes, Photoshop Import, Travelling Matte, Morphing, Stabilizing, Tracking, Offset Tracking, and 3D DVE Compositing. Prerequisites: DS-201

172 | Introduction to Avid NewsCutter

This two-day course is an introduction to Avid's Windows-based news editor Avid NewsCutter Effects. This course is designed to familiarize students with the concepts of nonlinear editing. It progresses through all the basic features of the Avid NewsCutter Effects system. Students will learn to identify and execute basic steps, to input information into the system, and to output a finished program. Topics include: Recording directly to the Timeline, tape-to-disk editing, audio with keyframe action, creating digital recordings, organizing source footage, trimming edits, editing audio and outputting work. Prerequisites: Students should have prior knowledge of editing in a news environment, and be familiar with the Windows operating system. Course is limited to two students per system, maximum eight students per class. Offered on-site at customer facility only.